Create a
COTTAGE GARDEN

Create a
COTTAGE GARDEN

RECIPES FOR BORDERS, BEDS AND CONTAINERS

KATHLEEN BROWN

ILLUSTRATED BY SIMON BUCKINGHAM

MICHAEL JOSEPH
LONDON

MICHAEL JOSEPH LTD

Published by the Penguin Group
27 Wrights Lane, London W8 5TZ
Viking Penguin Inc., 375 Hudson Street, New York, New York 10014, USA
Penguin Books Australia Ltd, Ringwood, Victoria, Australia
Penguin Books Canada Ltd, 10 Alcorn Avenue, Toronto, Ontario, Canada M4V 3B2
Penguin Books (NZ) Ltd, 182–190 Wairau Road, Auckland 10, New Zealand

Penguin Books Ltd, Registered Offices: Harmondsworth, Middlesex, England

First published in Great Britain October 1993
Second impression April 1994
First published in Mermaid Books 1997

Printed and bound in Singapore by Kyodo Printing Co.

ISBN 0 7181 3593 8

Contents

List of Recipes

GENERAL INTRODUCTION

The aim of this book is to show you, the reader, how to create your very own cottage garden. You will find fifty detailed garden plans and twenty-four containers to enjoy throughout the year.

Each one is presented in simple 'recipe' form, complete with a full list of plant ingredients, which may be combined together and arranged in a certain pattern, then left to develop and mature. An illustration accompanying the garden recipes reflects the planting scheme in a particular month or season. It is followed by a brief description of how the plan will look throughout the rest of the year. The containers mature much more quickly, so these have been specially planted and photographed. Additional details of all the plants used in both recipe sections are given in the plant lists.

Follow the recipes step by step, or adapt them to suit your own situation and taste. Try just one or two at first, then more as time and effort allow. Before long, you too can enjoy the cottage garden effect. It does not matter whether you live in a house or a flat, be it old or new. It is the style of gardening which you are trying to emulate, not the idealised rustic cottage.

What was this cottage style? It was a working garden – to be enjoyed not just from the road or house, but also from within – in which plants were closely packed to create a profusion of growth and a riot of colour. The cottage garden represented a scene of warmth and tranquillity. It was small and homely, informal and seemingly untamed. It made a stark contrast to the regimented rows of bedding plants which were the hallmark of so many Victorian, Edwardian and interwar gardens with their uniform heights and rules of colour.

What sort of plants were grown in the cottage garden? In many cases, there was a wholesome mixture of vegetables, fruit and flowers, but the accent was on the first two elements. By its very nature, the garden needed to provide food for the family. The vegetable patch in particular required hours of labour, and it was here that the cottager spent most of his 'spare' time.

Of necessity, therefore, the ornamental flowers and shrubs which were grown had to be largely undemanding. Easy annuals which flowered in just one summer grew side by side with the good old herbaceous plants which had stood the test of time. Annuals, such as marigolds, nasturtiums and larkspur, would probably seed themselves. Whereas perennials, such as peonies and Chinese lanterns, once planted, would remain untouched for years on end, with no need for division or renewal. Other perennials might be shorter lived, but were survivors nevertheless. They would seed themselves without

asking: lady's mantle in the path, hollyhocks underneath the washing line. Would they be allowed to stay? Lots of colourful climbers and scented shrubs clothed the walls, year after year, producing flowers and fluffy seedheads, fruit or berries. Numerous clumps of spring bulbs lay patiently waiting for their great moment of glory, and flowered without fuss or attention.

The cottage garden and its plants were very special in that they appealed to all the senses. To the eye, it was like a rich and glorious tapestry. Bright colours mixed happily together, with the pastel shades by their sides, often unplanned where the self-seeders were concerned. It is said that colour coding did not matter here. But did it matter anyway? There were often lots of blues and whites to break up the louder colours. Not too far away, there was the dominant green of the leaves of a tree, or a shrub or hedge, and the warm texture of a red brick wall or a wall of hewn stone. Paths and edgings were many and varied. The views were small in scale. The flowers might mingle or shout, but somehow they were absorbed into the scene, irrespective of colour.

The cottage garden was a great delight to the sense of smell. It contained a rich variety of plants renowned for their wonderful scents and aromas. Often the air would be filled with some special fragrance long before you sighted the plant from which it emanated. This provoked a moment of expectancy, and then a pleasure fulfilled. So many sweetly scented flowers spring to mind: violets, primroses, lily of the valley, old-fashioned roses and honeysuckle; the list could go on and on. They were all great favourites.

To the mouth, it was also deliciously rewarding. Fresh vegetables could be picked nearly the whole year round, and if winter brought snow and frost to the leeks and Brussels sprout patch, then there were still stores of carrots, onions and potatoes to be eaten, and copious quantities of salted beans and pickled mixtures. Nearly every garden would have a few fruit trees. Damsons, plums, apples and pears were common; greengages and cherries would also be grown. They were made into puddings and pies, or bottled and jammed, as were the soft fruits, including all the currants, strawberries and raspberries. In these respects the cottager and his family were largely self-sufficient.

What about the sense of touch? In many ways this was allied to the sense of smell. Just a gentle rub of a lemon verbena leaf was enough to release the powerful lemony smell. The foliage of rose-scented geraniums filled the air with the fragrance of roses. Bronze fennel gave off the smell of aniseed. The texture of the plant also played a part as you walked past. In early summer, the soft new leaves of the rosemary bush almost begged to be caressed as they stretched out by the gate; the same was true of the lavender flower spikes, still pliant but fragrant. Overhanging climbers and shrubs, narrow paths and a profusion of growth meant that touching plants was a natural and inevitable occurrence and a source of great pleasure.

The sense of hearing was well rewarded in the cottage garden, a haven for many forms of wildlife. There was shelter in the boundary hedges and trees, in the old walls and barns. There was plenty of food. Many of the plants produced fruit and berries, while the flowers were rich in nectar and offered a generous larder to the butterflies and bees. Animals, birds and insects all flourished together. In spring and early summer the early hours vibrated to the sound of the dawn chorus. The tuneful melody of the blackbird and song thrush, the chattering sparrows, the squabbling starlings, and the evocative cry of the cuckoo could all be heard. The honeybee buzzed as he fed on the nectar and gathered the pollen. Chances are he was not alone: many of his friends and relations would be there working the same plant, creating the same familiar drone.

But the cottage garden style was more than plants alone. It had to do with background fences and hedges, and the garden features themselves. Walls were particularly important, whether they were the low dividing walls between the road and garden, or the high walls of the house or barn. Both provided a framework for plants of various kinds. The front door was another 'prop'. It may have had a porch around it. Climbers and scented favourites were sure to have been growing there. Arches and pillars might have been found in the garden, simple rose arbours too. There might have been a ditch, or a stream or pond. There were likely to be paths and paving, and probably steps as well.

In order to recreate the cottage garden effect, choose from a variety of plants and put them together with the features. The style will soon develop and the senses will automatically be rewarded. Look through the recipes that follow and see which appeal most. Gradually the picture will emerge, in all its seasons and with all its joy.

Garden Recipes

INTRODUCTION

This chapter provides fifty recipes for different parts of the cottage garden. The size of your garden and your personal circumstances will suggest how many are relevant. No one garden could contain them all.

I have taken a visual, practical approach to cottage gardening in dealing with its many aspects. There are several recipes for borders: summer and winter ones, others for the whole year round and some to attract butterflies and bees. There are plans for hedges: neat clipped evergreen, or more informal and colourful deciduous. There are lots of schemes for rose arches, arbours and a pergola. There are ways to use trees. There are differing treatments for low and high walls. There are also recipes for wild flower areas of grassland and a cottage pond. The productive side of the cottage garden is represented here too, in working plans for the vegetable and fruit garden and an orchard.

Although a few of these plans cover a large area, in many cases the scale is deliberately small. This means that the plans adapt well to gardens of any size. Also, it is far easier to think in terms of only 2 or 3 m^2 (21 or 32 sq ft) per recipe, than to attempt to cover the whole garden at once. You then have the opportunity to add on extra units or to create other borders and features as appropriate. On a practical note, small-scale plans are cheaper to plant and easier to look after.

Many of the recipes have alternative treatments for sun and shade. One person's front door will be in shade for most of the day, while somebody else's will be in sunshine. The same holds true for the borders, walls and steps. Where possible, both situations are covered to take account of varying circumstances.

I have also allowed for different sized borders. Requirements can vary so much. As a result, I have designed sections which can be put together like a jigsaw. There are three 2-m (6½′) recipes for the sunny border and three more for shade. Use them in parts or as a whole depending on their suitability. The butterfly and bee border is on a larger scale. It involves tall shrubs like the butterfly bush and lavatera, and comprises two 5-m (16½′) sections. Again, they can be used together or separately.

The same flexible approach is taken to the front of the house. There are three garden recipes for the sunny front and three for the shady front. They refer to the door or porch and the windows on either side. Of course, some houses won't have a door in the middle, or borders under the windows, therefore all three plans will not be needed. But where they are appropriate, they fit together to produce colour and interest for as long as possible. They can easily be scaled down by the odd metre or two (3–6′) where dimensions vary. If extra planting is needed, just refer to the plans for the back door in sun and shade. These will provide further suitable schemes.

With so many ideas available, you can happily pick and choose the ones which suit you best. Sometimes, a plan might be suitable because you have the right 'props'. You might already have a rose arch with plants trained up it, but you might want to create a more exuberant 'cottage' look with lots of scent and colour. You might have a low wall but nothing growing on or beneath it. The front door might be bare on either side, just waiting to be planted. With new eyes you might now see your old apple tree as the perfect host to a rambling rose.

On the other hand, you might simply like the look of a recipe and be willing to make an entirely fresh start. You might plan a new winter border, a fern garden or a new hedge.

The scope is endless. This is really a cottage 'mix and match' type of gardening with something for everyone.

RECIPE

The recipe concept was first used in a book I co-authored with Effie Romain called *Creative Container Gardening*, originally published in 1987. Here I have applied the concept to garden plans as well, so that each one has an easy, straightforward approach, which includes all the relevant details. Each garden 'recipe' has a full list of ingredients, details on site and scale, a planting plan with timing information and aftercare instructions. Every one has its own painting, with the plant names and a description underneath. These recipes are easy to interpret and simple to follow. Either copy them plant by plant or use them as a basis from which to experiment. It is a matter of personal choice.

INGREDIENTS

This refers to the plants needed for the recipe, and gives the number required, a note of their colour, their size (*see* 'Planting Plan' below) and their flowering period (the months are indicated in figures). More detailed information about the plants is given in the plant lists in the third section of the book. An asterisk beside the plant name indicates that it is not shown in the illustration. This only occurs when a plant is lying dormant and cannot therefore be seen.

Where possible, common names have been used. They are far easier to pronounce and remember. However, gardeners use some strange names, and what may be common in one part of the country may be unheard of elsewhere. Therefore, the Latin name is given as well, so that there can be no mistake. On the whole, it is the Latin name which you will need in the garden centre.

Most recipes contain only eight different plant names, although more than one of each plant may be used in any one scheme (*see* the number required). This means that knowledge of the plants can be absorbed more easily. It would be tempting to add many more new species. Very soon, however, the list would become excessive, and the plans would be more complicated and expensive to execute. The limitation on numbers means that many cottage garden plants have not been included, so feel free to add other plants not mentioned here. If you feel that they fit into the general ethos of the cottage garden, use them by all means.

SITE

This is mentioned mainly with reference to sun or shade. In reality, many areas of the garden have both sun and shade for some part of the day throughout the year. Interpretation can sometimes be fairly loose. After all, lots of so-called shade-loving plants will grow well in a sunny spot if they have plenty of moisture.

SOIL

As a general rule, the plants are suited to most soils, unless it is stated otherwise.

Before planting, always prepare the borders well, adding plenty of compost and well-rotted manure. This will help to improve the texture of the soil as well as the humus content. As a result, it should be more water-retentive, and the plants should fare better in times of drought. They will also enjoy the higher nutritional element and grow into stronger, healthier specimens.

SCALE

This is measured in both centimetres or metres and inches or feet. As stated already, some plans link up with others to increase the overall scale.

Don't forget to allow a gap of about 25 cm (10″) beneath a wall where it will be too dry to plant successfully. All the measurements exclude this area, and refer only to that part of the border which is to be planted. Therefore, where walls are involved, add 25 cm (10″) to the depth of each border. Also leave a small gap at the front of the border, depending on the plants. You might want them to spill over the boundaries of the border, but be sure to allow them enough space to grow, in an area surrounded by good soil.

PLANTING PLAN

This has deliberately been kept simple, and refers mainly to the position of each plant in relation to the others, whether behind, in front, to the side, etc.

Allow the individual plants their natural area of spread as indicated in the ingredients section. Figures for height only are given for bulbs and climbers, while details of both height and spread are provided for other herbaceous plants and shrubs. The figures are approximations and depend on soil and rainfall; note that they refer to mature plants. Don't be afraid to prune back where there is excess growth and other plants are threatened. Practical details on planting distances and the depths for planting bulbs are given under the heading 'When to Plant'.

If the border looks very bare to begin with, don't panic. Just sow some summer annuals or buy some bedding plants and fill in the gaps. You should not have long to wait for a lovely show. Even in two years, growth on herbaceous plants can be rapid, while after three years, many will need dividing. The shrubs and trees will take longer to establish, but the butterfly bush and lavatera, for instance, can grow a surprising amount in just one season.

Further clarification of the plan is given by the illustration with the plant names listed underneath. This shows the positions of those plants actually visible at a particular moment in time. Of course, if it is a summer or an autumn picture, it won't show the leaves or flowers on the spring bulbs which will have disappeared beneath the ground.

WHEN TO PLANT

Each recipe gives its own detailed guide on the subject. However, unless specifically stated, *all container plants can be planted at any time of the year if the weather is favourable.* Obviously, planting in severe winter conditions of frost and snow should be avoided; it should on hot dry summer days too, unless you are willing to water the plants daily.

Bare-rooted specimens are much more rare these days now that the garden centres have become one of the main sources of plants to the general public. Nevertheless, the mail order business still thrives, particularly with regard to roses and some herbaceous plants, which will probably be sent out from the nurseries through the post in November or December. Follow the instructions given on the labels, or as stated in the text of each recipe.

Bulbs are usually purchased in a dry state without roots or leaves. They need to be planted in the autumn: some early, such as snowdrops, Madonna lilies and daffodils; some later, such as tulips. However, most daffodils, crocuses, scillas, hyacinths and tulips will survive whether they are planted in late September or late October. Snowdrops and Madonna lilies are perhaps the most temperamental. They do not like being out of the ground for too long, and many dry out too much before they are planted. Plant them as soon as they become available in the garden centres. Snowdrops can also be planted 'in the green', with their leaves still intact, after they flower in the spring.

AFTERCARE

Some plants need looking after more than others. Peonies may need staking but little else for the rest of their long lives. On the other hand, delphiniums will need lots of loving care and attention with regard to slugs, staking, feeding and division. Each recipe has its own special care plan and, although brief, all the salient facts have been included.

ILLUSTRATION

Each painting concentrates on just one period in time: the holly tree in December, the cottage path in May, the sunny porch in summer, or the high wall in autumn. The illustrations faithfully represent these features when they are looking particularly attractive.

It should be pointed out, however, that these plans will often be beautiful in other seasons as well. One quick glance at the 'Best' column in the ingredients list provides proof enough. Each of the three sunny border plans, for example, could have been painted in late spring, mid or late summer. The same is true of the shady borders. Indeed, most recipes are planted specifically so that they have colour and interest throughout the year, or over a long period.

The illustrations depict the plants in each recipe, but they also provide the background fences, walls and trees as well. They include the cottager, his wife, the postman, his friend and his children. His white West Highland terrier is never far away, neither is the cat. This is a book about practical cottage gardening with the cottager working in the garden. As in real life, people and animals are very much a part of the garden scene.

DESCRIPTION

This is based on the illustration, taking the season portrayed as the starting point. It moves on to describe the scheme throughout the rest of the year, thus completing the picture. It describes how the plants relate to each other, their colours, their uses, their strong points and their vices. The rich scents and aromas are described. Mention is also made of the garden visitors which they attract. Gradually the picture unfolds and captures the mood.

'Gardener' from *The Land*

When skies are gentle, breezes bland,
When loam that's warm within the hand
Falls friable between the tines,
Sow hollyhocks and columbines,
The tufted pansy, and the tall
Snapdragon in the broken wall,
Not for this summer, but for next,
Since foresight is the gardener's text,
And though his eyes may never know
How lavishly his flowers blow,
Others will stand and musing say
'These were the flowers he sowed that May.'

But for this summer's quick delight
Sow marigold, and sow the bright
Frail poppy that with noonday dies
But wakens to a fresh surprise;

Along the pathway stones be set
Sweet Alysson and mignonette,
That when the full midsummer's come
On scented clumps the bees may hum,
Golden Italians, and the wild
Black humble-bee alike beguiled:
And lovers who have never kissed
May sow the cloudy Love-in-Mist.

Nor be the little space forgot
For herbs to spice the kitchen pot:
Mint, pennyroyal, bergamot,
Tarragon and melilot,
Dill for witchcraft, prisoner's rue,
Coriander, costmary,
Tansy, thyme, Sweet Cicely,
Saffron, balm, and rosemary

VITA SACKVILLE-WEST

1   Wallflowers Beneath The Window

INGREDIENTS

No req	Name	Description	Ht × Spr (cm/m)	Ht × Spr ("/')	Best
20	Wallflowers *Cheiranthus cheiri* 'Fair Lady Mixed'	mixed	30 × 30 cm	1 × 1'	4–5
20	Tulips *Tulipa* 'Beauty of Apeldoorn'	yellow/rose	45 cm	18"	4–5
1	Spurge *Euphorbia characias* 'Lambrook Gold'	yellow-green	1.2 × 1 m	4 × 3¼'	4–5
1	Golden hop *Humulus lupulus* 'Aureus'	golden leaves	5 m	16½'	5–7, 9
1	Ceanothus *Ceanothus* 'Delight'	blue	3 m	10'	5–6
6	*Mignonette *Reseda odorata*	green	30 × 30 cm	1 × 1'	6–10
1	*Fuchsia *Fuchsia* 'Sealand Prince'	pink/violet	90 × 90 cm	3 × 3'	6–10
1	*Caryopteris *Caryopteris* × *clandonensis* 'Heavenly Blue'	blue	90 × 90 cm	3 × 3'	8–9

SITE
A sunny border in front of the house to the side of the front porch or door.

SCALE
3 m (10') and 90 cm (3') deep. *See also* Recipes 2 and 3.

PLAN
Left: Plant the spurge in front with the ceanothus and golden hop behind so that they can both be trained up the wall.
Beneath the window: Plant the caryopteris to the left and the fuchsia to the right with wallflowers and tulips in between. Replace the wallflowers with mignonette in summer.

WHEN TO PLANT
Plant the wallflowers 25 cm (10") apart in September or October each year. They can be grown from seed sown in May or purchased as bare-rooted plants in bunches. Where the soil is acidic, dress it with lime. Also in September or October, plant the tulips 15 cm (6") deep, 15 cm (6") apart. Plant the spurge from September to April. Choose a small specimen, as it will transplant better than a large one. The ceanothus and caryopteris may be planted in September or left until April. Allow the ceanothus three or four years to establish itself before planting the hop any time between September and April. The mignonette may be sown indoors in April or May or *in situ* in June when the wallflowers have been removed. Plant out the fuchsia in June.

AFTERCARE
Add plenty of compost each autumn when renewing the wallflowers; when they are newly transplanted they need lots of water. Remove the plants at the end of May after flowering and give the border a general fertiliser feed. Take away tulip petals as they fade, otherwise they can harbour disease; also remove yellow leaves and stems when they have died down naturally. Cut the old flower stems of the spurge down to ground-level to promote bushy growth. Prune the hop back to its base in early spring. The ceanothus will need wire supports up the wall to train it; after flowering trim any side shoots to restrict its spread. Discard the mignonette after flowering. The fuchsia is hardy, but give it a thick mulch at the end of October and be prepared to protect it with sacking in severe weather. Cut the stems down to within 15 cm (6") of the ground in March. At the same time, cut all the weak stems on the caryopteris down to ground-level, and prune the strong stems back to their healthy buds.

ceanothus
golden hop
spurge

tulips & wallflowers

jasmine
lavender

DESCRIPTION

A rich variety of colour lies under the cottage window in May. The wallflowers, which are called 'Fair Lady', are renowned for their delicious sweet perfume. They create a mass of apricot, yellow, rose, pink and mahogany, which show off beautifully against the sunny warm brick wall. They provide a wonderful setting for the tall 'Beauty of Apeldoorn' tulips which rise through them. These tulips are sturdy and reliable. They begin to flower at the end of April and will last until mid-May, when the once golden flower will be suffused with rose-pink. At the end of the wall a bold spurge erupts with large heads of yellow-green flowers. From April onwards it is a lively mass of colour, echoed in the golden hop above in May. The hop is climbing through a rich blue ceanothus which flowers through May and June. The bright golden foliage of the hop sets off the blue of the ceanothus and the two make a delightful picture.

Once the wallflowers and tulips have finished flowering, it is time to plant out the mignonette. This small annual was once the cottager's favourite. Its flowers are insignificant to look at, but the scent is memorable, just like that of lily of the valley, only it lasts all summer long. They provide a light green carpet for the hardy 'Sealand Prince' fuchsia which, by midsummer, has just begun its long season of flowering. The dark pink sepals and light violet skirts look lovely together and make a lively colour scheme, especially if combined with the lavender and jasmine in Recipe 2, which can just be seen to the right in the illustration above. By the end of August, the caryopteris begins to bloom in an outstanding display of rich blue flowers. It combines well with the fuchsia throughout September, and even then the quiet little mignonette will still be in flower. The fuchsia will perform beautifully until the first frosts, which could be as late as October.

2 A Scented Porch

INGREDIENTS

No req	Name	Description	Ht × Spr (cm/m)	Ht × Spr ("/')	Best
2	Garden pinks *Dianthus* 'Mrs Sinkins'	double, white	25 × 60 cm	10 × 24"	6
1	Climbing rose *Rosa* 'New Dawn'	pale pink	4 m	13'	6–7
1	Summer jasmine *Jasminum officinale*	white	6 m	19½'	6–10
2	Old English lavenders *Lavandula angustifolia* 'Grappenhall'	blue	90 × 90 cm	3' × 3'	7–9
20	*Snowdrops *Galanthus nivalis* 'Flore Pleno'	double, white	10 cm	4"	2–3
4	*Roman hyacinths *Hyacinthus orientalis albulus* 'Snow White'	white	15 cm	6"	4
10	*Spanish bluebells *Hyacinthoides hispanica*	pink	30 cm	1'	4–5
20	*Pheasant's eye daffodils *Narcissus poeticus recurvus*	white/orange	40 cm	16"	5

SITE
A sunny border on either side of the front door.

SCALE
1 m (3¼') wide on each side and approximately 90 cm (3') deep. *See also* Recipes 1 and 3.

PLAN
Left: Plant one lavender in the middle right of the plot with the jasmine behind. Beside the path, plant half the snowdrops and one 'Mrs Sinkins' with the Roman hyacinths behind and half the daffodils in a wide arc beyond them.
Right: Plant the other lavender in the middle left of the plot with the rose behind. Beside the path, repeat the pattern as on the left (above), substituting bluebells for the hyacinths.

WHEN TO PLANT
Snowdrops should be planted in August or early September, or left until March and planted 'in the green', 5 cm (2") deep, 8 cm (3") apart. A bare-rooted rose can be planted from October to March. October is best for the jasmine, lavender and pinks. The rest of the bulbs should be planted in September or October. Plant the hyacinths and bluebells 10 cm (4") deep, 10 cm (4") apart, and the daffodils 15 cm (6") deep and 15 cm (6") apart.

AFTERCARE
Apply a general rose fertiliser to the borders in early spring and then, avoiding the foliage of the pinks, mulch with compost or well-decayed manure while the ground is damp. Give the rose and the jasmine a second feed at the end of June to encourage late summer flowers. The climbers need supports.

Prune the rose in late February. Train a few horizontal growths near the bottom of the wall and aim to build up the shape gradually. Spray against greenfly and blackspot if necessary. Do not allow the rose to dry out in summer, and be particularly vigilant until it is well established.

Thin out the jasmine shoots after flowering, taking special care to keep the rose and the jasmine separate above the door. The pinks and hyacinths may need replacing every four or five years. The lavender flowers should be picked in July if you want to dry them, otherwise remove the flower stalks as they fade in late summer. The snowdrops, bluebells and daffodils should be left undisturbed.

jasmine
garden pink   lavender   rose
      lavender   garden pink

DESCRIPTION

By June the old-fashioned garden pink 'Mrs Sinkins' begins to spread over the path. She is by no means tidy, but her mass of large white blooms are all so powerfully scented that she is soon forgiven. Climbing above, the rose 'New Dawn' creates a wonderful display as the sweetly scented blooms cover the wall to the right of the front door. The flowers are a soft silvery pink; they are produced in a great mass and then continue to appear on and off all summer. They look particularly lovely beside the tiny white flowers of the summer jasmine which clambers up the other side of the door. With its powerful fragrance, pretty flowers and delicate leaf arrangement, it makes an excellent subject for planting in such a key position. Open the windows above and enjoy the rose and jasmine perfume inside the house as well.

Below, two old English lavender bushes stand sentinel on either side of the porch. Even in winter, just a pinch of an old leaf will release their evocative scent. But now, in late June, they have sprung into tender new growth, their silvery grey-green foliage making a perfect setting for the rose and jasmine above. Soon they will produce a blue haze which will last for many weeks. Lavender is one of the best sights in the cottage garden, and an old favourite both for its colour and fragrance. The bees visit with feverish interest as they gather the delicious nectar.

Snowdrops herald the start of the new year. They appear like long lost friends, always a delight, always welcome. Then, in April, come the scented Roman hyacinths. Their dainty flower spikes are rich with sweet fragrance. Next to show their heads are the Spanish bluebells (pink ones are used because they are not so invasive). They create a lovely clump beside the grey lavender. Last to appear among the bulbs are the much-loved white narcissi known as pheasant's eye. They have a delicate scent and multiply well, but they won't flower until May. By then the door is nearly ready for its summer mantle.

3 A Cottage Window in Summer

INGREDIENTS

No req	Name	Description	Ht × Spr (cm/m)	Ht × Spr (″/′)	Best
1	Bourbon rose *Rosa* 'Mme Isaac Pereire'	deep pink	4 m	13′	7–9
1	Perennial pea *Lathyrus latifolius*	magenta-pink	1.8 m	6′	6–9
1	Clematis *Clematis* 'Jackmanii Superba'	violet-purple	4 m	13′	7–10
2	Hollyhocks *Althaea rosea* 'Pinafore Mixed'	mixed	90 × 45 cm	36 × 18″	7–9
4	Bellflowers *Campanula persicifolia*	blue	90 × 30 cm	3 × 1′	6–7, 8–9
4	Cranesbills *Geranium sanguineum striatum* 'Splendens'	pink/crimson	12 × 30 cm	5 × 12″	6–9
4	Violas *Viola* 'Maggie Mott'	pale blue	15 × 25 cm	6 × 10″	5–9
8	*Polyanthus *Primula* × *polyantha*	mixed	10 × 20 cm	4 × 8″	4–5

SITE
A sunny border beneath the cottage window to the side of the door.

SCALE
3 m (10′) wide and 90 cm (3′) deep. *See also* Recipes 1 and 2.

PLAN
Border's edge: Alternate pairs of cranesbills and violas.
Left: Plant the clematis with the hollyhocks in front.
Beneath the window: Plant the bellflowers and polyanthus.
Right: Plant the rose with the perennial pea in front.

WHEN TO PLANT
November or December until March is ideal for planting the bare-rooted rose, clematis and the rest. However, if the hollyhocks are treated as hardy annuals and grown from seed sown in the spring, they can be transferred in May. Delay planting the perennial pea until the rose is well established.

AFTERCARE
Give the border a general rose fertiliser feed in early spring and then mulch while the ground is damp. The climbing plants need support to train them up the wall. Prune the rose in late February. Gradually build up a good open shape, removing anything that is weak or dead. Give 'Mme Isaac Pereire' another feed at the end of June to encourage late summer flowers. Guard against blackspot and greenfly. Do not allow the rose to dry out in summer, particularly in the first year after planting.

Bushy growth on the clematis is desirable. Cut it back to within 25 cm (10″) of ground-level in the second year after planting, then allow a few strong shoots to be trained horizontally about 45 cm (18″) above the ground. The new vertical shoots will then create a good wall of colour. In early spring, prune the shoots back to a pair of strong buds just above the horizontals, thus removing all the previous year's growth. Keep the clematis away from the rose above the window and the rose 'New Dawn' if planted, *see* Recipe 2.

Deadhead the perennial pea and cut growth back to ground-level at the end of October. Also cut back the bellflowers and cranesbills after the first flush to encourage later blooms. The bellflowers and hollyhocks may need support. Remove the hollyhocks after flowering. They are susceptible to rust, so it is probably best to use fresh plants each year. Deadhead the violas regularly and take cuttings, as they are not long-lived. Deadhead the polyanthus and keep them moist throughout the year.

clematis		bellflowers		rose
hollyhocks				perennial pea
cranesbills	violas	cranesbills	violas	

DESCRIPTION

The cottage window is framed with a striking picture of pinks and purples throughout July and August. To the right, the old-fashioned Bourbon rose 'Mme Isaac Pereire' produces a mass of bold deep pink flowers. They are large and full of perfume. Climbing up through her lower branches is a perennial pea, now smothered with small magenta-pink flowers. It is one of the most charming of all the cottage garden plants, and flowers profusely throughout the summer. To the left of the window is the 'Jackmanii' clematis with its rich violet-purple flowers. From July to October it creates a sensational mass of colour right at the heart of the cottage wall, with the deep pink rose 'Mme Isaac Pereire' on one side and the silvery pink blooms of the rose 'New Dawn' above the porch (*see* Recipe 2). Its tangled growth can be forgiven, for its contribution to the colour spectacle is almost without equal. Not surprisingly, it is an old favourite.

Like cathedral spires, the tall pink hollyhocks rise up into the clematis, growing even higher as the summer progresses. They flower for many weeks; the large ruffled blooms are both pretty and colourful. The cottage wall would hardly be complete without them. Lovely bellflowers provide a sea of colour under the window in June and early July, which continues on and off throughout the summer. Their spode-blue colouring adds variety to the pinks and purples elsewhere. At the very front of the border are the cranesbills with their small, delicate light pink flowers, crimson veins and dark centres. They bloom all summer, along with the old-fashioned viola 'Maggie Mott', which creates beautiful mounds of pale blue flowers spilling out onto the path.

By the middle of the following spring, the border is full of lovely bright polyanthus, which flower beneath the window for many weeks with a fragrant mixture of reds, scarlets, yellows and pinks. They will soon be joined by the violas and the long summer season will begin again.

4   The Autumn Window

INGREDIENTS

No req	Name	Description	Ht × Spr (cm/m)	Ht × Spr (″/′)	Best
1	Firethorn *Pyracantha rogersiana*	orange berries	3 m	10′	6, 9–3
2	Japanese anemones *Anemone × hybrida* 'Queen Charlotte'	pink	80 × 45 cm	32 × 18″	8–10
2	Japanese anemones *Anemone × hybrida* 'White Giant'	white	100 × 60 cm	3¼ × 2′	8–10
1	Hydrangea *Hydrangea* 'Preziosa'	pink	75 × 90 cm	30 × 36″	7–9
2	Elephant's ears *Bergenia stracheyi* 'Silberlicht'	white	30 × 45 cm	12 × 18″	4
1	Soft shield fern *Polystichum setiferum* 'Plumoso-divisilobum'	green	50 × 90 cm	20 × 36″	5–11
10	*Tenby daffodils *Narcissus pseudonarcissus obvallaris*	yellow	25 cm	10″	3–4
10	*Pheasant's eye daffodils *Narcissus poeticus recurvus*	white/orange	40 cm	16″	5

SITE
A shady border in front of the house with a window to the side of the door.

SCALE
3 m (10′) wide and 90 cm (3′) deep. *See also* Recipes 5 and 6.

PLAN
Left: Plant the firethorn at the back with the fern in front.
Beneath the window: Plant the white anemones at the back and the shorter pink ones in the middle, with groups of white and yellow daffodils on either side. Plant the elephant's ears in front along the path so that they will form a solid edge.
Right: Plant the hydrangea.

WHEN TO PLANT
October to March, although an April transfer is best for the fern. The daffodils should be planted in September or October, 15 cm (6″) deep and 15 cm (6″) apart.

AFTERCARE
Give the border a general rose feed in early spring and then mulch when the ground is damp. The firethorn needs a trellis or wires for support. It grows quite quickly and needs to be trained each summer so that it hugs the perimeter of the cottage window and forms a buffer at the end of the house. Tie in vigorous growths each year between July and September. Trim surplus growth between May and July. There will be some loss of potential berries, but by careful clipping many will still remain.

The Japanese anemones are best left undisturbed. Despite their height, they do not need staking. Cut the stems down to ground-level after flowering. The hydrangea needs plenty of moisture in summer; therefore, give it an annual mulch in April to help retain moisture later in the year and be prepared to water it in severe droughts. It needs little or no pruning, but remove dead flower heads in March.

Leave the elephant's ears alone except to cut off the stems after flowering. The fern needs no attention, nor do the daffodils but remove the dead leaves in midsummer.

firethorn

fern

white Japanese anemones
pink Japanese anemones
elephant's ears

hydrangea

honeysuckle

ivy

DESCRIPTION

In autumn the firethorn smothers the end of the cottage wall with its great clusters of warm orange berries. Blackbirds love them, but here, up against the house, most of the berries will probably last right through the winter months. Meanwhile, beneath the window, the Japanese anemones have been in bloom since August. The flowers are saucer-shaped, wide and delicate, and sway easily in the wind. The mixture of pink and white makes a lovely picture. The white are slightly taller and reach above the cottage windowsill, so that they are enjoyed as much from inside the home as out in the garden. They flower for such a long period, and are so graceful, that they easily rank as one of the great favourites.

From July to September the hydrangea is in full array with its mass of pink heads. The colour changes as they mature: from a light and creamy pink they deepen to a rich red and even crimson. The foliage has attractive tinting too; as the nights get colder, the purplish tones become more intense. Even in winter the mop heads remain; the colour almost disappears, but the shape and form add a great deal of interest to

the border at this bleak time of year. Picked in late summer, the heads may be used to great effect for dried flower arrangements. The honeysuckle and ivy from Recipe 5 show how the two planting schemes can be combined.

The elephant's ears and the fern make a valuable contribution to this shady spot. They are both evergreen and contrast wonderfully: the elephant's ears' large rounded leaves form an ever increasing bold clump in the centre of the border, while the fern has finely cut fronds, each one beautifully arranged and displayed magnificently as they spread out from the crown.

In spring, the bulbs make a lively show beneath the window: first, our native Tenby daffodil with its neat golden trumpet, and then the old-fashioned pheasant's eye with its gleaming white petals, frilly orange cup and sweet smell. In April, the elephant's ears begin to flower, their tall spikes laden with small white bells. Later, in June, the firethorn becomes a mass of creamy blossoms in readiness for its autumn show. Colourful and evergreen, it is good value all year round.

5 A Cheerful Shady Porch

INGREDIENTS

No req	Name	Description	Ht × Spr (cm/m)	Ht × Spr ("/')	Best
2	Ivies *Hedera helix* 'Heise'	silver	3 m	10'	all year
1	Winter-flowering jasmine *Jasminum nudiflorum*	bright yellow	3 m	10'	11–3
1	Christmas rose *Helleborus niger*	white	30 × 30 cm	1 × 1'	1–3
1	Elephant's ears *Bergenia stracheyi* 'Silberlicht'	white	30 × 45 cm	12 × 18"	4
20	Snowdrops *Galanthus nivalis* 'Flore Pleno'	double, white	10 cm	4"	2–3
4	*Hepaticas *Hepatica nobilis*	blue	10 × 25 cm	4 × 10"	2–4
6	*Foxgloves *Digitalis purpurea* and 'Alba'	purple, lilac, white	90 × 45 m	36 × 18"	6–7
1	Honeysuckle *Lonicera periclymenum* 'Serotina'	purple-red	3 m	10'	7–10

SITE
Shady borders on either side of the front door. Omit the ivies if you do not have a porch or pillars.

SCALE
1 m (3¼') wide and 90 cm (3') deep on either side. *See also* Recipes 4 and 6.

PLAN
Left: Plant the honeysuckle at the back with three foxgloves in front. Plant two hepaticas and twenty snowdrops near the path.
Right: Plant the winter-flowering jasmine at the back with three foxgloves in front. Plant the Christmas rose, elephant's ears and two hepaticas near the path. Allow the latter plenty of space so that they are swamped by the elephant's ears.
Pillars or porch wall: Plant the ivies.

WHEN TO PLANT
The snowdrops should be planted 5 cm (2") deep and 8 cm (3") apart, either as soon as they are available in August or early September or when they are 'in the green' in March. The other plants may be planted from late autumn to March.

AFTERCARE
The ivies will cling to the pillars, or porch walls, without assistance. Trim them in February or March, and again if necessary in midsummer, to keep them neat and within bounds. Don't be afraid to cut them back: new growth will soon appear. The winter-flowering jasmine needs supports to help it grow against the wall. It should be hard pruned after it has flowered. Cut off all flowering shoots to within 8 cm (3") of the base. Flowers will only appear on new growth, so this treatment ensures a good display for the following winter.

The Christmas rose will benefit from some leaf mould or manure in the spring, otherwise it likes to be left alone. The elephant's ears needs little attention, but remove dead flower spikes and tidy dead leaves. The snowdrops and hepaticas are best left to their own devices.

Foxgloves are biennial and so need to be replaced in the first year once they have flowered. However, they should seed themselves, so after two years the small colony should be self-perpetuating. Give a mulch of leaf mould or well-decayed manure to the honeysuckle in spring and then a light annual trim after flowering. Remove any dead wood.

honeysuckle   ivy   ivy   jasmine
snowdrops   Christmas rose   elephant's ears

DESCRIPTION

The front door of the cottage is often sheltered by a porch, particularly when it faces north or east. Here, a well-clipped ivy, trained up the supporting pillars, lends a homely air to the humble entrance. The silver-leaved ivy 'Heise' is one of the best choices for a shady site. Its colouring and soft variegation will give extra interest to the cottage entrance the whole year round. Beside the door to the right, the winter-flowering jasmine produces a cascade of yellow stars on its bare twigs from November through to March. It creates a golden corner, a bright and cheerful scene throughout the winter.

Growing on the right at the base of the porch is the Christmas rose which flowers sometimes as early as December, but more often in the new year, and lasts until early March. It has large white flowers with golden anthers. It is a priceless plant – no wonder it was so favoured in the cottage gardens of old. It shows up well against the dark background of the strong rounded leaves of the elephant's ears to its right. The latter is a plant which certainly lives up to its name. It maintains its solid, bold appearance all year and, like the ivy, acts as an anchor plant. In April it produces handsome white flowers on red-bronze spikes.

The winter scene would never be complete without beautiful double snowdrops. Here they are growing in a clump to the left of the porch. They brave the cold weather during January and February, at first just peeping through the hard ground, then growing taller as the days begin to lengthen. Always a welcome sight, no cottager would be without them.

As spring approaches, the first hepaticas begin to bloom, and by the end of February a mass of dainty bright blue flowers can be seen beside the path. They are one of the old cottage garden plants that went quite out of fashion for many years, but now at last they are available again. Once established, they are quite breathtaking.

By the middle of June the foxgloves begin to flower; their tall spires are so reminiscent of old-fashioned gardens. They vary in their colouring from purple and lilac to white, each one with the tell-tale spots inside their finger gloves. By the end of July the honeysuckle will be transformed. Its creamy flowers flush with purple-red, providing a display which will last until October. The perfume is most evocative, especially in the evening or after a rain shower. The shelter makes a perfect nesting place for a blackbird or thrush, and its berries are a favourite source of food.

25

6 The Lily of the Valley Window

INGREDIENTS

No req	Name	Description	Ht × Spr (cm/m)	Ht × Spr ("/')	Best
30	Pheasant's eye daffodils *Narcissus poeticus recurvus*	white/orange	40 cm	16"	5
25	Lily of the valley *Convallaria majalis*	white	15 cm	6"	5
1	Clematis *Clematis montana* 'Tetrarose'	pink	7 m	23'	5–6
1	Climbing rose *Rosa* 'Zéphirine Drouhin'	deep pink	3 m	10'	6–9
1	Cranesbill *Geranium wallichianum* 'Buxton's Variety'	blue	30 × 90 cm	1 × 3'	7–9
2	Cornish ferns *Polypodium vulgare* 'Cornubiense'	green	30 × 30 cm	1 × 1'	7–11
2	Hostas *Hosta* 'Thomas Hogg'	pale lilac	30 × 50 cm	12 × 20"	7
1	Fuchsia *Fuchsia* 'Chequerboard'	white/cerise	90 × 60 cm	3 × 2'	6–10

SITE
A shady border beneath the window to the side of the cottage door.

SCALE
4 m (13') wide (slightly longer than in Recipe 4) and 90 cm (3') deep. *See also* Recipes 4 and 5.

PLAN
Left: Plant the rose at the back, half the daffodils in the middle and the cranesbill at the front.
Beneath the window: Plant one Cornish fern and the fuchsia at the back, with the two hostas and the lily of the valley in front.
Right: Plant the clematis at the back, with the rest of the daffodils and the second fern in front.

WHEN TO PLANT
Plant the fuchsia at the end of May or in June – add a sprinkling of bonemeal. In September or October, plant the daffodils 15 cm (6") deep, 15 cm (6") apart, and the lily of the valley, with pointed crowns upwards, just below the surface of the soil, five to each group. Plant the bare-rooted rose and the rest of the ingredients from October to March.

AFTERCARE
The daffodils are late flowering. Let them die down naturally. The lily of the valley need a moist soil, so top dress them with leaf mould or compost in early autumn, otherwise leave them undisturbed. If they have spread too far, dig some up to be forced indoors or introduce them elsewhere in the garden. The clematis needs support. Put some wires up the wall around the window. After a few years you may want to restrict the growth, so prune it back immediately after the May flowering, as the new growth made in the summer will produce next year's flowers. In any case, be sure to keep it away from the rose. An annual mulch of well-rotted manure or compost is beneficial. Clematis like an alkaline soil, so add lime if necessary.

The rose needs support. Because it is thornless, it is easy to tie in each year. No pruning should be necessary in the first two years; thereafter prune it in late February. Remove any diseased or dead wood, and cut away any twiggy growth. Eventually you may want to cut back some of the older main growth to encourage new shoots. Mulch annually with decayed manure or compost and apply a good rose fertiliser in March and again in late June. Spray against blackspot and greenfly. Do not allow the rose to dry out in summer, especially in the first year of planting.

The cranesbill, ferns and hostas do not need special attention. The fuchsia is hardy, but give it a thick mulch at the end of October and protect it with sacking in severe weather. Cut the stems down to within 15 cm (6") of the ground in March.

rose				clematis
daffodils	hostas	fern	fuchsia	daffodils
cranesbill		lily of the valley		fern

DESCRIPTION

The cottage window creates a focal point in May, when it is framed by the two scented clumps of old-fashioned pheasant's eye daffodils which lie on each side. This is one of the last daffodils to flower, but its glistening white petals and frilly orange cups make it fully worth the wait. Right beneath the window, the lily of the valley emerge. Their unmistakable fragrance makes them one of the true cottage favourites. Just a few sprays of the pure white bells will perfume any room. High above the window, the 'Tetrarose' clematis creates a dainty pink cloud, smothering the cottage wall. Fortunately, it is not as rampant as some of its relatives, though it is just as pretty and welcome.

By June, the scene is transformed by the old-fashioned thornless rose, 'Zéphirine Drouhin'. Its deep pink flowers are all heavily scented and provide a wonderful spectacle from June to September. Down below, the glorious dome of a spode-blue cranesbill called 'Buxton's Variety' emerges, creating a blaze of intense colour throughout July and well into the autumn. The combination of pink and blue is particularly striking.

Further to the right, just beneath the window, is a group of interesting shapes produced by ferns and hostas. The crinkly edges of the evergreen Cornish ferns are a sharp contrast to the smoother line of the hostas with their creamy-white-edged leaves. Like most other hostas, 'Thomas Hogg' produces tall pale lilac flowers. The hostas make an excellent association with the fern and with their other neighbours. Earlier in the season they made a memorable bedfellow with the lily of the valley: their leaves are a similar shape, and as the two plants interweave, the creamy-white margins of the hosta leaves act like a variegated form of the lily of the valley. In so doing, they highlight the lily of the valley flowers.

Later in the summer, the same hosta presents a lively combination with the hardy fuchsia 'Chequerboard', renowned for its dainty white sepals and cerise skirt. Fuchsias are one of the best late summer plants in the cottage garden; they become taller and more elegant as the season progresses. This one is a great specimen; its warm colours make it a valuable plant for the narrow border. It does not matter if it grows as high as the windowsill, or trails over part of the path: the bigger it grows, the better the effect.

7 Cottage Tulips, Spurge and Granny's Bonnets

INGREDIENTS

No req	Name	Description	Ht × Spr (cm/m)	Ht × Spr ("/')	Best
20	Cottage tulips *Tulipa* 'Halcro'	red	75 cm	30″	5
1	Spurge *Euphorbia characias*	lime-green	1.2 × 1 m	4 × 3¼′	4–5
2	Golden feverfew *Tanacetum parthenium* 'Aureum'	white	30 × 30 cm	1 × 1′	6–7, or 7–9
2	Granny's bonnets *Aquilegia vulgaris* 'McKana Hybrids'	mixed	75 × 45 cm	30 × 18″	5–6
1	Peony *Paeonia lactiflora* 'Pink Delight'	pink	70 × 60 cm	28 × 24″	6
2	Lady's mantle *Alchemilla mollis*	lime-green	30 × 30 cm	1 × 1′	6–7, 9
1	Sea holly *Eryngium alpinum* 'Superbum'	blue-green	75 × 45 cm	30 × 18″	6–8
1	*Aster *Aster × frikartii* 'Mönch'	lavender-blue	90 × 40 cm	36 × 16″	7–10
1	Hollyhock *Althaea rugosa*	pale yellow	150 × 60 cm	5 × 2′	7–9

SITE

A sunny border.

SCALE

2 m (6½′) wide and 1.2 m (4′) deep. If the border is backed by a fence or low wall with a climbing pink or white rose and clematis, allow slightly more depth. *See also* Recipes 8 and 9.

PLAN

Back: Plant the spurge on the left, the aster in the middle and the hollyhock on the right.
Middle: Plant a broad band of tulips.
Front: Plant the peony on the left, the granny's bonnets in the middle, and the sea holly on the right, with feverfew and lady's mantle mixed in between.

WHEN TO PLANT

In October or November plant the tulips 15 cm (6″) deep, 15 cm (6″) apart. Plant all the herbaceous plants from October to March. Small spurge plants transplant best. Mix extra manure or compost beneath the peony, and plant the crowns just 3 cm (1¼″) deep. Then mix bonemeal around the surface area; use 100 g per 0.8 m² (4 oz per sq yd).

AFTERCARE

Apply a general rose fertiliser to the border in early spring and mulch while the ground is damp. Remove tulip petals as they fade. Allow leaves to die down naturally, then remove them. Support the peony at the end of April, and water it in dry spells. Deadhead the flowers. Cut foliage down in October. If the site is exposed, support the hollyhock in early summer. Cut faded flower stems of the spurge, feverfew, granny's bonnets, sea holly and hollyhock to ground-level after flowering. Otherwise, allow the granny's bonnets and feverfew to self-seed. Excess seedlings can be removed.

The feverfew may be prevented from flowering until later in the summer by regular trimming. Cut back the lady's mantle after flowering to encourage a second flush later. The aster should be cut down in late October.

spurge

                                              hollyhock

tulips & granny's bonnets

                                                                               rose

peony   *lady's mantle*   *golden feverfew*   *lady's mantle*   *sea holly*

DESCRIPTION

The border looks wonderful in May with its broad sweep of cheery tulips backed by the lime-green inflorescences of spurge. 'Halcro' is typical of the old cottage tulips, with its large oval flowers carried on long sturdy stems. Its brilliant red colour creates a bold statement, as do the large heads of the spurge just behind. This particular spurge makes a handsome winter plant whose glory lasts until early summer. It hangs its heads in early spring but with the warmer days it gradually straightens up to reveal masses of lime-green flowers, each with a distinctive dark brown centre. The spurge flowers from April to May, providing a solid mass at the back of the border. The feverfew's yellow leaves look extremely lively in front of the tulips. Beside them, the granny's bonnets are putting on a charming display: their tall spurred flowers combine a whole spectrum of rich colours from yellow to crimson and violet to orange. They are so elegant. Their blue-grey foliage is very dainty and remains attractive for the whole summer.

Meanwhile, the peony has been growing fast. Its young shoots are bronze at first, but turn green as the leaves mature. They provide a strong green background for the delicate colouring of the flowers. 'Pink Delight' is scented and extremely beautiful with its open cup-shaped blooms. Pale pink petals surround bold yellow stamens to make a simple yet delightful picture. By June the feverfew are bursting to bloom: their white daisy-like heads form great mounds. They always blend happily into the scene and provide interest for so much of the year. At the same time, the lime-green flowers of the lady's mantle spilling all over the path have a lovely softening effect. Both look charming beside the peony.

By strong contrast, the sea holly has steely blue thistle-like flowers and greeny-blue prickly foliage. It makes a distinctive display for many weeks from June to the end of August, gaining and retaining colour long before and after the flowers are in bloom. Further to the back of the border is the aster with its stout stems of lavender-blue flowers; on the other side, tall spires of hollyhock provide an evocative picture to last from July through to September. The single pale yellow flowers add a lovely touch to the scene as autumn approaches. Regular trimming of the feverfew through the summer could mean that its flowering is delayed until the autumn. The combination of white, yellow and lime-green would be most attractive and welcome, particularly if the border is continued with Recipes 8 and 9. The rose from Recipe 8 can be seen on the far right.

8 'Mrs Perry' and Her Friends

INGREDIENTS

No req	Name	Description	Ht × Spr (cm/m)	Ht × Spr ("/')	Best
1	Oriental poppy *Papaver orientale* 'Mrs Perry'	salmon-pink	90 × 60 cm	3 × 2'	6
3	Flag irises *Iris pallida*	lavender-blue	90 × 30 cm	3 × 1'	5–6
2	Delphiniums *Delphinium* 'Blue Tit'	dark blue	120 × 60 cm	4 × 2'	6–7
1	Rose *Rosa* 'Yvonne Rabier'	double, white	90 × 60 cm	3 × 2'	6–9
2	Baby's breath *Gypsophila paniculata* 'Rosy Veil'	double, pale pink	30 × 45 cm	12 × 18"	6–9
1	Perennial pea *Lathyrus latifolius* 'Pink Pearl'	pink	2 m	6½'	6–9
2	*Asters *Aster* × *frikartii* 'Mönch'	lavender-blue	90 × 40 cm	36 × 16"	7–10
1	Fennel *Foeniculum vulgare*	yellow	180 × 60 cm	6 × 2'	8–9
20	*Daffodils *Narcissus* 'February Gold'	yellow	15 cm	6"	2–4

SITE
A sunny border.

SCALE
2 m (6½') wide and 1.2 m (4') deep. If the border is backed by a fence or low wall with a climbing pink or yellow rose and clematis, allow slightly more depth. *See also* Recipes 7 and 9.

PLAN
Back: Plant the delphiniums on the left with the fennel to the right.
Middle: Plant the perennial pea in front of the delphiniums, then the daffodils and asters.
Front: Plant the rose on the left, three irises in the centre, and the poppy to the right with one baby's breath in front on either side.

WHEN TO PLANT
Plant the irises in early September with part of the rhizome lying just above the surface of the soil. Cut the leaves back by half to reduce transpiration and to prevent wind rock. Plant the daffodils 10 cm (4") deep and 10 cm (4") apart in September or early October. Plant the poppy in October or March to April. Plant the bare-rooted rose and the rest of the ingredients from October to March. Give the baby's breath extra lime if the soil is acidic.

AFTERCARE
In March apply a general rose fertiliser all round the border, then mulch with decayed manure or compost while the ground is still damp. Lightly trim the rose in late February. Remove dead or diseased growth. Feed it again at the end of June. Spray to guard against blackspot and greenfly. Do not allow the rose to dry out in summer, especially in the first year after planting.

Watch for slugs on the delphiniums from late winter onwards. Stake the plants in April. After flowering, cut the flower spikes back to the first healthy leaf. Divide and replant the delphiniums every three years in March or April. Deadhead the irises and fennel. Stake the poppy in early summer. Use sticks to support the asters and baby's breath. Encourage the perennial pea to climb over the delphiniums, not the rose. Cut the stems of the delphiniums, asters, fennel, perennial pea, poppy and baby's breath to ground-level in autumn. Let the daffodils die down naturally.

hollyhock   delphiniums   fennel
sea holly   perennial pea   poppy
rose   irises   baby's breath

DESCRIPTION

The poppy makes a wonderful show in June with its pretty green foliage and pale salmon-pink flowers. 'Mrs Perry' is an old favourite. The petals have a translucent quality and are particularly beautiful when seen with the sun striking them. Each petal has a black blotch at its base. As they drop, the seed capsules are fully revealed in all their intricacy. These may be cut and dried for winter use indoors. To the left, the scented flag irises are in bloom, with their silky lavender-blue flowers and tall thrusting leaves. By June, the 'Blue Tit' delphiniums are just beginning to show colour. From the end of June to the middle of July, they will be a glorious spectacle. The tall spikes of lovely dark blue flowers will completely dominate the back of the border. Beside them on the left, the hollyhock and the sea holly from Recipe 7 are also in bloom.

At the front of the border, the old-fashioned rose 'Yvonne Rabier' will soon make a delightful display with its shiny foliage and clusters of small double white flowers, each with a hint of lemon in the bud. It blooms continuously from late June to September; the flowers have a strong spicy fragrance which is at its best in the autumn. In July and August the baby's breath is in full array with its pink cloud of tiny flowers. Trained over the poppy patch, they help to fill the late summer gap. What a lovely contrast they make to the sword-like iris leaves which remain in the centre of the border.

The perennial pea begins to bloom as it scrambles up through the delphinium foliage. 'Pink Pearl' is the most beautiful soft pink, and by late July it is smothered with flowers. It is a show which lasts for many weeks. The asters are also in bloom by July. They have lovely tall lavender-blue flowers which continue to appear until October.

By early August the fennel has become a towering mass of thread-like leaves topped with tiny yellow flowers. The faint smell of aniseed is in the air and insects are in abundance.

All winter long the border lies at rest until the yellow 'February Gold' daffodils bring it to life again at the end of February. This is one of the best of the smaller daffodils, as it is both sturdy and long-lasting. It will probably still be in flower in early April.

9 The Charming 'Comte de Chambord'

No req	Name	Description	Ht × Spr (cm/m)	Ht × Spr ("/')	Best
1	Rose *Rosa* 'Comte de Chambord'	pink	90 × 60 cm	3 × 2'	6–9
2	Catmint *Nepeta* × *faassenii*	lavender-blue	45 × 45 cm	18 × 18"	6, 9
1	Caryopteris *Caryopteris* × *clandonensis* 'Heavenly Blue'	blue	90 × 90 cm	3 × 3'	8–9
2	Asters *Aster* × *frikartii* 'Mönch'	lavender-blue	90 × 40 cm	36 × 16"	7–10
3	Crocosmias *Crocosmia* 'Emily MacKenzie'	orange	70 cm	28"	8–9
2	Hollyhocks *Althaea rugosa*	pale yellow	150 × 60 cm	5 × 2'	7–9
20	*Tulips *Tulipa* 'Halcro'	red	75 cm	30"	5
1	*Lupin *Lupinus* 'Tom Reeves'	yellow	75 × 75 cm	30 × 30"	6
2	Lady's mantle *Alchemilla mollis*	lime-green	30 × 30 cm	1 × 1'	6–7, 9

SITE
A sunny border.

SCALE
2 m (6½') wide and 1.2 m (4') deep. If the border is backed by a fence or low wall with a climbing pink or yellow rose and clematis, allow more depth. *See also* Recipes 7 and 8.

PLAN
Back: Plant the lupin to the left with the hollyhocks to the right.
Middle: Plant the caryopteris on the left, the tulips in the middle and the rose with an aster on either side to the right.
Front: Plant the lady's mantle on the left, with the crocosmias in the middle and the catmint on the right.

WHEN TO PLANT
Plant the caryopteris from September to October or from March to April. Plant all the herbaceous plants from October to March. Plant the tulips in October or November 15 cm (6") deep and 15 cm (6") apart. Plant the rose in November or December, or any time up to March. Plant the crocosmias in spring, 8 cm (3") deep and 15 cm (6") apart.

AFTERCARE
In March apply a general rose fertiliser all round the border, except near the lupin, which will thrive better on a poor diet. Then mulch with decayed manure or compost when the ground is still damp. Prune the rose lightly in late February. Remove any dead or diseased growth. Feed it again at the end of June. Spray against blackspot and greenfly. Do not allow the rose to dry out in summer, especially in the first year after planting.

Prune the caryopteris in March. Remove all weak growth, and cut strong woody stems back to healthy young buds. Protect the plants in very severe weather if the border is not sheltered. The asters should be cut down in late October. Cut the crocosmia leaves to ground-level in the spring just before new growth starts. If the hollyhocks are exposed, stake them in early summer; cut down the flower stems after flowering. Treat them as perennials, but be prepared to replace the plants after three years. Purchase new seed, as it will not come reliably true from its seed here.

Remove the tulip petals and leaves as they die. Remove the lupin flower stems as they fade to prevent self-seeding. The lupin might flower again in late summer. Cut down all growth in November. Cut back the catmint and lady's mantle after flowering to encourage a second flush later.

fennel

          caryopteris

baby's breath   *lady's mantle*

crocosmias

hollyhocks

    aster   *rose*   *aster*

    catmint

DESCRIPTION

The autumn picture is a delightful mixture of pale and deep pink roses, catmint, fluffy blue caryopteris, lavender-blue asters, vibrant orange crocosmias and tall yellow hollyhocks. There are so many contrasting colours and shapes of leaves and flowers that the effect is as exciting as it is unexpected.

The rose 'Comte de Chambord' with its old-fashioned cup-shaped flowers and grey-green foliage has been in bloom since midsummer. The perfume is outstanding. At its feet, the catmint is performing for the second time, producing a welcome carpet of lavender-blue flowers. On either side of the rose, the asters are in bloom. They are one of the best perennials, refined and elegant, and colourful for months. They forge a strong link with the other parts of the sunny border. To the left, the soft blue heads of the caryopteris are breaking out, creating a wonderful dome of growth to complement the rose. It is one of the prettiest blues imaginable. These leaves, too, are grey-green. Further to the left, the fennel and the baby's breath from Recipe 8 connect the two planting schemes.

The late flowering crocosmias are in bloom, creating a fiery autumn glow right at the heart of the border. Their leaves are green and tapering, in stark contrast to the other plants. The flowers are rich and exciting with orange petals around a crimson throat. Behind them, tall yellow hollyhocks wave in the breeze; they have been in bloom throughout the summer and are now reaching the upper end of their flower spikes. They are so much a part of the cottage border, and are available in a wide range of colours. But of them all, this yellow seems one of the most resistant to rust, which otherwise can so often spoil the foliage. The lady's mantle on the left is in its second flowering.

Spring brings the brilliant red tulips, enhanced by the new growth on the lupin with its deeply divided leaves. In June 'Tom Reeves' has tall yellow flower spikes which will form a sumptuous display. Whatever the colour – and there are many to choose from – the effect will be wonderful. At the front of the border, the frothy flowers of the lady's mantle spill out over the path. The old-fashioned rose is about to bloom, surrounded by the blue catmint and asters. It is a beautiful summer scene buzzing with insects and deliciously scented.

10 Delightful Daphne

INGREDIENTS

No req	Name	Description	Ht × Spr (cm/m)	Ht × Spr ("/')	Best
30	Snowdrops *Galanthus nivalis* 'Flore Pleno'	double, white	10 cm	4″	2–3
1	Christmas rose *Helleborus niger*	white	30 × 30 cm	1 × 1′	1–3
1	Elephant's ears *Bergenia stracheyi* 'Silberlicht'	white	30 × 45 cm	12 × 18″	4
1	Winter-flowering daphne *Daphne mezereum*	pink	150 × 90 cm	5 × 3′	2–3
20	Anemones *Anemone blanda*	mixed	10 cm	4″	2–4
2	*Honesty *Lunaria annua* 'Alba'	white	75 × 30 cm	30 × 12″	4–5
4	*Granny's bonnets *Aquilegia vulgaris*	mixed	45 × 30 cm	18 × 12″	5–6
2	*Cranesbills *Geranium clarkei* 'Kashmir White'	white	30 × 30 cm	1 × 1′	6–9
2	*Japanese anemone *Anemone hupehensis* 'September Charm'	pink	75 × 45 cm	30 × 18″	8–9

SITE
A shady border.

SCALE
2 m (6½′) wide and 1.2 m (4′) deep. If the border is backed by a low wall or fence with honeysuckle or clematis trained over it, allow slightly more depth. *See also* Recipes 11 and 12.

PLAN
Back: Plant two honesty plants on the left, and the daphne to the right 50 cm (20″) away from back of border and underplanted with *Anemone blanda*.
Middle: Plant granny's bonnets to the left and right with cranesbills in the centre.
Front: Plant Japanese anemones and the snowdrops on the left, and the elephant's ears and the Christmas rose to the right.

WHEN TO PLANT
Plant the snowdrops in August or early September, or 'in the green' the following spring, 5 cm (2″) deep, 8 cm (3″) apart. Plant *Anemone blanda* in September or October, 3 cm (1¼″) deep, 8 cm (3″) apart. Plant the daphne in October or March to April. The rest of the ingredients should be planted from October to March.

AFTERCARE
Mulch the border in early spring with leaf mould or compost. The daphne may require winter protection in severe weather, particularly from cold east winds. Prune the straggly growths in March, then leave it alone. Give an extra mulch to the early spring *Anemone blanda* in autumn, otherwise leave them undisturbed.

Cut down the stems of the Japanese anemones in autumn. Leave the snowdrops and Christmas rose undisturbed. Remove dead flower spikes on the elephant's ears. The honesty and granny's bonnets will seed themselves all around the border. Remove unwanted seedlings or deadhead the flowers before the seeds mature. The honesty is biennial, so discard the old plants in either late autumn or late winter. If the cranesbills spread too rapidly, lift and divide them.

daphne

Anemone blanda

snowdrops   elephant's ears   Christmas rose

DESCRIPTION

Throughout the late winter and early spring the front of the border is very pretty, with graceful snowdrops on the one side and the beautiful white flowers of the Christmas rose on the other. In between, the great round leaves of the elephant's ears make a bold clump, like an anchor for the border, all through the year. But dominating the scene from February to March is the daphne with its brilliant show of pink blooms. It is an outstanding performance, matched by the most beautiful perfume. Underneath, there appears a low carpet of blue, mauve-pink and white anemones. The least bit of sun will transform them into wide open stars. They last for weeks.

Late spring and early summer is the time for the honesty to bloom. It grows very tall at the back of the border and produces a mass of fragrant white flowers. Just in front, the granny's bonnets appear: short spurred flowers in a whole range of blues, pinks and whites. Long after their flowers are over, their delicate foliage remains. What a delightful contrast to the bold outline of the elephant's ears with its rather stiff white flower spikes. The petals take on a tinge of pink with age and look very fine at the front of the border. From June to September the white cranesbills are in flower; they are attractive plants with deeply dissected leaves and delicate lilac veining to the blooms. They are not particularly showy, but they do perform continuously over a very long period.

By late summer, the honesty seedpods have turned from a green-purple to a translucent silver. They can be left to seed or picked for winter decorations indoors. The daphne is smothered in rich scarlet berries which are great favourites among the birds. One day the berries will be there, the next they will all have disappeared! By September, true to their name, the tall Japanese anemones are in full bloom. 'September Charm' has soft pink petals, with just a touch of salmon surrounding prominent yellow stamens. They make a lively and elegant group, bringing welcome colour and grace to the border throughout the early autumn.

11 Solomon's Seal, Bleeding Heart and Foxgloves

INGREDIENTS

No req	Name	Description	Ht × Spr (cm/m)	Ht × Spr ("/')	Best
2	Solomon's seal *Polygonatum × hybridum*	white	60 × 30 cm	2 × 1'	5–6
2	Lady's mantle *Alchemilla mollis*	lime-green	30 × 30 cm	1 × 1'	6–7, 9
1	Hosta *Hosta sieboldiana* 'Elegans'	lilac-white	75 × 60 cm	30 × 24"	7
1	Cranesbill *Geranium* 'Johnson's Blue'	lavender-blue	30 × 60 cm	1 × 2'	6–7
1	Bleeding heart *Dicentra spectabilis*	pink	60 × 45 cm	24 × 18"	4–6
4	Foxgloves *Digitalis purpurea*	purple, pink, white	90 × 45 cm	36 × 18"	6–7
6	*Primroses *Primula vulgaris*	pale yellow	15 × 20 cm	6 × 8"	3–4
20	*Tenby daffodils *Narcissus pseudonarcissus obvallaris*	yellow	25 cm	10"	3–4
20	*Spanish bluebells *Hyacinthoides hispanica*	pink	30 cm	1'	4–5

SITE
A shady border.

SCALE
2 m (6½') wide and 1.2 m (4') deep. If the border is backed by a low wall or fence with honeysuckle or clematis trained over it, allow slightly more depth. *See also* Recipes 10 and 12.

PLAN
Back: Plant the daffodils in two groups on the left and right, with foxgloves between and around them.
Middle, left to right: Plant Solomon's seal, three primroses, bluebells, three primroses, then the bleeding heart.
Front, left to right: Plant the two lady's mantle, the hosta, then the cranesbill.

WHEN TO PLANT
The daffodils should be planted 10 cm (4") deep and 10 cm (4") apart, and the bluebells 6 cm (2½") deep and 10 cm (4") apart, in September or early October.

The rest of the ingredients may be planted from October to March.

AFTERCARE
Apply a general rose fertiliser to the border in March. Then mulch it with leaf mould or compost while the ground is damp.

Bleeding heart needs shelter from strong winds in springtime. It does not like its roots disturbed, but it does enjoy plenty of moisture and additional liquid feed during the flowering period.

Bluebells will seed around the garden; deadhead them before the seeds are mature. The foxgloves, lady's mantle and primroses will also self-seed. If too many seedlings appear, simply transplant them elsewhere or discard. Deadhead the lady's mantle immediately after flowering to encourage a second flush in autumn. Solomon's seal may be attacked by sawfly larvae in spring. Control the larvae by spraying. Watch out for slugs on hosta leaves. Allow the daffodils to die down naturally. The cranesbill does not need special attention.

Solomon's seal
lady's mantle

foxgloves

hosta

bleeding heart
cranesbill

DESCRIPTION

By the middle of June, the border is bursting at the seams. Great wands of Solomon's seal stretch out towards the path. Each stem is topped with fly-away leaves, while groups of flowers dangle underneath. The flowers are small and white, tipped with green. It is an elegant arrangement. Below, the frothy lime-green flowers of the lady's mantle make a very pretty display as they tumble forwards and sideways. They are always welcome in the cottage garden. Just to the right, is bold *Hosta sieboldiana* 'Elegans'. Its sumptuous leaves are round, blue-grey and heavily puckered. What a wonderful clump it makes, here at the heart of the border. 'Johnson's Blue', one of the best-loved cranesbills, makes a beautiful mound to the right. It has a long succession of bright lavender-blue flowers which rise up high above the heavily divided foliage.

Stretching behind the cranesbill are the tall stems of bleeding heart with their exquisite pink flowers. Every bud is shaped like a heart, an intricate configuration which opens to reveal a white centre. They

will bloom from April through to May and June, growing taller and taller as the season advances. By June, the foxgloves begin to flower. They are such elegant yet homely plants and look so natural in the cottage garden. Here they appear in a whole range of colours, from purple to pink to white. Their tall stems make a marvellous backcloth to the border and will provide colour until the end of July. By then, dense lilac-white flowers will have appeared on the hosta, and by late summer or early autumn the lady's mantle will have concluded its second flowering.

After that, the border must lie in wait for the spring flowers. First the wild primroses bloom beside the path, and then the Tenby daffodils with their golden trumpets make a lovely display at the back of the border. This is a native daffodil, not too large yet rich in colour. After they fade it is the pink Spanish bluebells' turn. They make a lovely clump right in the centre of the border. Already the Solomon's seal is growing fast and soon the summer show will begin again.

12   The Green and White Fuchsia Border

INGREDIENTS

No req	Name	Description	Ht × Spr (cm/m)	Ht × Spr ("/')	Best
1	Fuchsia *Fuchsia* 'Hawkshead'	white	100 × 90 cm	3¼ × 3'	6–10
1	Hosta *Hosta* 'Thomas Hogg'	pale lilac	30 × 50 cm	12 × 20"	7
2	Japanese anemones *Anemone × hybrida* 'Honorine Jobert'	white	150 × 60 cm	5 × 2'	7–9
20	*Winter aconites *Eranthis hyemalis*	yellow	8 cm	3"	2–3
3	*Violets *Viola odorata*	white	8 × 25 cm	3 × 10"	2–4
2	*Hepaticas *Hepatica nobilis*	blue	10 × 25 cm	4 × 10"	2–4
1	Soldiers and sailors *Pulmonaria officinalis*	pink/blue	25 × 45 cm	10 × 18"	3–5
1	London pride *Saxifraga × urbium*	pink	30 × 30 cm	1 × 1'	5
3	Granny's pin cushions *Astrantia maxima*	pink	60 × 45 cm	24 × 18"	6–7

SITE
A shady border.

SCALE
2 m (6½') wide and 1.2 m (4') deep. If the border is backed by a low wall or fence with honeysuckle or clematis trained over it, allow slightly more depth. *See also* Recipes 11 and 12.

PLAN
Back, left to right: Plant one granny's pin cushion and the Japanese anemones with aconites in between.
Middle: Plant the fuchsia 45 cm (18") from the front on the left with violets underneath at the sides and back, and two granny's pin cushions to the right.
Front, left to right: Plant the hepaticas and London pride near the path underneath the fuchsia, then the hosta and soldiers and sailors.

WHEN TO PLANT
Plant the winter aconites 3 cm (1¼") deep and 8 cm (3") apart as soon as they are available in August or early September. Soak them overnight before planting them. Apart from the fuchsia, the rest of the plants may be planted from October to March. Plant the fuchsia in June, with a sprinkling of bonemeal, so that it will have a chance to establish itself before the winter.

AFTERCARE
Mulch the border in early spring with leaf mould or compost. Apply a general rose fertiliser feed in March. Cut the Japanese anemone and granny's pin cushion stems down to ground-level after flowering.

Water the fuchsia in very dry weather during the summer. Although it is a hardy plant, protect it during severe winter weather with sacking or a thick layer of bracken. Cut the stems down to within 15 cm (6") of ground-level in March. Protect the hosta leaves from hungry slugs. Deadhead it after flowering. The rest of the plants should be left undisturbed, but keep them tidy.

granny's pin cushion

Japanese anemones

granny's pin cushions

fuchsia

London pride

hosta

soldiers and sailors

DESCRIPTION

The hardy fuchsia gives a fine display from June until October. 'Hawkshead' makes an upright bush, and in a season will grow up to 1 m (3¼'). The leaves are quite dark but the flowers are white: they are small and narrow, and each petal is tipped with green. It is a beautiful combination and goes particularly well with the hosta 'Thomas Hogg' by its side. The hosta leaves are smooth, pointed and dark green with a creamy-white edge, and it is this which strengthens the happy association with the fuchsia. The hosta leaves make an attractive mound below the tall spires of pale lilac flowers which grow through them in July. To the far right, the Japanese anemones are in bloom. 'Honorine Jobert' dates back to 1858, yet she is still a great favourite, with her pure white petals and dark green leaves. She will flower gracefully for three whole months, from July right through to September.

In February, the back of the border comes to life with pretty yellow aconites. They are so welcome after the gloom of winter. A carpet of white violets begins to flower under the fuchsia; their tiny faces are sweetly scented. Near the path, the hepaticas are covered with starry blue flowers. Once upon a time, they were a common feature in all the old cottage gardens. The soldiers and sailors are in flower by February or March, and make an unusual combination of blue and pink. They produce a mass of blooms which look so pretty above their spotty leaves.

By May, the dark green rosettes of London pride which line the path become a mass of dainty pink flowers. It is an undemanding little plant, yet so effective as an edging. It will spread as far as you allow, but it is easy to stop. By June and July the granny's pin cushions reveal their pinkish star-like heads and collars of rose-pink. The leaves are bright green. They create a soft background for the young fuchsia and the clean-cut lines of the hosta.

13   A Clipped Evergreen Hedge

INGREDIENTS

No req	Name	Description	Planting Distance (cm)	Planting Distance (")	Height of young plants (cm)	Height of young plants (")
2	Ivies *Hedera hibernica*	black berries	30 cm	12"	45 cm	18"
4	Yews *Taxus baccata*	red berries	45 cm	18"	45 cm	18"
4	Hollies *Ilex aquifolium* 'Argenteo-marginata'	red berries	45 cm	18"	45 cm	18"
6	Box *Buxus sempervirens* 'Pyramidalis'	green	30 cm	12"	38 cm	15"

SITE
Sun or shade; this recipe is ideal for a front garden hedge, especially where the space between the house and road is limited. It can be grown over a low wall as here, but the wall is not necessary. In a sunny position, a golden variegated ivy and a golden variegated holly may be used.

SCALE
3.3 m (11') wide and 75 cm (30") deep on either side of the gate. This can be made larger by repeating the pattern. The hedge can be kept at 1 m (3¼') or allowed to grow to 2 m (6½') high; the depth can be controlled as well. It depends very much on individual circumstances.

PLAN
On either side of the gate, plant an ivy followed by two yews, two hollies and three box.

WHEN TO PLANT
Dig the trench deeply and prepare well. Add plenty of humus. An October or April planting would suit all four specimens. The holly would prefer the latter.

AFTERCARE
Keep the plants weed-free and be prepared to water them during dry spells for at least the first two years. The ivies need support, so erect a metal or wooden frame over the front gate. They will only flower and berry when the stems have reached the top of the support and the adult berry-producing growth has established itself. This will take several years to achieve, so patience is needed. Cut it back close to the support during February or March each year, but don't trim the top growth if berries are wanted.

The yews, hollies and box will all benefit from pruning before they reach the required height. Young yews especially should have their leading shoots pinched out to encourage a more bushy growth. Thereafter, trim to the required shape each July or August. Berries will only form on the previous year's growth on female bushes; inevitably most will disappear because of pruning. The hollies and box should be pruned in July each year. Fortunately the new holly leaves are not too spiky at this stage! As with the yews, some holly berries will be lost through pruning, but they will be in evidence even now, so try to leave just a few in order to give the hedge a festive look later.

Remember that any of these bushes can be made into topiary. Simple shapes, such as pyramids and balls, were often used, as well as more imaginative designs of animals and birds.

DESCRIPTION
The evergreen hedge in the middle of winter is carefully clipped. It produces a great range of foliage shapes and colourings. The spreading ivy leaf contrasts with the very thin leaves of the yew, the crinkly shape of the holly with its silver edge and the small round leaf of the box.

There is much more besides. With judicious pruning, the holly will have berries on it, rich shiny red ones nestling in amongst the foliage. They are so evocative of the cottage scene at this time of year. Fortunately, the birds will take longer to eat the ones

box   hollies   yews   ivy   ivy   yews   hollies   box

here beside the road than those on fully grown trees in the garden, but by the new year even these will disappear. The yews also produce red fruits, but they are a pinkier red and fleshy. Perhaps a few will survive the summer pruning – each one a bonus to add cheer to the dark green leaves. The ivy, too, will eventually produce proud clusters of berries: green and black ones at the top of the arch.

Although the hedge is entirely evergreen, it still has its seasons. Early summer brings fresh growth, transforming it. The young ivy leaves have a lustrous shine, which gives the arch a brand new look after the dreary months of late winter. The young holly leaves are all soft and pink – a lovely contrast to the older prickly ones behind them. The yews and box become quite fuzzy with the new growth, and look fresh and clean.

By midsummer, it is time for the annual haircut. Then a tidy, trimmed hedge appears. Only the top of the ivy arch can be missed out so as not to remove the source of flowers and berries. There is great satisfaction in looking at a beautifully ordered hedge. Solid and neat, it will provide a lasting feature between the house and the road.

14   Boxing Birds

INGREDIENTS

No req	Name	Description	Ht × Spr (cm/m)	Ht × Spr ("/')	Best
2	Box *Buxus sempervirens* 'Pyramidalis'	green	100 × 60 cm	3¼ × 2'	all year
1	Autumn cherry *Prunus subhirtella* 'Autumnalis Rosea'	pink	7 × 8 m	23 × 26'	11–3
10	Cyclamen *Cyclamen coum*	pink	5 cm	2"	1–2
40	Snowdrops *Galanthus nivalis*	white	10 cm	4"	1–3
1	Winter-flowering daphne *Daphne mezereum*	pink	150 × 90 cm	5 × 3'	2–3
2	Elephant's ears *Bergenia* 'Eric Smith'	salmon-pink	45 × 45 cm	18 × 18"	4
2	*Day lilies *Hemerocallis lilio-asphodelus*	lemon-yellow	75 × 45 cm	30 × 18"	5–6
2	*Day lilies *Hemerocallis fulva* 'Kwanso Flore Pleno'	double, orange	90 × 90 cm	3 × 3'	6–8

SITE
A partially shaded area beside the front garden gate.

SCALE
1.5 m (5') wide and 60 cm (2') deep on either side of the gate with a grass verge in front.

PLAN
Border: Plant one box on either side of the gate, with an elephant's ears beyond, and then all the cyclamen to one side. Plant the autumn cherry to the left and daphne to the right; here they are planted on the house side of the wall.
Grass verge: Plant the snowdrops in front of both elephant's ears. Plant the orange day lilies in front of the box, and the yellow ones nearer the road.

WHEN TO PLANT
Plant the snowdrops 5 cm (2") deep and 8 cm (3") apart in late August or early September, or buy them in March when they can be transferred 'in the green'. In September, plant the cyclamen 2–3 cm (¾–1¼") deep, 10 cm (4") apart. Plant the rest of the ingredients in September or October.

AFTERCARE
Box grows surprisingly quickly. Purchase medium to large specimens with a good compact form, and within three or four years the topiary can begin. Clip it in August or September. Daphne tolerates sun or partial shade, but will thrive best in a sheltered spot away from cold winds. Provide additional shelter during extreme weather. Pruning is unnecessary. Stake the autumn cherry when it is first planted.

Allow the snowdrop leaves to die down naturally before cutting the grass verge in the early summer. The cyclamen and elephant's ears need no attention, but tidy up the dead leaves of the latter. Cut away dead flower stems on the day lilies after they have flowered and remove dead leaves in the autumn.

autumn cherry

cyclamen   elephant's ears   box
       snowdrops

             daphne

box   elephant's ears
       snowdrops

DESCRIPTION

Box can be clipped into all sorts of shapes from homely birds to friendly bears. Whatever the style, topiary looks good the whole year round and provides a splendid backcloth for the seasonal colour surrounding it. One of the daintiest sights in the winter garden is the autumn cherry with its delicate tracery of branches reaching over the gate. In any mild spells between November and March the buds open to reveal pink blossoms. Down below, little cyclamen and pure white snowdrops are perfect partners in this winter scene. The cyclamen are tiny but exquisite with their nodding pink heads and finely marked leaves. The snowdrops gradually grow taller as the days grow longer, becoming ever more graceful in the process.

Scent is vital in the cottage garden; in the middle of winter there is no better place for sweet perfumes than beside the path. It is little wonder that this

daphne was such a favourite. Through the late autumn and into the new year it looks stiff and starchy, its upright stems quite bare of leaves. But in February the swollen flower buds break and it becomes smothered with deep pink blossoms. It fills the air with a powerful and delicious scent.

Two unusual elephant's ears flank the topiaried box. Their bold, crinkly leaves colour well in winter, and in spring they produce spikes of deep salmon-pink flowers. The new leaves look distinctive all summer, but by then the main display is focused on the day lilies. They are old favourites in the cottage garden. Each flower opens for only a day, but there is a succession which continues for many weeks. First the *Lilio-asphodelus* bloom in May and June with their beautiful fragrance and lemon-coloured flowers, then from June to August the double orange kind from Japan show up particularly well against the dark green topiaried box.

15 The Lilac and Laburnum Hedge

INGREDIENTS

No req	Name	Description	Ht × Spr (cm/m)	Ht × Spr ("/')	Best
1	Lilac *Syringa vulgaris* 'Katherine Havemeyer'	double, purple	5 × 5 m	16½ × 16½'	5
1	Clematis *Clematis montana rubens*	pale pink	6 m	19½'	5–6
1	Laburnum *Laburnum anagyroides*	yellow	7 × 7 m	23 × 23'	5–6
8	Honesty *Lunaria annua*	purple	75 × 30 cm	30 × 12"	4–5
1	Fuchsia *Fuchsia* 'Mrs Popple'	crimson/ purple	90 × 90 cm	3 × 3'	6–10
8	*Foxgloves *Digitalis purpurea* 'Alba'	white	90 × 45 cm	36 × 18"	6–7
1	Clematis *Clematis viticella* 'Alba Luxurians'	white	3.5 m	11½'	7–9
1	Viburnum *Viburnum tinus* 'Eve Price'	pink/white	3 × 3 m	10 × 10'	11–4

SITE

A shady front garden fence or wall. In the illustration, this recipe is shown as a continuation of Recipe 14.

SCALE

4 m (13') on each side of the gate, with a narrow 45 cm (18") border on either side of the fence or wall.

PLAN

House side of the fence: Plant the *Clematis montana rubens* and the lilac to the left of the gate; plant the viburnum, laburnum and *Clematis viticella* to the right. Interplant with one honesty and one foxglove on each side.
Road side of the fence: Alternate three honesty and three foxgloves on both sides of the gate; plant the fuchsia to the right of the gate.

WHEN TO PLANT

October to March. Leave the fuchsia until the end of May or June, then plant it deeply. Add a sprinkling of bonemeal. The two clematis are vigorous and are best left until the lilac and laburnum are well established. Mix extra compost into their planting holes. Add lime if the soil is neutral or acidic.

AFTERCARE

Stake the lilac. Remove most of the first season's flower buds. Deadhead as much as possible thereafter. Prune any weak or crossing branches from October onwards. Remove suckers in July. Both clematis need an annual mulch at their roots to help maintain moisture during the spring and summer. Train the *Clematis montana rubens* up the fence and allow it to scramble towards the gate. If it is needed, prune the clematis soon after it flowers, so the new growth can mature to produce next season's flowers. Take care it does not overpower the lilac; or the cherry in Recipe 14.

Stake, but do not prune, the laburnum. Allow the honesty and foxgloves to seed themselves, but remove excess seedlings in the autumn. They may be discarded or introduced elsewhere. The fuchsia is hardy, but cover its base in extreme winter conditions with sacking or a thick layer of bracken. Cut the stems down to within 15 cm (6") of the ground in March and then mulch well. Prune the *Clematis viticella*, before the new growth begins in February or March, to within 60 cm (2') of ground-level. Each year train it up into the laburnum. Trim the viburnum immediately after flowering if it outgrows its space.

DESCRIPTION

Despite its shady position, this scene is wonderfully bright and deliciously fragrant, particularly in the middle of May when the old-fashioned lilac is in full bloom, filling the air with its strong perfume. The flowers begin as a deep lavender-purple and fade to a

lilac
Clematis montana rubens
honesty

viburnum   laburnum
Clematis viticella
fuchsia   honesty

lovely pink. An old-fashioned *Clematis montana rubens* stretches out along the railings. It blooms for weeks on end, its mass of pale pink, scented flowers set off against the bronze-green foliage. On the far side of the gate the laburnum is just coming into its main flowering season. Its long yellow racemes form a cascade of colour which quite eclipse all else. It likes sun, but performs well even in a shady spot. Dotted beneath its feet, and along the fence, is a generous planting of purple honesty.

By June the fuchsia is beginning its long flowering season, which will last well into October and even November, if the season is kind. 'Mrs Popple' is a great favourite for her rounded display of crimson and purple flowers. White foxgloves play their part,

adding greatly to the informality of this front cottage border. They are self-seeders like the honesty, and in time find their own spot to grow. Their tall spikes add another dimension to the picture: they are both bold and elegant. By the end of July, the white *Clematis viticella* is also in flower. It scrambles up the trunk of the laburnum tree, where its dainty heads can be enjoyed to the full.

The viburnum is the last to flower, but it is well worth the wait. From November to April it will produce a mass of pink buds. These slowly open to reveal white flowers, giving a two-toned effect which looks delightful against its dark green leaves. It looks charming with the autumn cherry, cyclamen, snowdrops, elephant's ears and daphne from Recipe 14.

16 Roses and Lavender

No req	Name	Description	Ht × Spr (cm/m)	Ht × Spr ("/')	Best
2	Climbing roses Rosa 'Crimson Shower'	crimson	5 m	16½"	7–9
6	Lavenders Lavandula angustifolia 'Royal Purple'	purple	80 × 80 cm	32 × 32"	7–8
20	Love-in-a-mist Nigella damascena 'Persian Jewels Mixed'	mixed	40 × 20 cm	16 × 8"	6–8
30	*Dutch crocuses Crocus vernus 'Jeanne D'Arc'	white	10 cm	4"	3–4
30	*Dutch crocuses Crocus vernus 'Purpureus Grandiflorus'	purple-blue	10 cm	4"	3–4
30	*Wild daffodils Narcissus pseudonarcissus lobularis	pale yellow	15 cm	6"	3–4
4	*Cowslips Primula veris	yellow	15 × 15 cm	6 × 6"	4–5
1	Clematis Clematis macropetala 'Markhamii'	rose-pink	2 m	6½'	5–6
6	Sweet rockets Hesperis matronalis	mixed	45 × 15 cm	18 × 6"	6–7

SITE
A sunny front garden gate with a grass verge in front.

SCALE
The rose arch is 2.1 m (7') high. A low wall extends about 2 m (6½') on each side with narrow 60-cm (2') borders to the front and back. The grass verge is 1 m (3¼') deep.

PLAN
Arch: Plant the roses at the feet of the arch, on the outside, with the clematis to the left on the shadier side of the wall.
Wall: Plant the lavenders on the house side, and the sweet rocket and love-in-a mist on the other.
Grass verge: Mix the crocuses and plant them to the left of the gate. Plant the daffodils on the right with cowslips beyond.

WHEN TO PLANT
Plant the bulbs in September or October at the latest; the crocuses should be 5 cm (2") deep and 5 cm (2") or more apart, and the daffodils 10 cm deep (4") and 15 cm (6") or more apart. Plant the bare-rooted roses, lavenders, cowslips, clematis and sweet rocket from October to March. In March sow love-in-a-mist where you want it to flower, but thin the plants out later so that they are 25 cm (10") apart. Sweet rocket can easily be grown from seed.

AFTERCARE
Give the borders a rose fertiliser in early spring, then mulch while the ground is still damp. Train the roses and clematis up the supports. Prune the roses in late February, removing anything that is weak or dead. Try to create a dense covering over the outside of the arch. Give the roses extra rose fertiliser at the end of June. In some circumstances, this rose is susceptible to mildew. Either spray it with Nimrod T in May and again at the end of June, or use either the red rose 'Etoile de Hollande' or the purple/lilac rose 'Reine des Violettes' as an alternative. Spray against blackspot and greenfly if necessary. Do not allow the roses to dry out in summer, especially in the first year after planting. Do not prune the clematis unless it threatens to strangle the roses.

Trim the lavender after flowering to within 5 cm (2") of hard wood so that it will retain neat growth. Love-in-a-mist will self-seed; if it does not, sow more seed each March. Before mowing the grass allow the crocuses to seed, so that a rich mixture of lilac, purple and white will appear in future years. Do not mow until six weeks after the daffodils have flowered; give the cowslip patch time to self-seed. Give a late cut in autumn, so that the grass will be short when the crocuses flower. Sweet rocket is a short-lived perennial: remove the old flower spikes, leaving a few to self-seed, or replace them with seedlings – sown in April – from the nursery bed.

lavenders   clematis   rose   rose   lavenders
love-in-a-mist & sweet rockets   love-in-a-mist & sweet rockets

DESCRIPTION

The front gate is festooned with trusses of crimson roses which create a warm welcome to the cottage garden. 'Crimson Shower' is at its best in July, just as the lavender hedge on either side comes to its full glory. A multitude of deep purple flower spikes fill the air with their wonderful perfume. Watch the butterflies and bees enjoying the sweet nectar. Cut a generous bunch to dry indoors, and enjoy the scent all winter.

Beneath the wall lies a sea of love-in-a-mist with its finely cut foliage and saucer-shaped flowers. It blooms for many weeks, providing a mixture of colours for the roses and lavender above. Even when the flowering is over, lots of lovely seed pods remain to add interest to the border. Use them in dried winter arrangements.

In March the soft grey-green hedge is brought to life by a carpet of purple and white Dutch crocuses in the verge below. On a sunny day, the bees will pay their respects and soon cross-pollination will ensure a whole spectrum of beautiful tints. On the other side of the gate the wild daffodils with their pale yellow trumpets are in flower. They look quite at home in the grass, not in bold clumps, but in ones and twos, so that each one can be fully appreciated. Further along, the cowslips are growing. Soon they will flower, their delicate yellow bells held high above the grass. They are much loved for their sweet scent. Given time, they will spread and create an impressive group.

Throughout May and June, the 'Markhamii' clematis is a mass of rose-pink blooms. Silky seedheads follow to hide amongst the shiny dark green foliage of the rose. By June the old-fashioned sweet rocket is in bloom with a mixture of purple, mauve and white flowers stretching up above the lavender hedge. They have a lovely fragrance in the evening. As the month progresses, the love-in-a-mist will come into flower, and the scene will be set for the main summer show.

17   The Hedge of Hips and Haws

INGREDIENTS

No req	Name	Flowers	Berries/ Fruit	Planting Distance (cm)	Planting Distance (")
1	Sweet briar *Rosa rubiginosa*	pink 6–7	orange hips 8–11	30 cm	12"
1	Dogwood *Cornus sanguinea*	white 6–7	black fruit 9–11	30 cm	12"
2	Hawthorns *Crataegus monogyna*	white 5–6	red haws 8–11	30 cm	12"
2	Hollies *Ilex aquifolium* 'Argenteo-marginata'	white 4–5	red berries 9–12	45 cm	18"
1	Guelder rose *Viburnum opulus* 'Notcutt's Variety'	white 5	scarlet fruit 8–10	30 cm	12"
1	Hazel *Corylus avellana*	yellow catkins 2	nuts 9–10	30 cm	12"
1	Snowberry *Symphoricarpos albus* 'White Hedger'	pink 7–9	white berries 9–2	45 cm	18"
1	Dog rose *Rosa canina*	pink 6–7	scarlet hips 8–11	30 cm	12"

SITE
In sun or partial shade.

SCALE
3.5 m (11½′) wide and 1 m (3¼′) deep. This scale is very flexible, so reduce or expand it as necessary.

PLAN
Left to right: Plant the sweet briar, dogwood, hawthorns, hollies, guelder rose, hazel, snowberry and dog rose.

WHEN TO PLANT
October to March.

AFTERCARE
Keep the area of the hedge entirely weed-free, otherwise the weeds will soon smother the young hedging plants. Water the hedge thoroughly in spring and summer, especially during dry spells. A thick mulch of grass cuttings or leaf mould will help to keep the weeds down and reduce moisture loss. No feeding is required if the ground was well prepared with compost and well-decayed manure before planting.

In the first few years, light pruning of the young plants is necessary to establish bushy growth near the bottom of the hedge. Then the hedge can be pruned to shape and fully enjoyed for its hips, fruits and catkins. The annual pruning is best done in March.

sweet briar   hawthorns   guelder rose   snowberry

dogwood   hollies   hazel   dog rose

DESCRIPTION

The hedging plants have been particularly chosen for their rich variety of fruit and berries. At the far end of the hedge, sprays of orange hips from the sweet briar mingle with the fiery leaves and black berries on the dogwood. Further along, deep red haws are displayed on the hawthorns, red berries nestle in the hollies, scarlet fruits dangle on the guelder rose, and clusters of nuts lie hidden in the hazel. At the near end, scarlet hips on the dog rose are magnificent beside the glistening white snowberries.

The autumn harvest is very attractive to wildlife. The hazel is known to support seventy insect species – not all on one small hedging specimen, of course; nevertheless this figure shows just how important some shrubs can be to wildlife. The hawthorn and holly are great favourites with birds, both for the food they give and for the nesting places they provide. The dog rose and sweet briar offer welcome nectar to insects, and the hips are very popular during the colder days of autumn. The snowberry has tiny clusters of pink flowers from July to September, which the holly blue butterfly enjoys. However, the white berries which follow don't seem to find favour with birds or animals, and remain on the bush well into the new year.

From the first catkin on the hazel to the last lingering snowberry, there will be interest and colour in this hedge throughout the year. The dogwood, hawthorns, and guelder rose all have attractive blossoms but none compares with the soft pink flowers on the sweet briar and dog rose. In June and July they both provide a glorious picture, as the graceful trails reach out to befriend the neighbouring plants. Delicate and evocative of the countryside at its best, they create the prettiest scene of all.

After the hedge has become established, other plants, such as wild honeysuckle, can be introduced, and wild flowers can join the bulbs which might be planted at its base (*see* Recipe 18).

18 Beneath the Cottage Hedge

No req	Name	Description	Ht × Spr (cm/m)	Ht × Spr ("/')	Best
4	Primroses *Primula vulgaris*	pale yellow	15 × 20 cm	6 × 8"	3–4
4	Violets *Viola odorata*	white, purple	8 × 25 cm	3 × 10"	2–4
20	Daffodils *Narcissus* 'Van Sion'	double, yellow	35 cm	14"	3–4
2	Periwinkles *Vinca minor* 'Aureo-variegata'	blue	8 × 90 cm	3 × 36"	3–5
20	Bluebells *Hyacinthoides non-scripta*	mixed	30 cm	1'	4–5
4	Honesty *Lunaria annua*	purple	75 × 30 cm	30 × 12"	4–5
4	*Foxgloves *Digitalis purpurea*	purple	90 × 45 cm	36 × 18"	6–7
1	*Honeysuckle *Lonicera periclymenum*	creamy yellow	5 m	16½'	6–9

SITE
In partial shade, under an established hedge.

SCALE
3.5 m (11½') wide and 1 m (3¼') deep. Leave a 30-cm (1') gap at the foot of the hedge before planting.

PLAN
Back, from left to right: Plant one honesty, half the bluebells, the honeysuckle (centre), more bluebells and another honesty.
Middle, from left to right: Plant two foxgloves, one periwinkle, two honesty (centre), the second periwinkle and two more foxgloves.
Front, from left to right: Plant half the daffodils to the left of the first periwinkle, then the primroses and violets (centre), with the rest of the daffodils to the right of the second periwinkle.

WHEN TO PLANT
Fork the soil as well as possible without disturbing the hedge roots. Try to incorporate some leaf mould into the planting area.

Plant the daffodils and bluebells in September or October; each bulb should be planted 10 cm (4") deep and 10 cm (4") apart. Plant the rest of the ingredients from October to March or as they become available in containers. The herbaceous plants may be introduced three or four years after the hedge is first planted, but the honeysuckle should be planted only when the hedge has reached its required height and is well established.

AFTERCARE
Give the plants a dressing of leaf mould in early spring. These plants need little attention. However, make sure that they do not get too dry, especially in spring and early summer. Keep the weeds out to reduce competition. Deadhead the bluebells to prevent seeding, if you want to restrict their spread elsewhere. Like daffodils, their bulbs will increase naturally over the years. The primroses, violets and periwinkle will spread and establish themselves well. The honesty and foxgloves are biennials and will seed themselves. The honeysuckle may be pruned after it flowers if it becomes overgrown or straggly.

honesty   bluebells   bluebells   honesty
periwinkle   *honesty*   *periwinkle*
daffodils   *violets & primroses*   *daffodils*

DESCRIPTION

In March and April a carpet of colour transforms the bottom of the hedge with familiar flowers and scents. Pale primroses show their pretty faces, and provide food for the early brimstone butterfly and the night moths. Beside them, tiny violets peek out, glistening white and purple faces crowding together to see the spring. Behind them, two groups of old-fashioned daffodils, the double yellow 'Van Sion' with their ruffled yellow trumpets, are in flower. Periwinkles send out their long trails with evergreen variegated leaves, which provide interest and ground cover the whole year round. Now, in spring, they produce lovely blue flowers over a period of many weeks. At the same time, new shoots appear which are often covered with ladybirds. From end to end, the bluebells are just coming into flower; they look like pink, blue and white fountains.

Honesty makes a striking display for many weeks. Its purple flowers grow tall under the hedge; their nectar is popular with butterflies and bees alike. Watch the papery seed pods form; a greenish purple to begin with, they turn silvery with age until at last you can rub the outer layer off and they become transparent. In the middle of winter they look lovely arranged against the cottage window.

In June, the foxgloves enjoy their season of triumph; their tall spires of purple speckled flowers look so attractive and fit into the hedgerow scene so well. It is here that the bumblebees call, wanting to inspect every little compartment with their long tongues; they start at the bottom and work upwards before flying on to the next plant. The wild honeysuckle is also in its full glory, as it scrambles along the hedge top with its mass of creamy yellow flowers. The perfume is truly wonderful, especially in the evening or after a shower of rain; it seems to last for weeks and weeks as new flowers unfold.

19   A Sunny Low Wall

INGREDIENTS

No req	Name	Description	Ht × Spr (cm/m)	Ht × Spr ("/')	Best
3	Aubrietas *Aubrieta deltoidea* 'Dr Mules'	violet-purple	15 × 45 cm	6 × 18"	4–6
2	Alyssum *Alyssum saxatile*	yellow	25 × 45 cm	10 × 18"	4–6
3	Houseleeks *Sempervivum tectorum*	pink	10 × 20 cm	4 × 8"	all year
1	Ivy *Hedera helix* 'Buttercup'	golden	1 × 1 m	3¼ × 3¼'	all year
30	*Dutch crocuses *Crocus vernus* 'Remembrance'	purple	10 cm	4"	3–4
30	Daffodils *Narcissus* 'King Alfred'	yellow	45 cm	18"	4
6	Flag irises *Iris pallida*	lavender-blue	90 × 30 cm	3 × 1'	5–6
3	Ice plants *Sedum spectabile* 'Autumn Joy'	pink	60 × 60 cm	2 × 2'	8–10

SITE
A sunny low wall with a narrow border at its base.

SCALE
Approximately 4 m (13') wide with a 60-cm (2') deep border in front.

PLAN
In pockets of soil along the top of the wall: Interplant aubrietas, houseleeks and alyssum, leaving 1 m (3¼') at the far end for the ivy to cover.
Border: Plant crocuses and daffodils in three broad groups towards the back of the border with the ivy at the far end. Leave space for the ivy to spread. Plant two groups of irises at either end of the border with three ice plants in between.

WHEN TO PLANT
Prepare the soil well, incorporating plenty of compost to help retain moisture. Add bonemeal at the rate of 100 g per 0.8 m² (4 oz per sq yd). In early September or October, plant the crocuses 5 cm (2") deep and 5 cm (2") apart, and the daffodils 10 cm (4") deep and 10 cm (4") apart. Plant the irises in early September. Part of the rhizomes should lie just above the surface of the soil, facing the direction from which they will receive maximum sunshine. Cut the leaves by half to reduce wind rock and to discourage slugs. Plant the aubrieta, alyssum, houseleeks, ivy and ice plants in the autumn or any time until the following March.

AFTERCARE
Deadhead the aubrieta, alyssum and irises. Remove the old core of the houseleeks after flowering, and replant the plantlets which will have developed all round. Prune the ivy in early March if growth is excessive. Allow the bulb foliage to die down naturally after flowering, then remove it when it turns yellow. Keep it away from the ice plants in front. Feed the irises with a low nitrogenous fertiliser each March; allow 100 g per 0.8 m² (4 oz per sq yd). The fertiliser will also be good for the daffodils. Remove the old flowering stems of ice plants in early spring. After a few years the irises will need dividing and replacing. Be ruthless with the excess rhizomes.

alyssum, aubrieta & houseleeks
daffodils

irises

ice plants

ivy
irises

DESCRIPTION

Aubrieta and alyssum go hand in hand on old cottage walls, and flower for weeks on end throughout the spring and early summer. They are never short of visitors, for the butterflies and bees love them both. The aubrieta 'Dr Mules' is deep violet-purple and contrasts well with the yellow alyssum by its side. In-between there are clumps of fleshy houseleeks. Their tight green rosettes redden in different seasons, and eventually they flower themselves to death. But that does not matter – they produce lots of babies to take their place!

The end of the wall is festooned in the 'Buttercup' ivy with bright yellow leaves. It creates a focal point all year round and revels in its sunny home. What a rich setting it made for the mass of purple crocuses which flowered along the base of the wall in March. Now, in April, the crocus leaves are hidden by the golden daffodils. 'King Alfred' is very robust. It is strong and tall with large yellow flowers, and has been well loved for over a hundred years.

By the time the daffodils are over, the irises will be growing fast. There are many to choose from, but the ancient blue flag iris, *Iris pallida*, remains a great favourite. The silky flowers are a clear lavender-blue and have a wonderful scent. They live quite contentedly alongside the daffodils, whose foliage dies down by the time the iris rhizomes want to bask in the sunshine. It is a happy arrangement that brings weeks of colour to the old wall.

The sword-shaped leaves of the irises retain their beauty all summer, and are joined in the later months by the fleshier, rounder leaves of the old ice plant. By August, the ice plants begin to flower. Their heads are green at first, but they slowly turn a rich pink as autumn approaches. They are broad and flat, and offer a sumptuous spread to the butterflies, who love to feed on the nectar. They can remain all winter, along with the colourful ivy and starry houseleeks, until, at last, spring brings colour to the wall again.

20 A Shady Low Wall

INGREDIENTS

No req	Name	Description	Ht × Spr (cm/m)	Ht × Spr ("/')	Best
1	Clematis *Clematis alpina* 'Ruby'	pink	2.5 m	8'	4–5
2	Comfrey *Symphytum × uplandicum* 'Variegatum'	lilac	30 × 60 cm	1 × 2'	4–5
3	Foam flowers *Tiarella cordifolia*	white	15 × 30 cm	6 × 12"	5–6
2	Cranesbills *Geranium macrorrhizum* 'Walter Ingwersen'	rose-pink	30 × 60 cm	1 × 2'	5–8
1	Soft shield fern *Polystichum setiferum* 'Acutilobum'	green	60 × 60 cm	2 × 2'	5–11
3	Bellflowers *Campanula poscharskyana*	lavender-blue	30 × 60 cm	1 × 2'	6–7
2	Ivy-leaved toadflax *Cymbalaria muralis*	pink	5 × 45 cm	2 × 18"	5–9
3	Biting stonecrop *Sedum acre* 'Aureum'	yellow	3 × 15 cm	1¼ × 6"	3–6

SITE
A low wall in partial shade, with a narrow border at its base.

SCALE
Approximately 4 m (13') wide with a 60-cm (2') deep border in front.

PLAN
In pockets on top of the wall: Alternate bellflowers, ivy-leaved toadflax and stonecrop, leaving 90 cm (3') at the end for the clematis to cover.
Border, left to right: Plant the fern, cranesbills, comfrey and foam flowers, with the clematis behind.

WHEN TO PLANT
Be sure to prepare the soil well, incorporating plenty of compost to help retain moisture. The foam flowers and comfrey will not thrive if the soil is too dry. Where the soil is neutral or acidic, the clematis and fern will benefit from extra lime. The foam flowers and comfrey should be planted from October to November or March to April; the fern should be planted in April. The rest of the ingredients can be planted from October to March.

AFTERCARE
Provide support for the clematis to clamber over the wall. Do not prune it. Mulch the border with compost or leaf mould each spring. The herbaceous plants should spread by themselves and form a dense carpet beneath the wall. If the foam flowers die back, fill in the gaps with young outside growths. The bellflowers, ivy-leaved toadflax and stonecrop multiply easily, so within a few years you should have growth tumbling all the way down the wall.

bellflowers, ivy-leaved toadflax & biting stonecrop

fern   cranesbills   comfrey   clematis
                                                               foam flowers

DESCRIPTION

The *Clematis alpina* makes a very delicate covering for a shady old wall where its pretty pink lanterns can be fully appreciated. It flowers profusely in April and May and then produces silky seedheads. At its feet a soft carpet of lilac, pink and white is coming to fruition. The variegated comfrey is in full raiment with its bright new leaves and drooping lilac bells. Like the clematis, it is at its best in April and May. Meanwhile, the foam flowers are just coming into season; their creamy white flower spikes are held well above mid-green leaves. They flower from May to June.

At the other end of the wall, the cranesbills make a lovely show with their clear pink flowers, which appear over a long period from May to August. Their leaves are aromatic when crushed, and turn from light green to bright russet in autumn. They are almost evergreen, while those of the foam flower are fully so. The soft shield fern is evergreen too. It takes pride of place to the left of the wall, where its graceful new fronds twist and turn in the most delightful manner.

They are upright and arching throughout the summer, though in mid-winter they lie prostrate.

The top of the wall is a mass of bright blue bellflowers for the whole summer. They spread into thick mats smothered in little bells which flower unabated in June and July and even later. It is one of the most common of all cottage garden plants, as it gives a fine display with no trouble at all, except perhaps that it can be rather too friendly. The ivy-leaved toadflax and biting stonecrop are persistent too. The toadflax produces tiny pink flowers like miniature snapdragons from May to September. It hugs the wall and sends its roots far into the crevices. The stonecrop is a long-suffering plant which is often seen hanging from the top or half-way down the side of old walls. Bright yellow star-like shoots emerge in spring and early summer which create a lovely fresh look to the wall. Small yellow flowers are produced later.

These three wall plants will colonise the wall from top to bottom. They look so natural and all are welcome.

21   The Wisteria Wall

No req	Name	Description	Ht × Spr (cm/m)	Ht × Spr (″/′)	Best
1	Japanese wisteria *Wisteria floribunda*	violet-blue	9 m	30′	5–6
1	Clematis *Clematis* 'General Sikorski'	blue	3 m	10′	6–7
1	Climbing rose *Rosa* 'Pink Perpétue'	deep pink	3.5 m	11½′	6–9
5	Garden pinks *Dianthus* 'Letitia Wyatt'	double, pink	30 × 30 cm	1 × 1′	5–9
2	Lavenders *Lavandula angustifolia* 'Royal Purple'	purple	80 × 80 cm	32 × 32″	7–8
6	*Guernsey lilies *Nerine bowdenii*	pink	60 cm	2′	9–11
20	*Grape hyacinths *Muscari armeniacum* 'Heavenly Blue'	blue	15 cm	6″	3–4
6	*Hyacinths *Hyacinthus orientalis* 'Lady Derby'	pink	20 cm	8″	4

SITE

The sunny high wall of a garden or house with a border underneath.

SCALE

The wall should be 3 m (10′) or more in height. The border underneath is approximately 4 m (13′) wide and 90 cm (3′) deep.

PLAN

Left: Plant the rose, then the clematis, with one lavender in front.

Centre left: Plant two garden pinks along the front of the border with the third behind to form a broad triangle. Plant an arc of ten grape hyacinths, three hyacinths and three Guernsey lilies around the pinks.

Centre right: Plant the wisteria with the second lavender in front.

Right: Plant two garden pinks along the front of the border, and repeat the planting scheme for the bulbs as on the centre left.

WHEN TO PLANT

Before planting, wire the wall at 50-cm (20″) intervals. Allow the rose to establish itself before the wisteria and the clematis are planted. Plant the garden pinks in October or March. Plant the Guernsey lilies as soon as they become available in August or April, 10 cm (4″) deep and 15 cm (6″) apart. Plant the hyacinths 10 cm (4″) deep, 10 cm (4″) apart and the grape hyacinths 6 cm (2½″) deep, 6 cm (2½″) apart from August to October. October to March will suit the wisteria, rose, clematis and lavenders.

AFTERCARE

Tie the wisteria and the rose to wire supports. Cut back the wisteria in February to within two buds of the base of the previous year's growth. Prune it again in July, removing the long vegetative growths to within five buds of its base. Be careful that the wisteria does not entangle itself around the rose; training and pruning will prevent this. Prune the rose in late February. Gradually build up a good open shape so that flowers appear all the way up.

In the second spring after planting, cut back all clematis shoots to within 25 cm (10″) of ground-level to promote bushy growth at a lower level. Thereafter, as buds start to swell in the spring, remove all weak and dead wood and tie in replacement shoots. Keep the clematis away from the rose.

Replace the pinks every three years. Take side-shoot cuttings in June or July to produce spare plants. Remove autumn debris to prevent rot. Trim the lavender after flowering to within 5 cm (2″) of the old wood. In early spring give the plants a general rose fertiliser and then mulch the rose, clematis and wisteria, but avoid the garden pinks. Feed the Guernsey lilies with bonemeal in May. In early July, give a liquid feed to the Guernsey lilies, the rose and the garden pinks. Allow the bulbs to die down naturally, then remove any dead leaves.

rose   *clematis*   *wisteria*
lavender   *garden pinks*   *lavender*   *garden pinks*

DESCRIPTION

The wall is dominated in May and June by the long violet-blue racemes of the Japanese wisteria. Fragrant and graceful, they cascade down the wall like a beautiful waterfall, naked at first, but then joined by a leafy background. It is a memorable sight. The bigger the wall, the larger the display can be, but height is not the only criterion: wisteria can be trained right round the cottage! A rich blue clematis called 'General Sikorski' takes on the colour theme as it climbs up the left side of the wall. He grows beside the 'Pink Perpétue' rose. The blue and pink flowers look stunning together. The rose is only slightly fragrant, but it repeats well, and its deep pink flowers are so beautifully formed that it is certainly a rose to treasure.

In the small border below are the garden pinks, with their soft pink flowers and delightful fragrance. They seem to bloom all summer, reaching out over the path and creating a lacy carpet around the base of the two lavenders. It is July before the lavenders begin to make their full impact. They love the warm dry spot at the foot of the wall and produce masses of slender purple spikes filled with lovely scent. Pick them as they first open and dry them indoors, where they will bring back happy memories of summer for the rest of the year.

As autumn approaches, the frilly pink flowers of the Guernsey lilies come into bloom. Their leaves appear later, but for now the silvery foliage of the garden pinks suffices and lends an air of softness to their base. They make a worthy display for several weeks and, even if the weather is poor, they can be cut and brought indoors, where they will last surprisingly well.

It is the end of March before there is colour again. The spring bulbs look lovely behind the grey foliage of the garden pinks. Lots of bright blue grape hyacinths appear with the old-fashioned pink hyacinths so well loved for their rich colour. They are very fragrant, as are so many of the other plants grouped together against the wall.

22   The Wall of Fire

INGREDIENTS

No req	Name	Description	Ht × Spr (cm/m)	Ht × Spr ("/')	Best
1	Virginia creeper *Parthenocissus quinquefolia*	crimson leaves	15 m	50′	10
1	Winter-flowering jasmine *Jasminum nudiflorum*	bright yellow	3 m	10′	11–3
1	Parsley ivy *Hedera helix* 'Manda's Crested'	crinkly leaves	2 m	6½′	10–3
4	Elephant's ears *Bergenia stracheyi* 'Silberlicht'	white	30 × 45 cm	12 × 18″	4
4	Cornish ferns *Polypodium vulgare* 'Cornubiense'	lacy green fronds	30 × 30 cm	1 × 1′	7–11
30	•Daffodils *Narcissus* 'Van Sion'	double, yellow	35 cm	14″	3–4
1	Climbing rose *Rosa* 'Zéphirine Drouhin'	deep pink	3 m	10′	6–9

SITE
This recipe is ideal for a shady north or east wall with a narrow border at its base.

SCALE
The wall should be 3 m (10′) or more high, with a border underneath approximately 4 m (13′) or more wide and 90 cm (3′) deep.

PLAN
Back, left to right: Plant the Virginia creeper, winter jasmine, rose and ivy.
Middle: Plant three groups of daffodils.
Front: Interplant the elephant's ears with ferns.

WHEN TO PLANT
Make sure plenty of well-rotted manure and compost has been added to the site before planting, as it is important to create a moisture-retentive soil. Wire the wall at 50 cm (20″) intervals to a height of 3 m (10′). Plant the daffodils in September or October, 10 cm (4″) deep, 10 cm (4″) apart. Plant the climbers and elephant's ears from November to December through to March. In April or May, plant the ferns very shallow, and anchor the rhizomes with bent wires or stones.

AFTERCARE
Give the border a general fertiliser in March and then mulch while the ground is damp. The Virginia creeper should have its new upward growth pinched out in the first year to encourage side shoots to form. It will need support to begin with. Keep it away from the rose and do not allow it to reach roof height. Cut back the new growth in midsummer so that it remains within bounds. It is more difficult to remove the mature clinging tendrils, so act while they are still young.

The climbing rose will need support, so tie it in with garden string as it reaches the various wires. Prune it in late February. Aim to build up a good open shape, but do it gradually to encourage flowering lower down as well as higher up. Give it extra rose fertiliser at the end of June. Spray against blackspot and greenfly. Do not allow the rose to dry out, especially in the first year after planting.

Support the winter-flowering jasmine, and prune the flowering shoots to within 8 cm (3″) of the base in early spring. New flower buds form on growths made the previous summer. The ivy and ferns need no attention. Allow the daffodils to die down naturally. Remove the old flower spikes and any untidy leaves on the elephant's ears in late spring.

Virginia creeper   jasmine   rose   ivy
elephant's ears & ferns

DESCRIPTION

The Virginia creeper takes on its fiery mantle in October. As the month progresses, the wall gradually changes into a cascade of crimson leaves. They create one of the unforgettable autumn sights, warm and rich and all-pervading.

As the last leaves fall, the winter-flowering jasmine comes into bloom. It is studded with tiny yellow stars, a charming display which will last for many months throughout the winter. On the other side, the crinkly green leaves of the 'Manda's Crested' ivy have changed to a warm copper. They make an attractive display, combining well with the yellow jasmine to the left. Down below, the great round leaves of the elephant's ears create a handsome effect. As the plants mature, they form an excellent edging to the border, as do the lacy green fronds of the ferns. Both retain their leaves throughout winter.

Spring is heralded by the 'Van Sion' daffodils which make a lovely show at the foot of the wall amidst the contrasting foliage of the ferns and elephant's ears. This double daffodil has rich golden heads; it makes a bold and welcome contribution to the scene. In April, the elephant's ears produce their flower spikes; they are white at first, then tinged with pink as they age. They are such valuable plants, tolerant of both dry and shady conditions.

As the Virginia creeper reclothes itself for the summer, its pointed leaves contrast sharply with the round crinkly leaves of the ivy. The climbing rose comes into leaf, ready for its summer display in June. Deep pink, well-perfumed, semi-double flowers provide a wonderful show that continues on and off until the autumn. The thornless 'Zéphirine Drouhin' suits this eastern or northern aspect, free from mildew.

By the time October comes round again, the wall will have been clothed each season in colour and interest, like a rich and beautiful tapestry.

23 'Paul's Himalayan Musk' in an Old Apple Tree

INGREDIENTS

No req	Name	Description	Ht × Spr (cm/m)	Ht × Spr ("/')	Best
1	Rambling rose *Rosa* 'Paul's Himalayan Musk'	pale pink	10 m	33'	7
5	Foxgloves *Digitalis purpurea*	mixed	90 × 45 cm	36 × 18"	6–7
40	*Snowdrops *Galanthus nivalis* 'Flore Pleno'	double, white	10 cm	4"	2–3
40	*Crocuses *Crocus chrysanthus* 'Blue Pearl'	blue/white	8 cm	3"	2–3
20	*Snake's head fritillaries *Fritillaria meleagris*	pink, purple, white	25 cm	10"	4–5
20	*Pheasant's eye daffodils *Narcissus poeticus recurvus*	white/orange	40 cm	16"	5
4	Honesty *Lunaria annua*	purple	75 × 30 cm	30 × 12"	4–5
3	*Solomon's seal *Polygonatum × hybridum*	white	60 × 30 cm	2 × 1'	5–6

SITE
In sun or partial shade. Use an existing large tree. An old apple tree is ideal, but other mature trees may also be suitable. NB: This rose is rampant, so it is inappropriate to grow it up a newly planted tree.

SCALE
The tree should have a height and spread of 7 m (23'). Prepare a wide 'eye' for the rose and herbaceous plants around the base of the tree, 2 m (6½') long and 1 m (3¼') across.

PLAN
In the eye: Plant the honesty, rose and foxgloves along the front, with the Solomon's seal behind.
In the grass: Plant the snowdrops and crocuses in two separate but adjacent groups about 1 m (3¼') from the eye. Plant the snake's head fritillaries about 2 m (6½') from the eye, with the daffodils in two groups on either side.

WHEN TO PLANT
Plant the bare-rooted rose in October to March. Take the bottom out of an old bucket and bury it just below the surface of the soil about 45 cm (18") away from the base of the tree. Then, using a good rich loam such as John Innes No 3, plant the rose in the bucket with the union of the rootstock and crown just beneath soil-level. Plant the snowdrops, 5 cm (2") deep, 8 cm (3") apart, as soon as they are available in August or September. Alternatively, plant them 'in the green' in March. Plant the other bulbs in September or October. Plant the crocuses 5 cm (2") deep, 8 cm (3") apart; the snake's head fritillaries 10 cm (4") deep, 10 cm (4") apart; and the daffodils 15 cm (6") deep, 15 cm (6") apart. Plant the Solomon's seal, honesty and foxgloves from September to March.

AFTERCARE
The rose needs extra care with watering until it is well established. Water the soil in the bucket for the first year until the roots are able to search out the food and moisture below. After planting it, retain only about 30–45 cm (12–18") of the strongest growths, and prune the weaker shoots to within 10 cm (4") of the base. Thereafter, prune it to establish good flowering shoots right up the trunk of the tree. Pruning the rose in the tree is not necessary, although untidy excess growth can be cut away immediately after the rose flowers, or it may be left until February. Apply a rose fertiliser in March.

The early bulbs will show off better if the grass is mown in late autumn. But do not mow it again for at least six weeks after the daffodils have finished flowering. The honesty and foxgloves will self-seed. Thin out the excess seedlings. The Solomon's seal does not need special attention.

honesty
    foxgloves

apple tree   honesty
rose   foxgloves

DESCRIPTION

'Paul's Himalayan Musk' is one of the prettiest sights of the summer garden. It can climb up through the old apple tree, producing long trails of growth which fall almost to the ground. In early July each one is adorned with great clusters of flowers so profuse that the effect is like a bubbling pale pink fountain. The musk scent wafts down on a gentle summer breeze.

Foxgloves live in the shade at the base of the tree, with their tall spires reaching up towards the rose. They make a homely scene, waving in the summer breeze. Rich shades of purple, maroon, pink and white mix happily. As time passes, a whole colony will establish itself. They will flower for several weeks; as each spotted glove opens up in June and July, the bees will call to pay their respects. By autumn the honesty plants are a mass of silvery seed pods, and apples lie rotting on the ground, providing food for the distinctive red admiral butterfly. Just watch them trying to scare away the wasps so that they can wine and dine alone.

All winter the apple tree stands stark and bare.

Then, at the end of January, the snowdrops begin to appear, shy at first and then bolder as the weeks pass. By the end of February, their dainty nodding heads have formed a beautiful white carpet. Growing beside them are the 'Blue Pearl' crocuses. Each flower is a pale silvery-blue on the outside and white within – an exquisite association of colours. They make a wonderful combination with the snowdrops. By April the snake's head fritillaries are in flower. They are one of our outstanding wild flowers. Each nodding flower, chequered white, pink or purple, is held high on a slender stem; the leaves are hardly noticeable.

It is May before the pheasant's eye daffodils open. The orange centre is surrounded by small glistening white petals. They are sweetly scented and provide a lovely picture framed by fragrant purple honesty and great wands of sweet-smelling Solomon's seal. Together, they make a memorable show now that the old apple tree is in full bloom. Beautiful pink buds open up into white delicate flowers. Before long the tree will be covered in a canopy of light green leaves, and it will be time for the rose to flower again.

24 'Wedding Day' for the Weeping Birch

INGREDIENTS

No req	Name	Description	Ht × Spr (cm/m)	Ht × Spr ("/')	Best
1	Weeping birch *Betula pendula* 'Youngii'	yellow catkins	7 × 4 m	23 × 13'	4–5
1	Rambling rose *Rosa* 'Wedding Day'	white	6 m	19½'	6–7, 9
3	Hostas *Hosta fortunei* 'Marginato-alba'	lilac	75 × 60 cm	30 × 24"	7
8	*Colchicum *Colchicum speciosum* 'Album'	white	15 cm	6"	9–10
40	*Snowdrops *Galanthus nivalis*	white	10 cm	4"	1–3
40	*Winter aconites *Eranthis hyemalis*	yellow	8 cm	3"	2–3
30	*Anemones *Anemone blanda*	blue	10 cm	4"	2–4
30	*Daffodils *Narcissus* 'Rip Van Winkle'	double, yellow	15 cm	6"	4

SITE
In the sun. The weeping birch should be reasonably mature – at least eight to ten years old – before it is used to support the rose. However, other deciduous trees, such as silver birch, apples, pears or laburnum could be used instead. The weeping birch has wide-spreading surface roots, so keep it away from fences or borders. This recipe is ideal for the centre of a lawn.

SCALE
Eventually the birch will have a spread of about 4 m (13'), although this may be restricted somewhat by pruning. There is no border: the grass within a 2-m (6½') radius of the trunk is used for planting.

PLAN
45 cm (18") from the tree: Plant the rose in an old bucket (*see below*).
1 m (3¼') from the tree: Plant the hostas on the shadier side and the colchicums on the sunnier side.
1.5 m (5') from the tree: Plant the snowdrops and winter aconites in alternate groups of ten bulbs each.
2 m (6½') from the tree: Plant three groups of daffodils, with an arc of anemones in front.

WHEN TO PLANT
Plant a new birch tree from October to March and the bulbs at the times given below, but leave the rose for eight to ten years until the birch becomes well established and can bear its weight. Plant the bare-rooted rose from October to March. Remove the bottom of an old bucket and bury it, just below the surface of the soil, about 45 cm (18") away from the base of the tree. Use a rich loam, such as John Innes No 3, and plant the rose in the bucket with the union of the rootstock and crown just beneath soil-level.

Plant the hostas from October to March; plant the colchicums in August, or as soon as they are available, 15 cm (6") deep, 25 cm (10") apart. Plant the snowdrops and winter aconites at respective depths of 5 cm (2") and 3 cm (1¼"), and 8 cm (3") apart, in August or as soon as they become available. Alternatively, plant them 'in the green' in March. Plant the anemones 4 cm (1½") deep, 10 cm (4") apart, and the daffodils 10 cm (4") deep, 10 cm (4") apart in September or October.

AFTERCARE
Take extra care with watering until the rose is well established. Prune to establish two or three strong leading shoots low on the plant. Remove any weak growths. Pruning the rose in the tree is not necessary, although excess growth can be removed immediately after flowering. However, this will incur the loss of hips. Feed it with a rose fertiliser in March and then mulch while the ground is damp. Watch for slugs on the hosta leaves. Allow six weeks after the daffodils have finished flowering before mowing the grass. The early spring bulb display will be better if the grass is cut in late autumn, but avoid the colchicum flowers.

weeping birch & rose
hostas

DESCRIPTION

During the first half of July, the weeping birch is dramatically transformed. Hundreds of tight apricot rosebuds have been waiting to open, and now they do so in great clusters. They form a remarkable cascade of dainty white flowers, each with prominent yellow stamens. Their scent wafts down in the gentle summer breeze. Even without a host tree to scramble through, the 'Wedding Day' rose would create a mound of arching sprays. Here we have the perfect partner, a weeping tree with the same pattern of growth, which lifts the main stems off the ground and allows the rose to trail down naturally. Fortunately, the rose leaves are small and do not swamp the dainty birch.

Below, the hostas form a handsome group with their bold sage-green leaves. Each leaf has a broad white edge; the flowers are pale lilac. They make a charming picture against the white bark of the tree.

In autumn the tiny rose hips turn orange-red – an attractive sight amongst the yellowing leaves of the birch. They are popular with blackbirds and mice. Soon the colchicums will be in bloom; their pure white petals stand up well to the October weather.

They, too, are striking against the white bark of the birch and look lovely surrounded by the yellow carpet of autumn leaves. Their foliage appears in the spring.

By February, the snowdrops and winter aconites are in flower, creating a wonderful pool of sunshine beneath the naked birch. They will flower for many weeks through the most dreary of days. The snowdrop flower peeps out at the end of January, gradually becoming bolder as the days grow longer. The winter aconite has a bright little yellow flower, which is also shy at first, and emerges on the shortest of stems. As it matures, it grows to about 8 cm (3″) and its pale green leaves become evident.

In early April the anemones are in bloom, a sea of blue around the golden daffodils. They open like little stars in the sunshine and form a mass of lovely bright colour, beginning in February and lasting for many weeks. It is here that 'Rip Van Winkle' is to be found. It is one of the oldest daffodils and quite a talking point with its strange dandelion-type flowers. Before long, the birch will spring into new life, to show off its mass of yellow catkins. The fresh green leaves follow and the summer zenith is upon us again.

25 Underneath the Holly Tree

INGREDIENTS

No req	Name	Description	Ht × Spr (cm/m)	Ht × Spr ("/')	Best
1	Holly *Ilex aquifolium* 'Pyramidalis'	red berries	6 × 5 m	19½ × 16½'	10–12
12	Cyclamen *Cyclamen coum*	pink	5 cm	2"	1–2
1	Periwinkle *Vinca major* 'Variegata'	pale blue	20 × 90 cm	8 × 36"	3–5
24	˙Daffodils *Narcissus* 'February Gold'	yellow	15 cm	6"	2–4
24	˙Wood anemones *Anemone nemorosa*	white	15 cm	6"	3–4
24	˙Spanish bluebells *Hyacinthoides hispanica*	white, pink	40 cm	16"	4–5
2	Male ferns *Dryopteris filix-mas*	green fronds	90 × 90 cm	3 × 3'	5–9
3	Hard ferns *Blechnum spicant*	evergreen	45 × 45 cm	18 × 18"	5–11
2	Elephant's ears *Bergenia cordifolia* 'Purpurea'	magenta	60 × 75 cm	24 × 30"	4
3	Bellflowers *Campanula latiloba* 'Highcliffe'	violet-blue	90 × 45 cm	36 × 18"	6–8

SITE
The difficult, dry area beneath an existing holly tree.

SCALE
A semi-circular border with a 2 m (6½') radius.

PLAN
50 cm (20") from the tree: Plant the male ferns on either side, with the periwinkle to the front.
1–1.5 m (3–5') from the tree: Plant the bluebells, daffodils and anemones in three groups on either side and at the front. Interplant with bellflowers.
2 m (6½') from the tree: Plant the elephant's ears at either end with three hard ferns and three groups of cyclamen in between.

WHEN TO PLANT
To grow a new holly tree, it is preferable to plant it in late April to May or September to October. 'Pyramidalis' is one of the few hollies that does not need a pollinator in order to produce berries. If there isn't a male holly nearby, this variety would be an excellent choice. Improve the soil where possible by mixing in compost or leaf mould. Substitute *Polypodium vulgare* 'Cornubiense' for the hard fern if the soil is limey.

Plant the cyclamen 2–3 cm (¾–1¼") deep, 10 cm (4") apart, as soon as it is available in early autumn. Alternatively, buy it in pots and transfer it slightly later. Mix in plenty of leaf mould. A mature tuber will produce lots of flowers, so just a few tubers eventually make an impressive display.

Plant the bulbs in groups of eight in September or October at the latest. Plant the daffodils 10 cm (4") deep, 10 cm (4") apart, the anemones 5 cm (2") deep, 15 cm (6") apart, and the bluebells 15 cm (6") deep, 15 cm (6") apart. Plant the periwinkle, ferns, elephant's ears and bellflowers from October to March.

AFTERCARE
The soil beneath a mature holly will be shaded and dry, so provide an annual autumn mulch of leaf mould to encourage a more moisture-retentive soil. The holly can be left to grow into a mature specimen or it can be pruned in July or August. Don't be afraid to cut additional sprigs in December: the seasonal gathering will do it no harm. Allow the leaves of the cyclamen and spring bulbs to die down naturally. Restrict the periwinkle if it becomes too rampant. The ferns, elephant's ears and bellflowers are best left undisturbed, but remove dead flower spikes.

male fern   holly male fern elephant's ears
  elephant's ears periwinkle bellflowers
     hard ferns & cyclamen

DESCRIPTION

By December, the holly berries have turned a vivid red and the tree takes on its crowning glory. When the pale sun shines and the berries glisten, there can be few finer sights in the winter garden.

The holly is evergreen and a mature specimen will create arid shady conditions around its trunk for the whole year. This presents problems for some plants, so special care is needed. Little cyclamen will cope beneath the outer branches, emerging to greet the new year in a pretty frill. Their dainty nodding heads are a rich pink. The leaves are shaped like ivy, and are silver-grey in colour, with varying patterns marked on them.

The periwinkle will thrive here quite happily. It has attractive pale blue flowers from the end of March to May, which make a delightful picture against its variegated evergreen leaves. Beside it, 'February Gold' daffodils make a vivid splash of early spring colour. They are one of our first daffodils to bloom, and are so sturdy and long-lasting. Dainty wood anemones flower nearby, and by the end of April the Spanish bluebells are in full colour. Pink and white bluebells look lovely against the blue flowers of the periwinkle.

Behind the bluebells, the male fern is slowly unfurling. Soon it will create bold clumps of finely divided fronds. It thrives quite close to the tree-trunk and produces a lovely backdrop throughout the long summer months. Near the path, the small evergreen hard fern makes a welcome display throughout the year. It does not much care whether the ground is wet or dry, so it will be quite at home here. Both of these pretty native ferns associate well with the bold rounded leaves of the elephant's ears. 'Purpurea' has bright magenta flowers in the spring and leaves which are tinged purple throughout the winter.

Another dependable plant for these conditions is the violet-blue bellflower known as 'Highcliffe'. Three together make a wonderful sight in midsummer which will last well into July and August. Their tall spikes bear wide cup-shaped flowers. Long after they have finished blooming, their neat evergreen rosettes of leaves give pleasure during the autumn and winter months. Then it will be time to enjoy the holly berries again.

26 Madonna Lilies and Climbing Roses

INGREDIENTS

No req	Name	Description	Ht × Spr (cm/m)	Ht × Spr ("/')	Best
1	Climbing rose *Rosa* 'Mme Grégoire Staechelin'	double, pink	5 m	16½'	6–7, 9–12
1	Climbing rose *Rosa* 'Lady Hillingdon'	apricot-yellow	5 m	16½'	6–9
1	Clematis *Clematis* 'The President'	purple-blue	2.5 m	8'	6–7
4	Madonna lilies *Lilium candidum*	white	1.5 m	5'	6–7
2	Hollyhocks *Althaea rugosa*	pale yellow	150 × 60 cm	5 × 2'	7–9
2	Erigerons *Erigeron* 'Darkest of All'	violet-blue	60 × 40 cm	24 × 16"	6–8
2	Erigerons *Erigeron* 'Quakeress'	lilac	60 × 40 cm	24 × 16"	6–8
4	Valerian *Centranthus ruber*	pink	60 × 30 cm	2 × 1'	6–7, 9–10
15	*Cottage tulips *Tulipa* 'Queen of Night'	black	65 cm	26"	5
6	*Forget-me-nots *Myosotis alpestris*	blue	15 × 15 cm	6 × 6"	4–5

SITE
A sunny back door, or, alternatively, a sunny front door.

SCALE
1.75 m (5½') on either side of the door with narrow 90-cm (3') deep borders.

PLAN
Left: To the back of the border, plant the 'Mme Grégoire Staechelin' rose with the two hollyhocks in the middle. Along the front from the far left, plant *Erigeron* 'Quakeress', then *Erigeron* 'Darkest of All', with two valerian next to the door.
Right: To the back of the border, plant the clematis and the 'Lady Hillingdon' rose. In the middle, plant the Madonna lilies, tulips and forget-me-nots. Along the front, plant two valerian next to the door, then *Erigeron* 'Darkest of All' and *Erigeron* 'Quakeress'.

WHEN TO PLANT
Plant the herbaceous and climbing plants from October to March. Plant the tulips in November, 10 cm (4") deep, 10 cm (4") apart. Plant the Madonna lilies just beneath soil-level 25 cm (10") apart, as they become available in August or September. However, it may be safer to leave them until the following autumn when all the other planting has been completed. Madonna lilies and clematis thrive best on alkaline soil, so add lime if the soil is acidic or neutral.

AFTERCARE
Give the border a general rose fertiliser in March, then mulch with decayed manure or compost while the ground is damp. The roses and clematis need supports to train them up the wall. Prune the roses in late February. Keep 'Mme Grégoire Staechelin' in careful balance: she is a vigorous rose and in this situation needs far stronger medicine than 'Lady Hillingdon'. Spray against blackspot and greenfly. 'Mme Grégoire Staechelin' is sometimes prone to rust, so treat it as necessary. Give 'Lady Hillingdon' extra rose fertiliser at the end of June. Make sure the roses do not dry out in summer.

Prune the clematis in early spring before the new growth begins. In its second year, cut it back to within 25 cm (10") of its base; thereafter reduce the shoots by up to one-third, cutting back to where the strong leaf axil buds can be seen. Take care it does not strangle young rose shoots. Leave the Madonna lilies undisturbed. If exposed, stake the hollyhocks in early summer, then after flowering cut their flowering stems to within 15 cm (6") of the ground. Give the

'Mme Grégoire Staechelin' rose
hollyhocks
erigerons   valerian

clematis   'Lady Hillingdon' rose
Madonna lilies
valerian   Erigeron 'Darkest of All' & 'Quakeress'

erigerons support with twigs in May. Deadhead them to encourage further flowers, and cut the stems to ground-level in autumn. Deadhead the valerian in June to encourage later flowering. Clear away tulip petals as they fade, as they can harbour disease. Remove the yellow leaves and stems when they have died down naturally. Forget-me-nots are biennial but they will self-seed. Remove excess seedlings in spring.

DESCRIPTION

Old-fashioned scented roses frame the back door and give colour for most of the summer. 'Mme Grégoire Staechelin' produces one magnificent flush of clear pink flowers in June and July. The flowers are large and hang down in great clusters; they have a delicious scent of sweet peas. Although the rose has only the one season of flowering, its foliage is excellent and it produces great buff yellow hips in the autumn. 'Lady Hillingdon', on the other hand, flowers regularly all summer with large apricot-yellow blooms which are richly scented. Its foliage is dark green.

Climbing up the rose to the right is 'The President' clematis. It creates a pillar of purple-blue flowers,

each with a paler stripe down the centre of its eight petals. It makes a memorable combination with the yellow rose above and provides a wonderful background for the tall Madonna lilies which grow next to it. These lilies have long white trumpets and golden stamens. Their perfume is outstanding. They are typical cottage garden plants, and thrive against a warm south-facing wall where they can be left undisturbed.

On the other side of the door, tall yellow hollyhocks are beginning to flower. Like the lilies, they are one of the great cottage favourites. At their feet, the daisy-like erigerons are both in bloom, with their lilac and violet-blue flowers providing colour from June to August. The butterflies and bees love them, and bring extra interest to the cottage door. The pink valerian have the same effect. They flower from June to July, and from September to October if they are cut back earlier. The butterflies just can't resist them.

In spring, the garden comes alive again with forget-me-nots. Their bright blue flowers provide a carpet of colour for the velvety black tulips. Together they put on a sumptuous display. Soon the roses will bud and the main season will begin once more.

27 Shady Scented Climbers

INGREDIENTS

No req	Name	Description	Ht × Spr (cm/m)	Ht × Spr ("/')	Best
1	Climbing rose *Rosa* 'Mrs Herbert Stevens'	white	3.5 m	11½'	7
1	Clematis *Clematis* 'Perle d'Azur'	blue	3 m	10'	6–7
3	'Yellow Edge' Hostas *Hosta fortunei* 'Obscura Marginata'	mauve	75 × 60 cm	30 × 24"	7
1	Honeysuckle *Lonicera × heckrottii* 'Goldflame'	orange-pink	4 m	13'	7–9
1	Stinking hellebore *Helleborus foetidus* 'Wester Fliske'	yellow-green	60 × 60 cm	2 × 2'	3–5
20	˙Daffodils *Narcissus* 'February Gold'	yellow	15 cm	6"	2–4
2	Soldiers and sailors *Pulmonaria saccharata* 'Margery Fish'	pink/blue	30 × 60 cm	1 × 2'	3–5
1	Clematis *Clematis alpina* 'Frances Rivis'	lavender-blue	2 m	6½'	4–5

SITE
A shady back door, or, alternatively, a front door.

SCALE
1.5 m (5') on either side of the door with a narrow 90-cm (3') border in front.

PLAN
Left: To the back of the border, plant the rose, and the 'Perle d'Azur'. In the middle, plant the soldiers and sailors on either side of a group of ten daffodils. Plant two hostas in front.
Right: To the back of the border, plant the honeysuckle, and the *Clematis alpina*. Plant the rest of the daffodils in a group in the centre, with the hellebore and one hosta in front.

WHEN TO PLANT
November or December until March for the rose. October to March for the clematis and herbaceous plants. September or early October for the daffodils; plant them 10 cm (4") deep and 10 cm (4") apart.

AFTERCARE
The honeysuckle, rose and clematis need supports to train them up the wall. Give the border a general rose fertiliser in March, then mulch with well-decayed manure or compost while the ground is damp. Prune the rose in late February. Build up a good open shape, gradually removing any weak or dead growth. Retie as necessary. Prune again after flowering to remove some of the very long shoots. Spray against blackspot and greenfly. Do not allow the rose to dry out in summer, particularly in the first year after planting.

The 'Perle d'Azur' clematis should be pruned in early spring before the new growth begins. Cut all the previous season's growth down to a pair of strong leaf axil buds 15 cm (6") above the ground. Prune the *Clematis alpina* lightly after flowering to encourage new growth to be produced and ripened for next year's show.

Prune the honeysuckle after flowering if it outgrows its space. Do not allow it to tangle with the rose. It is not quite as hardy as some of our native honeysuckles, which is why the evergreen hellebore is planted right in front of it for protection. If it is cut back by frost, remove affected parts and allow it to grow up again. Watch out for aphids on the honeysuckle and slugs attacking the hostas. The hellebore, soldiers and sailors and daffodils should be left undisturbed.

rose   'Perle d'Azur' clematis
soldiers and sailors
hostas

honeysuckle
Clematis alpina
hellebore   hosta

DESCRIPTION

'Mrs Herbert Stevens' is a climbing hybrid Tea rose, much loved for its long elegant pointed buds. The flowers are fragrant white with a touch of green, making this a beautiful specimen for a shady spot. Climbing beside its lower and middle stems is the 'Perle d'Azur' clematis, with its azure blue petals and creamy green anthers. It is truly one of the old favourites, and dates back to the last century. It flowers over a long period from late June possibly until August. On the ground below, the sumptuous hostas spread over the path. A broad creamy band surrounds each broad leaf. Tall mauve flowers emerge in July.

The 'Goldflame' honeysuckle dominates the other side of the doorway. From July to September it is a mass of scented flowers, a vibrant mixture of orange, pink and purple. It creates a striking spectacle, with another 'Yellow Edge' hosta and a hellebore at its

feet. These are both handsome plants, particularly the hellebore with its dark green leaves, which are deeply divided and have reddish-purple stems similar in tone to the honeysuckle above. It is at its best in early spring. Graceful clusters of pale yellow-green flowers hang down from the tall stems, each one with a fine edge of reddish-purple. Its display lasts for many weeks.

Beside the hellebore a group of golden daffodils appear sometimes as early as February; they can last until the first week of April. Another clump of 'February Gold' grows beneath the rose on the other side and is surrounded by a carpet of spotty-leaved soldiers and sailors, whose flowers change from pink to blue as they age. Next to bloom is the *Clematis alpina*, with its lantern-shaped petals. It forms a delicate wall of blue as it scrambles through the honeysuckle. Later it will be covered with fluffy seedheads.

28 The Walled Herb Garden

INGREDIENTS

No req	Name	Description	Ht × Spr (cm/m)	Ht × Spr ("/')	Best
1	Bourbon rose *Rosa* 'Louise Odier'	double, pink	1.5 × 1.2 m	5 × 4'	6–9
1	Rosemary *Rosmarinus officinalis*	pale blue	1.8 × 1.5 m	6 × 5'	4–5
1	Narrow-leaved sage *Salvia lavundulifolia*	blue	60 × 45 cm	24 × 18"	6–7
1	Purple sage *Salvia officinalis* 'Purpurascens'	blue	45 × 60 cm	18 × 24"	6–7
1	Thyme *Thymus vulgaris*	mauve	12 × 25 cm	5 × 10"	6
2	Golden marjoram *Origanum vulgare* 'Aureum'	pink	30 × 30 cm	1 × 1'	7–8
1	Bronze fennel *Foeniculum vulgare* 'Purpureum'	yellow	180 × 60 cm	6 × 2'	5–10
1	Apple mint *Mentha* × *rotundifolia*	furry leaves	60 cm	2'	5–8

SITE
Against the shelter of a warm south-facing wall, or beside the back door of the cottage.

SCALE
Allow for a border 4 m (13') wide and 1 m (3¼') deep.

PLAN
Left: Plant the rosemary with the purple sage in front to the left. (Chives and parsley can be added directly in front of the rosemary until it establishes itself fully, but note that the rosemary has a 1.5-m (5') spread.)
Centre: Plant the rose with thyme and marjoram in front.
Right: Plant the narrow-leaved sage, followed by mint and fennel.

WHEN TO PLANT
March and April will give the best start to the herbs, particularly the rosemary, marjoram and thyme, which will then be better rooted and acclimatised for the following winter. For ease in planting the whole scheme, plant the rose in March. The mint will spread rapidly unless it is confined to a sunken container. Bury a bucket, but leave a rim of 5 cm (2") or more.

AFTERCARE
Prune the rose in late February. Trim it to the right shape by cutting half the length of the shoots, or merely remove the tips of the shoots and allow the branches to intermingle with the plants on either side. Remove any weak, diseased or dead wood. Spray for blackspot and greenfly as necessary. Apply a rose fertiliser in March and again at the end of June to encourage further blooms throughout the summer.

The sages and thyme should be trimmed regularly in the spring to induce fresh new growth, otherwise they can become straggly. Deadhead both to keep them neat. The bronze fennel will seed itself endlessly, so remove old flower heads to prevent this from happening. Every three years, take cuttings of the rosemary, sages and thyme so that they can replace older specimens if they are damaged by frost or age. The golden marjoram, fennel and mint should be cut down in late autumn. These three can be forced in the greenhouse for winter use. Divide the roots and pot up: it is one way of dealing with stray mint! Mulch the border in spring while the soil is damp.

rosemary   rose   apple mint

purple sage   *thyme*   *golden marjoram*   *narrow-leaved sage*   *bronze fennel*

DESCRIPTION

The herb garden is full of colour and interest in June and July, when it embraces a rich mixture of colours and textures, both of foliage and flowers. The contrasting scents and aromas are a living pot-pourri to be enjoyed and appreciated.

'Louise Odier' looks extremely beautiful with its warm pink flowers. This is one of the best of all the Bourbon roses, richly fragrant and continuously in flower throughout the summer. The flowers are double and cup-shaped, and are produced in dense clusters. The rose has strong bushy growth and looks particularly pleasing with the spiky grey-green rosemary on the one side and the upright pale grey sage on the other. Its perfume is welcome anywhere, but especially here, where it can be associated with many other culinary flowers, such as the pale blue rosemary that blooms in April and May and the sages and thyme that are blooming now.

Both sages have brilliant blue tubular flowers which are scented just like the leaves. They make a lovely contrast to the pink of the rose. The thyme has mauve flower spikes; these are not so showy but are pleasing and fragrant nevertheless. Later in the year the pink heads on the golden marjoram and the tiny clusters of yellow flowers on the fennel can also be picked. Gather the flowers as often as the leaves, and use them to decorate or add flavour to salads and pâtés, jellies, cakes and savoury biscuits. They will transform the simplest of dishes.

By late summer the bronze fennel has grown to its full height, creating a fountain of polished stems and graceful thread-like foliage. The colour balances well with the dusky appearance of the purple sage at the other end, now completely wrapped around the far side of the rosemary. Elsewhere, the hairy mint leaves, soft and pretty and full of flavour, add another dimension. Like the thyme and marjoram, this mint has been chosen for utility as well as for appearance. Here is a herb garden for the entire year. It looks wonderful in high summer and in the middle of winter with the evergreen rosemary, thyme and sages. What is more, by late winter or early spring there will be fresh growth on the marjoram and fennel.

29 The 'Herbalist' Garden

INGREDIENTS

No req	Name	Description	Ht × Spr (cm/m)	Ht × Spr ("/')	Best
2	Roses *Rosa* 'The Herbalist'	deep pink	90 × 90 cm	3 × 3'	6–9
1	Hyssop *Hyssopus officinalis*	blue	45 × 45 cm	18 × 18"	7–9
2	Golden marjoram *Origanum vulgare* 'Aureum'	pink	30 × 30 cm	1 × 1'	7–8
6	Parsleys *Petroselinum crispum*	green	30 × 25 cm	12 × 10"	5–10
2	Lemon thymes *Thymus × citriodorus* 'Aureus'	pink	20 × 30 cm	8 × 12"	6
2	Chives *Allium schoenoprasum*	lavender	15 × 15 cm	6 × 6"	6–7
4	Lemon balms *Melissa officinalis* 'Variegata'	green/gold leaves	60 × 45 cm	24 × 18"	5–10

SITE
A sunny plot with a path in front or all the way round.

SCALE
3 m (10') wide and 1.2 m (4') deep.

PLAN
Back, left to right: Plant two lemon balms, a rose, the hyssop, another rose and two more lemon balms.
Front, left to right: Plant one thyme and three parsleys. Plant the chives in the centre with a marjoram behind on either side, then another three parsleys and the second thyme.

WHEN TO PLANT
October to March for all the ingredients, including the bare-rooted rose but excepting the parsley, which can be sown indoors and planted out in April or May or purchased as small plants in a strip and planted out when available. Alternatively, pot it up and grow it on in the greenhouse before planting it out in late May. The lemon balm can be invasive so segregate it by using a sunken bucket or tiles.

AFTERCARE
Apply a rose fertiliser to the whole border in early spring, then mulch generously while the ground is damp. Prune the roses in late February. Remove about half of the previous season's growth. Feed them again at the end of June. Use an organic spray for blackspot and greenfly. Do not allow the roses to dry out in summer, particularly in the first year.

The hyssop should be cut to within 8 cm (3") of the ground in early spring. Cut down the golden marjoram in late autumn. Remove the flower stalks on the parsleys before they develop properly. Cut the plants down in September to encourage new leaf before the winter. Plant with fresh stock in spring. The thyme should be divided every three years in March, April or September or replaced. Remove dead flower heads to keep the plants dense and healthy.

Divide the chives every three years in September, and replant in freshly manured ground. Renew the old practice of giving the variegated lemon balm a close shearing every two or three weeks during the summer to retain a low clumpy appearance and good colouring on the leaves; this is useful if it is growing near a path. Do not allow it to encroach on the roses.

lemon balms	rose		hyssop		rose	lemon balms
		golden marjoram	golden marjoram		
lemon thyme	parsleys		chives		parsleys	lemon thyme

DESCRIPTION

'The Herbalist' is a modern rose grown from old parents. It inherits attributes of the famous old 'Apothecary's Rose' (otherwise known as the 'Red Rose of Lancaster') but it blooms throughout the summer. The rich deep pink flowers are semi-double and fragrant, and have prominent golden stamens. They look particularly lovely next to the vibrant blue hyssop, which is a mass of colour for many weeks from July to September. It is one of the bees' favourite plants and is teeming with activity throughout this period. Both the bees and the butterflies enjoy the marjoram when it flowers in July and August. The two mounds of fresh golden growth are topped with pretty pink heads which are as fragrant as the leaves. These are attractive plants from spring right through to late autumn.

The main edging plants at the front of the herb garden are the parsleys, thymes and chives. The thymes are evergreen. Although not long-lived, they make excellent cornerpieces throughout the year, until in summer they are smothered with pretty pink flowers, which are just as tasty as the leaves. But it is the curly dark green parsley leaves which dominate the front path. They always look wonderful contrasted with rich colours, especially here with the deep pink rose. Clumps of chives with grass-like leaves grow in the centre. These can be cut several times before the pretty lavender flowers are allowed to bloom.

Variegated lemon balm grows beneath the roses. Their bright green leaves are splashed with gold. Treated as a low edger, with their stems cut back to within a few centimetres (1″) of ground-level, they will retain their bright colouring far longer than otherwise; they make a good contrast next to the rose.

30 The Privy

INGREDIENTS

No req	Name	Description	Ht × Spr (cm/m)	Ht × Spr ("/')	Best
2	Chinese lanterns *Physalis alkekengi franchetii*	orange lanterns	60 × 90 cm	2 × 3'	9–11
1	Cotoneaster *Cotoneaster horizontalis*	orange berries	2 × 2 m	6½ × 6½'	10–3
2	Winter-flowering jasmines *Jasminum nudiflorum*	bright yellow	3 m	10'	11–3
1	*Japanese quince *Chaenomeles speciosa* 'Apple Blossom'	white/pink	2 × 2 m	6½ × 6½'	3–4
1	*Forsythia *Forsythia suspensa sieboldii*	yellow	2 × 2 m	6½ × 6½'	3–4
24	*Daffodils *Narcissus* 'Van Sion'	double, yellow	35 cm	14"	3–4
20	*Lily of the valley *Convallaria majalis*	white	15 cm	6"	5
2	*Day lilies *Hemerocallis fulva*	orange-red	90 × 90 cm	3 × 3'	6–8

SITE
Any small building, such as a privy, barn or garage.

SCALE
2–3 m (6½–10') wide, 3 m (10') deep and 2–3 m (6½–10') tall.

PLAN
South (entrance door): Plant a jasmine and Chinese lanterns on either side, with day lilies in the grass in front.
East: Plant the cotoneaster with the daffodils below in the grass.
North: Plant the forsythia.
West: Plant the Japanese quince with lily of the valley in the border below.

WHEN TO PLANT
Prepare a border for the lily of the valley, adding lots of leaf mould. The daffodils can be planted directly into the grass. The rest of the ingredients should have planting holes 30 cm (1') away from walls. Mix compost and well-rotted manure in each one.

Plant the lily of the valley in September or October, in four clumps, 20 cm (8") apart, pointed ends uppermost just below soil-level. Plant the daffodils at the same time in three groups, 10 cm (4") deep and 8 cm (3") apart. Plant the rest of the ingredients from October to April.

AFTERCARE
Keep the area free of weeds and trim the grass around the base of the plants. Winter-flowering jasmine needs support in order to be trained up the wall. Prune it immediately after flowering. Cut it back to within two or three buds of the old wood. It thrives in any aspect, although it will perform earlier on a south-facing wall than on a shady north wall. The cotoneaster needs little attention; it thrives on any wall. The Chinese lanterns may, in time, become invasive. They spread by a running root system. Dig up the excess in March or April to keep them within bounds. Cut a few of the stems when the lanterns first begin to show colour and hang them upside-down in a light airy shed to dry so that they can be used in winter arrangements. Although tolerant of most conditions, they perform best in a sunny position.

Train the Japanese quince on wires fastened to the wall. Prune it after it flowers in May by cutting back the previous season's growth to two or three buds. It can cope with any aspect. The forsythia is particularly suited to an east- or north-facing wall. After flowering, prune its trailing lateral growths to within two buds of the old wood. Allow the lily of the valley to spread undisturbed, just mulch annually with leaf mould to keep the soil moisture-retentive. Cut the flowering stems of the day lilies to ground-level once they have finished blooming. Do not mow the grass around the daffodils for six weeks after flowering.

jasmine jasmine cotoneaster
Chinese lanterns Chinese lanterns

DESCRIPTION

Beautiful autumn colours transform the privy walls. The Chinese lanterns have been in rich array since September. Three or four – maybe more – orange papery pods dangle from each stem; after just a few seasons there will be plenty to cut for the cottage vase and to enjoy outside in the garden. The cotoneaster is smothered with tiny orange berries and its once glossy green foliage turns a rich red. Soon the leaves will fall, leaving the branches with their well-defined herring-bone pattern even more obvious. The berries will stay throughout the winter months, and will still be there when the new leaves appear in March. Meanwhile, the winter-flowering jasmine is just beginning to flower, its bare stems trained round the privy door. Each flower appears like a little yellow star, so simple yet so effective. It blooms from November to March in all but the worst weather, providing a cheerful welcome throughout the dreariest of winter days.

By March, the Japanese quince is in full bloom covering the western wall. It creates a beautiful display, with small clusters of white flowers, each one tinged with pink. Later, yellow fruits will appear; they are excellent for making jelly. This variety of forsythia lacks all the stiffness of its upright relatives.

Instead, its branches trail down, creating a cascade of yellow flowers in March and April. Left to its own devices it creates quite a large shrub, but grown against the wall it is best pruned to shape. Enjoy its dense clusters of bright yellow flowers and its graceful habit. Also flowering in April is the old 'Van Sion' daffodil, which has lovely double yellow flowers. It will naturalise well beneath the cotoneaster, where it will create a bold and arresting sight.

Next to appear are the lily of the valley, nestling under the opposite wall beneath the Japanese quince. The pointed spikes push through the soil and gently reveal the daintiest of flowers, smelling so sweetly – you can never have too many. Here, under the privy wall, they can roam to their hearts' content. Try digging up a few and forcing them in the greenhouse. Even five or ten stems will scent a room.

By the end of June the orange-red day lilies are in flower. Two large clumps on either side of the privy door will give a colourful welcome for weeks on end. Each flower only lasts for a day but the succession goes on and on. They thrive in grass and make a good foil for the Chinese lanterns behind. These have been unspectacular all summer, but by the time the day lilies are over, the papery pods have turned bright orange and the autumn season has returned.

31 Crown Imperials Beside the Cottage Path

INGREDIENTS

No req	Name	Description	Ht × Spr (cm/m)	Ht × Spr (″/′)	Best
4	Crown Imperials *Fritillaria imperialis* 'Aurora'	orange	75 cm	30″	4
12	Golden feverfew *Tanacetum parthenium* 'Aureum'	white	30 × 30 cm	1 × 1′	6–7, or 7–9
4	Primulas *Primula* × *pruhonicensis* 'Wanda'	claret	8 × 25 cm	3 × 10″	3–5
2	Auriculas *Primula auricula* 'Old Yellow Dusty Miller'	yellow	15 × 15 cm	6 × 6″	4–5
4	Heartsease *Viola tricolor*	purple/yellow	8 × 25 cm	3 × 10″	4–9
2	Daisies *Bellis perennis* 'Dresden China'	pink	5 × 12 cm	2 × 5″	3–6
4	Cowslips *Primula veris*	yellow	15 × 15 cm	6 × 6″	4–5
3	Fuchsias *Fuchsia* 'Chequerboard'	white/cerise	90 × 60 cm	3 × 2′	6–10

SITE
A narrow border beside the cottage path. These plants will tolerate partial shade or a sunny position.

SCALE
3 m (10′) wide and 1.2 m (4′) deep. The border can be continued using the same plants.

PLAN
Along the path from left to right: Plant two primulas, two auriculas and two heartsease, followed by another two primulas, all the cowslips (two deep), both daisies and the two remaining heartsease.
45 cm (18″) back: Plant the feverfew in four groups.
60 cm (2′) back: Plant the three fuchsias spaced out behind the feverfew, with the four Crown Imperials in between.

WHEN TO PLANT
Plant the Crown Imperials in September or October, 20 cm (8″) deep, 60 cm (2′) apart, slightly on their side, with some sharp sand underneath each bulb. Plant the rest of the ingredients at the same time as the Crown Imperials or any time until March. The fuchsias should be planted the following June.

AFTERCARE
Apply a high potash fertiliser to the Crown Imperials in early spring before the new shoots can be seen. Remove old stems when they have died off in summer. Elsewhere, provide a general rose fertiliser in early spring and then mulch while the ground is damp. The feverfew, heartsease and cowslips will seed themselves. If the feverfew gets too unmanageable, simply pull out the excess seedlings or cut off the flowers before they have had a chance to seed. The heartsease may be used to replace existing specimens; it would also look pretty under the fuchsias. Allow the cowslips to spread further along the border or move the excess elsewhere.

Divide *Primula* x *pruhonicensis* 'Wanda' and the auriculas every three years shortly after they flower. Divide the daisies in March each year and replant them, otherwise they will not flower in such great profusion.

Water the fuchsias – and the other plants – in very dry weather during the summer months. These fuchsias are hardy, but give them extra protection in severe weather. Cover their roots with a deep mulch of ashes or bracken and cut them back to within 15 cm (6″) of ground-level in the spring.

Crown Imperials & fuchsias
  golden feverfew
    primulas   *auriculas*   *heartsease*   *cowslips*   *daisies*

DESCRIPTION

The straight line of Crown Imperials makes a dramatic display beside the old garden path. These stately plants were often seen in cottage gardens where, undisturbed, they flowered and multiplied year after year. Their tall stems support large orange bells which are fully out in April. Between each plant, humble golden feverfew grow. Their bright green leaves looked cheerful throughout the winter, but now in spring their golden foliage seems particularly welcome as it weaves an attractive carpet for its lofty neighbours.

Right beside the cottage path are a lovely mixture of old-fashioned plants including the claret flowers of *Primula* x *pruhonicensus* 'Wanda', which seems to bloom endlessly from February or March until May. Next to them are yellow auriculas. These were once so common. Their simple flowers are most endearing and make a delightful picture beside the purple and yellow heartsease with their cheeky little faces. They

are such friendly little plants, it would be hard to keep them out of the border even if you wanted to! Next along the path is the soft pink 'Dresden China' daisy which will also flower over a long period, from very early spring until midsummer. The cowslips make a very pretty display with their tall stems of tiny yellow bells, sweet smelling and very welcome here with primroses on one side and more heartsease at the end. The edgers make a vivid show in front of the feverfew and Crown Imperials.

As the spring flowers fade, the feverfew grow bigger and bigger until they burst into flower. Their simple white daisy-type blooms last for weeks as the Crown Imperials die down and the fuchsias take on their summer mantle. 'Chequerboard' has dainty white fly-away sepals with lovely rich cerise bells. It gives a prolific display which in a good year will last from June until October. It is quite low growing and will form an impressive bank of colour as the season matures.

32   *The Forget-me-not Path*

INGREDIENTS

No req	Name	Description	Ht × Spr (cm/m)	Ht × Spr (″/′)	Best
3	Moss phlox *Phlox subulata* 'Alexander's Surprise'	pink	8 × 45 cm	3 × 18″	4–5
2	Violas *Viola* 'Mollie Sanderson'	blue-black	15 × 25 cm	6 × 10″	4–10
30	Tulips *Tulipa* 'Clara Butt'	salmon-pink	60 cm	2′	5
12	Forget-me-nots *Myosotis alpestris* 'Blue Ball'	blue	15 × 15 cm	6 × 6″	4–5
3	Garden pinks *Dianthus* 'Valda Wyatt'	lavender-pink	30 × 25 cm	12 × 10″	6–9
2	Dwarf bellflowers *Campanula cochleariifolia*	white	8 × 25 cm	3 × 10″	6–8
3	•Erigerons *Erigeron* 'Quakeress'	lilac	60 × 40 cm	24 × 16″	6–8
3	•Ice plants *Sedum spectabile*	pink	45 × 45 cm	18 × 18″	8–10

SITE
A narrow sunny border beside the cottage path.

SCALE
2.5 m (8′) wide and 90 cm (3′) deep.

PLAN
Along the path from left to right: Alternate the phlox with the groups of violas, garden pinks and bellflowers. Plant forget-me-nots immediately behind.
45–90 cm (18–36″) from path: Plant the tulips in groups of ten (three deep) with forget-me-nots, erigerons and ice plants on either side.

WHEN TO PLANT
Plant the tulips in October or November, 10 cm (4″) deep, 15 cm (6″) apart. There are many other tulips from which to choose. Plant the rest of the ingredients between October and March.

AFTERCARE
Apply a general rose fertiliser in early spring when the ground is damp and then mulch. Support the erigerons with twiggy sticks in May before the new growth appears. Deadhead the erigerons to encourage further flowering, and cut them down to ground-level in autumn. Leave the seedheads on the ice plant until spring, then snap them off.

The moss phlox should be trimmed after flowering. The violas and garden pinks need replacing every three or four years; they propagate easily from side shoots. The tulip bulbs should be left undisturbed. Discard tulip petals and leaves as they fade and die. The bulbs may need replacing in three or four years.

Treat the forget-me-nots as biennials. They will seed themselves. Remove the seedlings in early spring if too many appear around the pinks and violas. The bellflowers will also seed themselves and spread. They are easily pulled up if they get too invasive.

tulips
forget-me-nots
moss phlox   *violas, bellflowers & moss phlox*   *garden pinks*   *moss phlox*

DESCRIPTION

The little plants that line the path are all sun-lovers and give a beautiful display from spring to late summer. The first to bloom are the old moss phlox with their neat mats of spiky leaves covered in pink flowers. They create lovely patches of colour all along the path throughout April and May. Right beside them are small groups of 'Mollie Sanderson' violas, which flower from April or May right through the summer. Their little blue-black faces have tiny yellow centres. Behind the phlox and violas, tall pink tulips rise up out of a sea of blue forget-me-nots which flower prolifically for many weeks. 'Clara Butt' is a very old bedding tulip dating back to the last century. It is a strong, late-flowering variety which makes a perfect companion for the forget-me-nots. The spring border is a lovely mixture of pinks, deep blue-black and rich blue.

The summer scene is quite different. The violas continue to perform well, but now the garden pinks are their companions. 'Valda Wyatt' is a modern hybrid which creates low mats of spiky silver foliage which is both vigorous and compact. The flowers are a delicate lavender-pink. They are heavily scented and last for many weeks throughout the summer, with bursts of colour from June to September. They are greatly valued here beside the cottage path where they cannot escape notice. By midsummer the dwarf bellflowers are covered in tiny white bells dangling on wiry stems. They flower for many weeks, giving a dainty and very pleasing display.

Right behind these summer edgers are the erigerons and ice plants. 'Quakeress' is an old but worthy erigeron with soft lilac flowers which open like daisies from June to August. They create a good bank of colour for the bees and butterflies, who love to hover overhead and gather the nectar. But the butterflies will soon forsake them when the ice plants are in bloom. Their flat heads are dense with tiny flowers. They gradually change colour from green to pink as the autumn days get shorter. What a treat it is to watch a tortoiseshell butterfly sipping nectar on a warm autumn morning, wings outspread, as still as can be.

33   The Peony Steps

INGREDIENTS

No req	Name	Description	Ht × Spr (cm/m)	Ht × Spr ("/')	Best
2	Peonies *Paeonia officinalis* 'Rubra-plena'	double, red	75 × 75 cm	30 × 30"	5
2	Peonies *Paeonia lactiflora* 'Sarah Bernhardt'	double, pink	90 × 90 cm	3 × 3'	6–7
2	Valerian *Centranthus ruber*	pink	60 × 30 cm	2 × 1'	6–7, 9–10
2	Mexican daisies *Erigeron karvinskianus*	pink	10 × 30 cm	4 × 12"	6–10
2	Cheddar pinks *Dianthus gratianopolitanus*	pink	15 × 30 cm	6 × 12"	5–7
2	Baby's breath *Gypsophila repens*	pink, white	15 × 30 cm	6 × 12"	6–8
2	Thrift *Armeria maritima* 'Dusseldorf Pride'	pink	15 × 30 cm	6 × 12"	6–8
1	Rock rose *Helianthemum nummularium* 'Wisley Pink'	pink	25 × 60 cm	10 × 24"	6–8

SITE
Sunny steps with paving above and below.

SCALE
Adaptable to any flight of steps.

PLAN
Above the top step: Plant the old red peony on either side.
Below the bottom step: Plant one 'Sarah Bernhardt' peony and one valerian in the ground on either side.
Steps: Plant the rock rose in the paving at the top of the steps on the left close to the wall. Plant the Mexican daisies along the base of the middle steps; they will soon colonise down below.
Walls: Plant one of the cheddar pinks, one baby's breath and one thrift on one side and the second thrift, another baby's breath and a cheddar pink on the other in reverse order.

WHEN TO PLANT
October to March. Prepare large planting holes for the peonies, adding lots of well-rotted manure. The peony crowns should be set no more than 3 cm (1¼") deep. They should remain undisturbed and are likely to flower happily for fifty years or more! Create pockets of soil in the crevices near the top of the walls for planting the cheddar pinks, baby's breath and thrift. The rock rose will benefit from sand or grit.

AFTERCARE
Mulch the peonies in April, and stake them with a wire hoop. Deadhead them after flowering and cut down foliage in October, otherwise leave them undisturbed. Cut back the valerian after flowering in July to avoid it setting seed and to encourage a later show in September. Remove seedlings as they occur. The Mexican daisies will flower all summer, then multiply profusely. So much the better, for in future years they will appear all down the steps.

The baby's breath and rock rose should be cut back after flowering to keep them tidy and to further the production of flowers. Deadhead the thrifts and cheddar pinks to make the plants look neater.

red peony	rock rose	red peony
thrift		cheddar pink
baby's breath	Mexican daisies	baby's breath
cheddar pink		thrift
pink peony & valerian		valerian & pink peony

DESCRIPTION

The peonies look enchanting in late spring and early summer. The red ones appeared first; their sweetly scented flowers guard the top step. Now 'Sarah Bernhardt', with her exquisite double pink blooms, frames the steps down below in June. She is younger than the old double red peonies by several hundred years, nevertheless she is about to reach her centenary! Both remain trusted favourites. Peonies have a relatively short flowering time – just a few weeks each – but by using these two together the period is extended from May to June or early July. The heavily dissected foliage remains attractive well into the autumn.

By late June the valerian has come into full flower with a prolific show of pink blooms much loved by the butterflies who flit to and fro, then rest awhile, gathering the nectar. Up and down the steps the Mexican daisies are in bloom, from June to October. Each flower is tiny, but there are so many of them, in various shades of white and red and pink, that the effect is most pleasing.

Meanwhile, on top of the walls, the sweet little cheddar pinks have been flowering since May. They will give two or three months of soft colour. Right next to them, the creeping baby's breath with its dainty pink and white flowers appears from June to August. The thrift will be in flower at the same time. Their tight green hummocks are transformed by their upright, rich pink flowers. Together these plants create a beautiful summer tapestry.

Planted between the paving at the top is a small pink rock rose which basks in the sunshine and flowers from June to August. Like the valerian, if it is cut back earlier, it will flower again in the autumn. The butterflies, particularly the beautiful tortoiseshells, love them both. Even in September, while the sun still has some warmth in its rays, the steps are a place to linger and watch. The insect life will always add lots of interest.

34   The Fern Steps

INGREDIENTS

No req	Name	Description	Ht × Spr (cm/m)	Ht × Spr ("/')	Best
2	Male ferns *Dryopteris filix-mas*	green fronds	90 × 90 cm	3 × 3'	5–9
2	Day lilies *Hemerocallis* 'Stella D'Oro'	yellow	55 × 60 cm	22 × 24"	6–7, 9–10
1	Creeping Jenny *Lysimachia nummularia*	bright yellow	2 × 60 cm	¾ × 24"	6–7
2	Bellflowers *Campanula poscharskyana*	lavender-blue	30 × 60 cm	1 × 2'	6–7
2	Cranesbills *Geranium wallichianum* 'Buxton's Variety'	blue	30 × 90 cm	1 × 3'	7–9
1	Corydalis *Corydalis lutea*	yellow	15 × 30 cm	6 × 12"	4–11
2	London pride *Saxifraga* × *urbium*	pink	30 × 30 cm	1 × 1'	5
2	*Violets *Viola odorata*	purple	8 × 25 cm	3 × 10"	2–4

SITE
Steps in partial shade with paving above and below.

SCALE
Adaptable to any flight of steps.

PLAN
Top step: Plant a day lily on either side, with a violet and a cranesbill beside the one on the left.
Bottom step: Plant a fern on either side, with a creeping Jenny on the left and a violet and a cranesbill on the right.
In the crevices between the steps and in the walls: Plant the bellflowers at the base of a step next to the wall, one at the bottom left and one near the top right. Plant the corydalis on the left. London pride is best on the level; plant it at the base of the middle step and let it colonise sideways.

WHEN TO PLANT
October to April. Prepare the planting holes well for the day lilies, cranesbills, ferns, creeping Jenny and violets, adding lots of compost or leaf mould.

AFTERCARE
Mulch the ferns and day lilies in early spring while the soil is damp. The ferns, bellflowers and violets will not need attention. Cut the day lily stems almost to ground-level after flowering, otherwise do not disturb them. The creeping Jenny may need restraining, as it roots along its runners, but it is easily pulled up. Cut the old flowering stems of the cranesbills to ground-level to encourage further flower production. The corydalis will seed itself, so keep it in check by removing unwanted seedlings. London pride may also need keeping within bounds. If it spreads too far, introduce it to another step.

day lily   cranesbill

corydalis
London pride
fern   bellflower
creeping Jenny

day lily

bellflower

fern
cranesbill

DESCRIPTION

The shady steps are full of character in summertime, with the lush green ferns standing guard at the bottom and the yellow day lilies at the top. The male fern is one of the most long-suffering plants and will thrive in the most difficult spots, even here in the deep shade at the foot of the wall. In early summer its new fronds make a wonderful picture as they slowly unfurl, quite strange and beautiful. Around the feet of the fern on the left, the creeping Jenny sends out long runners, each bearing a string of bright yellow flowers. Directly behind it, the starry lavender-blue bellflower provides a pretty background as it roams the area below the bottom step.

The cranesbill known as 'Buxton's Variety' provides a mass of colour from July onwards. Its spode-blue flowers have large white centres and look charming beside the right fern. It is echoed at the top of the steps, where its partner lives next to the yellow day lilies. The lilies flower unceasingly during the summer months, often with another show in the autumn.

The steps and walls are attractive too, clothed in pretty yellow corydalis, which flowers from April to November without any fuss or help. Its dainty evergreen leaves provide interest the whole year round and greatly help to soften the hard outline. Dark green rosettes of the London pride have the same effect. They don't mind how shady it is and will happily colonise right across the steps if they are allowed to do so. Delicate sprays of pink flowers shoot up in May to form a pretty haze. It is such a common plant and yet so useful. Another bellflower climbs up the wall to the right, smothering everything around it and creating a lovely effect. It might seem out of place in other spots in the garden, but not here where it is free to clamber as it likes. Only the violets hold back their display, waiting for spring, when they produce their tiny, sweetly scented purple flowers.

35   The Honeysuckle Arch

INGREDIENTS

No req	Name	Description	Ht × Spr (cm/m)	Ht × Spr ("/')	Best
1	Honeysuckle *Lonicera periclymenum* 'Belgica'	purple/red/ yellow	4 m	13'	5–6, 9
4	Granny's bonnets *Aquilegia vulgaris* 'Snow Queen'	white	75 × 45 cm	30 × 18"	5–6
4	Solomon's seal *Polygonatum × hybridum*	white	60 × 30 cm	2 × 1'	5–6
2	Granny's pin cushions *Astrantia maxima*	pink	60 × 45 cm	24 × 18"	6–7
5	Foxgloves *Digitalis purpurea* 'Alba'	white	90 × 45 cm	36 × 18"	6–7
1	Climbing rose *Rosa* 'Paul's Scarlet Climber'	double, scarlet	3 m	10'	6–7, 9
6	˙Primroses *Primula vulgaris*	pale yellow	15 × 20 cm	6 × 8"	3–4
2	Soldiers and sailors *Pulmonaria officinalis*	pink/blue	25 × 45 cm	10 × 18"	3–5

SITE
Partial shade.

SCALE
The arch is approximately 2.1 m (7') high, 1 m (3¼') wide and 1 m (3¼') deep, with a narrow path through the middle and borders 90 cm (3') wide on either side. The arch will be much more successful if the path leads somewhere of interest.

PLAN
Left: Plant the rose with three primroses, a granny's pin cushion and one soldiers and sailors along the path. Plant two Solomon's seal and two granny's bonnets behind.
Right: Substituting the honeysuckle for the rose, repeat the pattern as on the left.
Plant the foxgloves to stand guard outside the entrance posts with an extra one to the front right.

WHEN TO PLANT
If it is bare-rooted, the rose is best planted any time between October and March. The rest of the ingredients may be planted from September to March.

AFTERCARE
Give a general rose fertiliser to all the plants in early spring and then mulch with compost or leaf mould while the ground is damp. This helps to prevent drying out later.

The honeysuckle and rose need to be trained up the framework. Prune the honeysuckle after flowering if it gets too overgrown. Cut out the dead wood and reshape the plant. It will soon grow back. Make very sure it is not allowed to twine itself around the rose. Unravel it and cut it back as necessary. Prune 'Paul's Scarlet' in late February. Aim to get a good dense rose covering up one side of the arch. Spray against greenfly and blackspot. Keep the rose well watered for the first year, until it is established.

The granny's bonnets might need twiggy supports or they will flop forward and spoil. As with the foxgloves, they can seed themselves, but they probably won't produce all-white offspring. You can let them spread or remove them and replant. The Solomon's seal, primroses and soldiers and sailors need little attention, but they should be kept moist. Cut the granny's pin cushion stems down to ground-level after flowering.

rose
foxglove, Solomon's seal, granny's bonnets
soldiers and sailors

honeysuckle
granny's bonnets, foxglove
foxgloves, granny's pin cushion

DESCRIPTION

The honeysuckle is the early Dutch variety which flowers throughout May and June, its purple, red and yellow flowers cascading around the top and sides of the arch. Birds love to perch amongst the foliage and nest amongst its bushy branches. It is highly scented but especially so in the evening or after a shower of rain. It is a valuable addition to any garden and certainly creates a focal point here.

In the shadier parts down below, a dainty array of granny's bonnets are in flower with their lovely white spurs. Another old name for them was columbines. The shape of their flowers is a strong contrast to the little white bells which dangle in clusters from the arching stems of the Solomon's seals. These reach out right over the path, creating a lovely woodland feel. Growing beside them are the creamy, greenish-pink flowers of the granny's pin cushions, wonderful plants which go on flowering throughout June and July and

often later. They do not shout out amongst the rest, rather they blend the others together. The same cannot be said for the elegant white foxgloves which dominate the scene in June and July, as they flower on their tall spikes and create a link between the plants below and the climbers above. By late June it is time for the old-fashioned rose to flower.

'Paul's Scarlet' has large clusters of double scarlet flowers which create a cheerful effect in this shady area. It is almost thornless, so it is a good subject for an arch. It has one main flowering period in late June and July, and follows on well from the honeysuckle.

By early autumn, the frame of the arch is bright with orange honeysuckle berries. The birds find them very tasty and they soon disappear. Spring brings the arch to life again. Then, all along the path, the primroses can join ranks with the pink and blue flowers of the soldiers and sailors until the honeysuckle comes into bloom once more.

36   Climbing Roses and a Purple Vine

No req	Name	Description	Ht × Spr (cm/m)	Ht × Spr (″/′)	Best
2	Climbing roses *Rosa* 'Gloire de Dijon'	yellow/pink	4.5 m	15′	6–10
1	Grape vine *Vitis vinifera* 'Purpurea'	purple	7 m	23′	6–10
30	˙Glory of the snow *Chionodoxa luciliae*	blue	10 cm	4″	2–3
3	Perennial wallflowers *Cheiranthus* 'Bowles Mauve'	mauve	50 × 30 cm	20 × 12″	5–7
2	Lady's mantle *Alchemilla mollis*	lime-green	30 × 30 cm	1 × 1′	6–7, 9
4	˙Violas *Viola labradorica* 'Purpurea'	mauve-blue	10 × 20 cm	4 × 8″	4–6
2	Purple sages *Salvia officinalis* 'Purpurascens'	blue	45 × 60 cm	18 × 24″	6–7
1	Bronze fennel *Foeniculum vulgare* 'Purpureum'	yellow	180 × 60 cm	6 × 2′	8–9

SITE
In full sun. The arch can be of wood or metal.

SCALE
The arch should be approximately 2.1 m (7′) high, 1 m (3¼′) wide and 1 m (3¼′) deep, with a path through the middle. The borders should be 60 cm (2′) wide on either side.

PLAN
On each side of the arch: Plant a rose, two violas and a lady's mantle, with half the glory of the snow just behind.
Right: Plant the grape vine at the base of the arch, with the bronze fennel and a wallflower nearby.
Front entrance: Plant a purple sage on either side.
Rear entrance: Plant one wallflower on either side.

WHEN TO PLANT
The roses and vine are best planted from November to March. Plant the glory of the snow in the autumn, 8 cm (3″) deep and 8 cm (3″) apart, in two wide groups. The wallflowers and sage should be left until March or April. Plant the rest of the ingredients any time between September and March.

AFTERCARE
Give a general rose fertiliser to all of the plants in early spring and mulch while the ground is damp. The roses and vine need to be trained up the arch by tying in young growths. Prune the roses in late February. Aim to get a good dense covering of the arch on both sides. Growth is vigorous so tie it in repeatedly to get a good shape. Spray against greenfly and blackspot. Keep the roses well watered for the first year until the plants are well established. Give them another feed at the end of June.

Initially prune the vine back to within 25 cm (10″) of ground-level. Thereafter, allow only two stems to develop. Thin out old growths and shorten young ones by two-thirds in late summer. It will take several years to cover the frame but it should fruit well.

Trim the sage in early spring to encourage new growth; after four years take cuttings in September as it is not long-lived. For the same reason, take cuttings of the wallflowers in August. Cut back the flower stems on the lady's mantle after the first flush is over in order to encourage further flowering. The glory of the snow, lady's mantle, violas and bronze fennel will self-seed. Remove the seedheads of the bronze fennel before they ripen if self-seeding poses a problem.

lady's mantle   *rose*   *grape vine*   *rose*   *bronze fennel*
       purple sage   *purple sage*   *wallflower*

DESCRIPTION

The rose 'Gloire de Dijon' has beautiful large flowers, even in September. They are buff yellow, tinged with salmon and pink. The blooms are heavily scented and hang down from the arch amidst a mass of foliage. The main flush is in July but the flowers continue to appear on and off right through to October. Its principal partner is a purple vine whose leaves change from claret-red to dusky purple as the season progresses. They look sumptuous with the sun shining through them, whether in summer or later, but in September they are highlighted by bunches of purple grapes all covered in a blue bloom. Seen alongside the rose flowers, they make an exciting combination of tones and shapes.

After a quiet winter, the arch comes to life again with the glory of the snow. This is a small but showy bulb with light blue flowers, each with a white centre. They create a carpet of colour in February and March. In early summer the perennial wallflowers produce tall spikes of mauve and purple flowers. They contrast well with the tiny lime-green flowers of the lady's mantle which spill out over the path. Look at their leaves after a shower of rain: little drops of water will be trapped amongst the hairs.

A purple-bronze theme runs through the rest of the plants at the bottom of the arch which lie in wait for the grapes to swell and for the vine leaves to take on their rich autumn colours. The flowers and the leaves of the violas are tinged with purple; so is the dusky foliage of the purple sage which wraps itself around the base of the arch. Even more striking is the bronze fennel which produces a delicate haze of thread-like foliage, erupting ever higher as the summer progresses, until at last it stands nearly 2 m (6½') high and is topped by dainty yellow flowers. It smells and tastes faintly of aniseed and is a great attraction for bees and other small insects. It creates a wonderful focal point in its own right, and yet manages to blend with all the other plants which surround the arch.

37　The Scented Tunnel

INGREDIENTS

No req	Name	Description	Ht × Spr (cm/m)	Ht × Spr (″/′)	Best
1	Rambling rose *Rosa* 'Albertine'	copper-pink	5 m	16½′	6–7
1	Rambling rose *Rosa* 'Leontine Gervaise'	salmon	5 m	16½′	7
4	Lady's mantle *Alchemilla mollis*	yellow-green	30 × 30 cm	1 × 1′	6–7, 9
2	Cranesbills *Geranium himalayense* 'Grandiflorum'	violet-blue	30 × 60 cm	1 × 2′	6–7, 10
2	Cranesbills *Geranium endressii* 'Wargrave Pink'	salmon-pink	60 × 90 cm	2 × 3′	6–9
1	*Clematis *Clematis* 'Jackmanii Superba'	violet-purple	3 m	10′	7–9
4	Crocosmias *Crocosmia masonorum* 'Firebird'	flame orange	80 cm	32″	7–9
4	Flag irises *Iris pallida*	lavender-blue	90 × 30 cm	3 × 1′	5–6
2	Clematis *Clematis* 'Miss Bateman'	white	2.5 m	8′	6–7

SITE
In the sun. The arch will be appreciated more if it leads somewhere interesting, with a definite path through the middle.

SCALE
The double rose arch should be approximately 2.1 m (7′) high, wide and deep. The borders should be 60 cm (2′) wide.

PLAN
Right: Plant two irises to stand guard outside the entrance. Inside, plant a blue cranesbill, a lady's mantle, the 'Albertine' rose in the centre, another lady's mantle, a pink cranesbill, a 'Miss Bateman' clematis, and two crocosmias outside the second entrance.

Left: Plant two irises to stand guard outside the entrance. Inside, plant a 'Miss Bateman' clematis, a pink cranesbill, one lady's mantle, the 'Leontine Gervaise' rose in the centre, another lady's mantle and a blue cranesbill, then the 'Jackmanii' clematis. Plant two crocosmias outside the second entrance.

WHEN TO PLANT
Plant the roses, clematis and herbaceous plants from October to March.

AFTERCARE
Apply a rose fertiliser to all the plants in early spring, and mulch while the ground is damp. The roses need training and pruning. Tie the shoots to the framework to get a good dense covering. Thereafter, prune as necessary in late February and autumn to restrict growth, and remove any dead wood. Spray for greenfly and blackspot. Keep the roses well watered for the first year, until the plants are well established.

Both of the clematis flower on the current season's growth. Prune in early spring before the new growth has started. A bushy growth is wanted on the 'Miss Bateman', so cut her back to 25 cm (10″) from ground-level in the second year after planting. Thereafter, cut back by one-third to where strong leaf axil buds are visible. Remove all dead and weak growths and tie in replacement shoots. The 'Jackmanii' clematis needs a similar second-year treatment, but after that allow a few strong shoots to be trained horizontally about 45 cm (18″) above ground-level. The new vertical shoots will then create a good wall of growth. Prune all the vertical shoots back early each spring to a pair of strong buds just above the horizontals, thus removing the previous year's growth. Make sure the clematis, especially the 'Jackmanii', do not strangle the roses. The rest of the plants will spread well to form good clumps and need little attention.

'Miss Bateman' clematis   'Leontine Gervaise' rose   'Albertine' rose   'Miss Bateman' clematis
irises   pink cranesbill   lady's mantle, blue cranesbill, crocosmias
irises   blue cranesbill, lady's mantle, pink cranesbill, crocosmias

DESCRIPTION

The old-fashioned rambling roses make the arch a focal point in the cottage garden throughout most of June and July. One side is dominated by 'Albertine', with its rich salmon-pink buds which open up to a faded copper-pink flower. They are very fragrant and make lovely long sprays. The other side is covered with 'Leontine Gervaise'. It has similar colouring to the 'Albertine' with its deep salmon flowers, but the main show is slightly later and will probably continue through to the autumn. It is a graceful rose, with good glossy foliage.

Down below, the yellow-green flowers of the lady's mantle make an easy colour association with the roses above and the cranesbills by their side. The 'Grandiflorum' cranesbill is a wonderful intense violet-blue with strongly marked veins, and provides a vivid colour scheme with the salmon and copper roses. It has daintily cut leaves, which contrast well with the spiky irises just in front. Further back is the 'Wargrave Pink' cranesbill, with its bright little salmon-pink flowers, which appear for weeks on end. It forms itself well into dense weed-free clumps.

By late summer the 'Jackmanii' clematis is in full bloom. The rich violet-purple blooms completely smother the sides and top of the arch. 'Jackmanii Superba' is one of the old favourites, and has been grown for over a hundred years. Rightly so, for its display is quite magnificent and lasts from July to September. It makes a stunning contrast to the fiery arching spikes of the crocosmias which stand sentinel at the far entrance to the arch. They are a brilliant orange-red and last as long as the clematis above.

The cranesbill leaves turn russet in autumn, and all the plants go into hibernation until late spring. Then, in May, the irises come into bloom. They stand with their sword-like leaves like guards at the entrance. Their flowers are a pale lavender-blue, crinkly and silky, with a sweet fragrance like orange blossom. These irises are among the best known; they have been cultivated since ancient times, and are so easy to look after. Unlike many others, their grey leaves remain beautiful until the autumn, thereby earning them their prominent position.

The clematis 'Miss Bateman' is in her full glory in June. Her single white flowers have slender red anthers like the stems of the 'Albertine' rose, and where they are in shade a green stripe can be seen down the centre of each petal. She looks exquisite beside the opening rosebuds.

38 The 'May Queen' Rose Arbour

INGREDIENTS

No req	Name	Description	Ht × Spr (cm/m)	Ht × Spr ("/')	Best
2	Rambling roses *Rosa* 'May Queen'	lilac-pink	4.5 m	15'	6–7
2	Provence roses *Rosa* 'Fantin-Latour'	double, pink	1.5 × 1.2 m	5 × 4'	6–7
4	Delphiniums *Delphinium* 'Blue Dawn'	blue	150 × 90 cm	5 × 3'	6–7
4	Foxgloves *Digitalis purpurea* 'Excelsior Hybrids Mixed'	pink, purple	150 × 60 cm	5 × 2'	6–7
6	Bellflowers *Campanula persicifolia* 'Alba'	white	90 × 30 cm	3 × 1'	6–7, 8–9
6	Catmints *Nepeta* 'Six Hills Giant'	lavender-blue	90 × 90 cm	3 × 3'	6, 9
1	Mock orange *Philadelphus* 'Beauclerk'	white	2 × 2 m	6½ × 6½'	6–7
1	Butterfly bush *Buddleja davidii* 'Empire Blue'	violet-blue	2.5 × 2.5 m	8 × 8'	7–8

SITE

The rose arbour can be in full sun or a little shade.

SCALE

The two borders on either side of the rose arbour should each be 3 m (10') wide and 3.5 m (11½') deep.

PLAN

Back: Plant the mock orange to the left and the butterfly bush to the right, with one foxglove off to the side in front of each shrub.
Middle: Plant the 'Fantin-Latour' roses in the centre of each border, with two delphiniums near the centre and three bellflowers forming an arc just in front.
Front: Plant three catmints.
Arbour: Plant 'May Queen' roses at the base on both sides.

WHEN TO PLANT

October to March for all the herbaceous plants and the bare-rooted roses.

AFTERCARE

Apply a general rose fertiliser in early spring and then mulch while the ground is damp. Prune the roses in late February, removing any growth that is weak or dead. Prune so as to build up a good open shape.

The arbour should be rampant with growth and flowers. Tie the shoots to the framework to get a good dense cover. With the shrub roses, aim to get a good shape, remove all weak growths and some of the old central wood from time to time to make way for fresh new growth. Spray against blackspot and greenfly. Do not allow the roses to dry out in the summer, particularly in the first year after planting.

Prune the mock orange after flowering. Thin out the old wood but take care to retain young shoots that will flower the following year. Prune the butterfly bush in March to within 8 cm (3") of the old wood. If it threatens to spoil the shape of the plants in front, cut it back. There will be no shortage of flowers elsewhere. Place prickly rose stems or berberis in amongst the catmints early in the season to stop cats from rolling in it.

Support the delphiniums and bellflowers in late April or May. Beware of slugs on young delphinium growth. Deadhead the delphiniums to the nearest healthy leaf below the raceme; a second crop of flowers might then appear. Cut back the bellflowers to encourage a second show later. Cut the catmints, delphiniums and bellflowers down to ground-level in the late autumn. The foxgloves should self-seed.

mock orange
Provence rose
foxglove, bellflowers, delphiniums, foxglove
catmint

rambling roses

butterfly bush
Provence rose
bellflowers, foxglove, delphiniums, foxglove
catmint

DESCRIPTION

'May Queen' is an old-fashioned rambling rose with quartered lilac-pink blooms which are held in abundance against neat and shiny foliage. It is easy to train and so makes a good subject for the rose arbour. The flowers have a delicate fragrance and are similar in colour to the lovely Provence rose 'Fantin-Latour' which grows on either side. This, too, has good foliage. It also has a pervading perfume and is justly renowned as one of the most famous of all the old roses.

The delphiniums flower for several weeks at the end of June and early July and make a notable contribution with their tall spikes as well as their blue colouring. Pink and purple foxgloves bow to greet the visitor at the entrance to the arbour, while more appear towards the back of the border. They don't mind whether they are in sun or shade. The bees will still find them and investigate each speckled glove. They are old favourites and blend perfectly with the roses and delphiniums. Not so showy, but lovely nevertheless, are the white bellflowers which reach up amongst the pinks and blues. Theirs is a gentle presence which is much appreciated. Lazy catmint spreads itself in a haze of lavender-blue, spilling right out over the path. Bees buzz round ceaselessly, as if their work will never end.

At the back of the left-hand border is the mock orange. 'Beauclerk' is an arching deciduous shrub with large single white flowers, each strongly scented. It blooms at the same time as the roses and provides an excellent setting for them. The milky white flowers show through above the lovely pinks and blues of the plants in front. On the other side, the violet-blue flowers of the butterfly bush 'Empire Blue' are just beginning to open. They have a strong orange eye and are attractive to a whole host of butterflies in July and August. It is a delightful cottage scene, full of colour and fragrance, and humming with insects. The old bench is aptly placed in the centre of it all.

39 Hops and Hips on the Cottage Pergola

INGREDIENTS

No req	Name	Description	Ht × Spr (cm/m)	Ht × Spr ("/')	Best
1	Clematis *Clematis tangutica*	yellow	5 m	16½'	8–10
1	Rambling rose *Rosa* 'Rambling Rector'	double, white	6 m	19½'	6–7, 9
1	Climbing rose *Rosa* 'Mme Alfred Carrière'	white	6 m	19½'	6–7, 9
1	Golden hop *Humulus lupulus* 'Aureus' (female form)	golden leaves	5 m	16½'	5–7, 9
40	Golden feverfew *Tanacetum parthenium* 'Aureum'	white	30 × 30 cm	1 × 1'	6–7, or 7–9
2	Perennial peas *Lathyrus latifolius* 'White Pearl'	white	2 m	6½'	6–9
1	Clematis *Clematis* 'Vyvyan Pennell'	double, violet	3 m	10'	5–7, 9–11
1	Clematis *Clematis* 'Mrs Cholmondeley'	pale blue	2.5 m	8'	5–10

SITE
Sunny.

SCALE
You'll need a substantial pergola 6 m (19½') wide and 2 m (6½') deep with a 1-m (3¼') path in the middle. Use eight posts 2–2.5 m (6½–8') high, separated at 2 m (6½') intervals. The borders should be 60 cm (2') deep on either side. Cover the top of the pergola with strong wire mesh or a wooden trellis so that the plants do not obstruct the pathway. A support system – plastic or wire netting, or simple wires – should be attached to each post to help the plants climb. The narrow grass strip can be avoided by placing the border right next to the path. More plants can be included here along with the feverfew.

PLAN
Far side: At the base of the four posts, plant 'Vyvyan Pennell', 'Rambling Rector', a perennial pea and 'Mme Alfred Carrière'.
Near side: At the base of the four posts, plant *Clematis tangutica*, another perennial pea, the hop, then 'Mrs Cholmondeley'.
Both sides: Plant six feverfew between each post and one at either end where they will shade the three clematis roots.

WHEN TO PLANT
November to December, and up to March. The clematis will benefit from extra lime if the soil is acidic or neutral.

AFTERCARE
Give the plants a general fertiliser in March and mulch while the ground is damp. Give another feed again at the end of June to help the autumn flowerers. Train the roses to establish a good fan shape so that they flower from top to bottom, not just along the pergola top. After she flowers, cut back the new long shoots of 'Mme Alfred Carrière'. This will encourage further flowering later in the season. Tie in growths with garden string. In midsummer, just before flowering, 'Rambling Rector' sends out long shoots. Prune them off. This will channel all its energy back into producing flowers. Do the same again in early autumn so the energy goes into the hips.

Train *Clematis tangutica* horizontally at first, then allow verticals to grow up the sides. Every spring, cut the verticals back to a pair of plump buds near the horizontals. Prune the other two clematis in spring. In their second year, cut them back to within 25 cm (10") of their base; thereafter, reduce the shoots by up to one-third. Remove weak and dead wood and tie in replacement shoots. Prune the hop back to its base

'Vyvyan Pennell' clematis

rambling rose

climbing rose

Clematis tangutica

perennial pea   golden hop   'Mrs Cholmondeley' clematis

golden feverfew

in early spring. Keep alternate feverfews clipped all summer, so that some flower in June and July, and some in early autumn. Replant them in spring with new seedlings. Deadhead the perennial peas and cut them down in late October.

DESCRIPTION

The cottage pergola looks wonderful even in September. *Clematis tangutica* is in full array with its dense mass of twining feathery foliage and citrus-yellow flowers which are shaped like lanterns. They are produced over such a long period from August to October that flowers appear at the same time as fluffy seedheads. Reaching out through its yellow heads are long delicate sprays of small orange hips belonging to the rose 'Rambling Rector'. It flowered in great profusion in June and early July; now its autumnal display is very different. Further along the pergola, the rose 'Mme Alfred Carrière' is still in bloom. The flowers are white with a touch of pink, large and well scented. This is a strong climber which will grow right along the pergola top, mingling with all the other climbers, including the golden hop. The hop naturally grows upwards first and then cascades down with a profusion of foliage creating curtains along the pergola. The bright golden foliage looked wonderful

with the two white roses in midsummer, but the leaves have now turned to more of a mid-green. There might be a few trusses of pale green hops, but the golden form is less generous than its common relative.

Beneath the pergola is a low 'hedge' of golden feverfew with their white daisy-like flowers bright with yellow centres. Keep half of them well clipped throughout the summer, so that they retain their golden foliage. Then, at last, let them free and they will burst into a mass of flowers, looking so fresh against the finely divided leaves. The perennial pea has been flowering since June, clambering up the supports, with its mass of green stems and pretty white clusters of flowers. The two together provide a white and green carpet which blends beautifully with the rose and clematis above.

At the front of the pergola, the clematis 'Vyvyan Pennell' climbs up to produce a mass of double violet flowers. In June and July it makes a sumptuous combination amongst the creamy white clusters of the 'Rambling Rector'. Further back, 'Mrs Cholmondeley' is still in bloom with her large pale blue flowers. Both of the clematis produce flowers throughout the summer and well into the autumn, a hint of blue amongst all the white, yellows and pale greens.

40   *The Winter Garden*

INGREDIENTS

No req	Name	Description	Evergreen	Ht × Spr (cm/m)	Ht × Spr ("/')	Best
1	Mahonia *Mahonia japonica*	yellow	yes	3 × 3 m	10 × 10'	1–3
1	Viburnum *Viburnum × bodnantense* 'Dawn'	pink	no	3 × 2 m	10 × 6½'	11–2
1	Daphne *Daphne odora* 'Aureomarginata'	white/purple	yes	1.5 × 1.5 m	5 × 5'	2–4
4	Winter heathers *Erica carnea* 'Springwood White'	white	yes	20 × 45 cm	8 × 18"	1–3
60	Snowdrops *Galanthus nivalis*	white	no	10 cm	4"	1–3
4	Lenten roses *Helleborus orientalis*	mixed	yes	45 × 60 cm	18 × 24"	2–3
1	Garrya *Garrya elliptica*	green catkins	yes	4 × 3 m	13 × 10'	1–3

SITE
An open sunny border, accessible by a path, and near a window so that it can be seen throughout the winter whatever the weather.

SCALE
4 m (13') wide and 2 m (6½') deep.

PLAN
Back, left to right: Plant the mahonia, viburnum and garrya.
Middle: Plant a quarter of the snowdrops and a Lenten rose on either side of the daphne.
Front: Plant two heathers at each end, with a Lenten rose and the rest of the snowdrops on either side of the centre.

WHEN TO PLANT
Planting in either early October or early April suits most of the plants. However, snowdrops are best planted in August or early September, or left until March and then planted 'in the green'. Plant them 5 cm (2") deep, 8 cm (3") apart in groups of fifteen. *Garrya elliptica* prefers the April planting and must be protected during the first winter. It also needs the protection of a fence or wall. If this is not possible, substitute *Viburnum tinus*.

AFTERCARE
Mulch in autumn while the ground is damp. The shrubs do not need any regular pruning, only enough to remove dead wood and to maintain shape. April is the best time to prune, but feel free to cut stems during the winter for indoor arrangements. This will help to confine them to the space available. Cut back the heathers after they flower in the spring, as this will help to maintain a neat appearance. The Lenten roses and snowdrops should be left undisturbed.

mahonia   viburnum   garrya

Lenten rose   daphne   Lenten rose

snowdrops

heathers   Lenten roses   heathers   snowdrops

DESCRIPTION

This winter garden has a wonderful abundance of flowers and fragrance. It might seem surprising to find such small flowers with so strong a perfume. However, the mahonia, the 'Dawn' viburnum and the daphne all have a scent which is powerful beyond expectation.

The mahonia flowers have a beautifully sweet fragrance, just like lily of the valley. They appear from January through to March in great abundance, and are much loved by the bees. Each tiny yellow flower is shaped like a miniature daffodil; together they line the long drooping racemes. Even four or five stems in a little vase on the table can scent an entire room. It is a sculptural plant with dark green spiny leaves which remains attractive throughout the year. The rich pink flowers of the 'Dawn' viburnum are another show-stopper. They are deliciously fragrant and extremely attractive. They appear throughout the winter on dark bare twigs. This is one of the most frost-resistant of all the winter-flowering shrubs. The daphne is altogether much smaller and more compact. Its white, sweetly scented blooms are tinged with red and purple. They show off well against the gold-rimmed leaves.

Not all the winter flowers have a strong scent, but any plant which produces colour in the garden at this time of year is very much appreciated, especially the 'Springwood White' heathers, with their abundance of white blooms which last for weeks and weeks from mid-winter until spring. The little snowdrops with their dainty nodding heads are always welcome. Particularly noteworthy are the Lenten roses with their cup-shaped heads. They may be maroon or crimson, pink or white; some are spotted inside and flushed with green. They all have great charm and poise. What about the long grey-green catkins of the *Garrya elliptica*! They dangle like silky tassels and look lovely alongside the pink viburnum flowers.

Of all the shrubs only the 'Dawn' viburnum is deciduous; it flowers on naked stems. Its spring leaves are bronze, while its autumn leaves have purple tints.

41 A Summer Rose Garden

INGREDIENTS

No req	Name	Description	Ht × Spr (cm/m)	Ht × Spr ("/')	Best
2	Old Velvet Moss roses *Rosa* 'William Lobb'	double, magenta-purple	2 × 1.5 m	6½ × 5'	6–7
1	Damask rose *Rosa* 'Mme Hardy'	double, white	1.5 × 1.5 m	5 × 5'	6–7
3	Striped roses *Rosa gallica* 'Versicolor' (Rosa Mundi)	crimson/white	90 × 90 cm	3 × 3'	6–7
2	Baby's breath *Gypsophila paniculata* 'Snow White'	white	90 × 120 cm	3 × 4'	6–9
4	Hostas *Hosta sieboldiana* 'Elegans'	lilac-white	75 × 60 cm	30 × 24"	7
2	Meadow rue *Thalictrum aquilegifolium* 'Thundercloud'	lilac	100 × 60 cm	3¼ × 2'	6–7
4	Foxgloves *Digitalis purpurea* 'Alba'	white	90 × 45 cm	36 × 18"	6–7
2	Bellflowers *Campanula lactiflora* 'Loddon Anna'	lilac-pink	1.2 × 1.5 m	4 × 5'	6–8
3	Bear's breeches *Acanthus spinosus*	mauve/white	120 × 60 cm	4 × 2'	7–9

SITE
A sunny border.

SCALE
4.5 m (15½') wide and 3 m (10') deep.

PLAN
Back: Plant the 'Mme Hardy' 75 cm (30") from the back of the border, with the two 'William Lobb' 1.5 m (5') away on either side.
Middle: Plant the meadow rue and foxgloves to the left, with bellflowers in the centre and bear's breeches to the right.
Front: Plant the Rosa Mundi along the centre of the border, allowing the full 90-cm (3') spacing. Plant one baby's breath on either side of the roses, with two hostas at each end to make a bold statement at the corner.

WHEN TO PLANT
November to March.

AFTERCARE
Apply a rose fertiliser to the whole border in early spring and then mulch generously while the ground is damp. Prune all the roses in late February, removing about one-half of the previous season's growth. Try to cut out congested growth in the centre of the bushes and any superfluous thin shoots. Spray against blackspot and greenfly. Do not allow them to dry out in summer, particularly in the first year after planting. 'William Lobb' may need extra support, although 'Mme Hardy' will give some support in the centre. Metal rose hoops would be ideal, or prune rather more tightly than otherwise.

Baby's breath likes limey soil, so if the soil is neutral, apply lime, 50 g per 0.8 m² (2 oz per sq yd). Use twiggy sticks for support early in the growing season. Support the meadow rue at the same time. Cut it down in November. The foxgloves are biennial and will seed themselves. Cut the flowering stems of the bear's breeches, hostas and bellflowers almost to ground-level after flowering.

'William Lobb' rose		'Mme Hardy' rose		'William Lobb' rose
meadow rue	foxgloves	bellflowers		bear's breeches
hostas	baby's breath	Rosa Mundi	baby's breath	hostas

DESCRIPTION

Many beautiful aspects of old-fashioned roses are encapsulated here in this one setting: perfume, fullness of bloom, rich colouring and mossing.

Two Old Velvet Moss roses called 'William Lobb' dominate the scene, providing a wealth of magenta-purple flowers. They are borne in such large clusters that they cascade downwards and intermingle with all around them. One of the main attractions is the heavy moss-like growth around the flowers, which is particularly noticeable in the bud stage. It is this occurrence which adds to the rich perfume.

'Mme Hardy' is the elegant white rose in the centre. Her vigorous light green growth offers useful support to the laxer growth of 'William Lobb'. She is smothered in flowers, each strongly scented, with inner petals that remain incurved around a tiny green eye even though the outer ones turn down with age. A little distance in front are the ancient Rosa Mundi roses with their crimson, blush-pink and white stripes. They form an attractive low hedge. On either side there is a wonderful cloud of tiny white flowers belonging to the baby's breath. It has a lovely softening effect on the dark flowers of 'William Lobb' and the showy stripes of Rosa Mundi. In stark contrast, bold hostas form the cornerpiece on either side. Their sumptuous blue-grey leaves are crinkled and deeply veined, and create great fans of foliage.

The groups of plants between the high roses and the lower front hedge add a considerable variety of colours and shapes. On the left, tall fluffy heads of meadow rue rise up from a dainty mass of foliage. The flowers are a deep lilac and look very fine with the glaucous hosta leaves and white baby's breath just in front. Further back, tall white foxgloves tower upwards, standing out so beautifully against the deep crimson blooms of 'William Lobb'. In the centre, the pale lilac-pink bellflower called 'Loddon Anna' forms one great mass which will go on flowering for many weeks. Beside it are bold spikes of bear's breeches with their tall heads of mauve and white flowers, and deeply divided arching leaves. They make a stately group, contrasting well with the laxer growth of 'William Lobb' behind, and softened at the front by the billowing white cloud of baby's breath. It is a delightful midsummer scene.

42   The Fern Garden

INGREDIENTS

No req	Name	Evergreen	Ht × Spr (cm/m)	Ht × Spr ("/')	Best
2	Lady ferns *Athyrium filix-femina*	no	70 × 70 cm	28 × 28″	5–9
1	Victorian lady fern *Athyrium filix-femina* 'Victoriae'	no	80 × 80 cm	32 × 32″	5–9
3	Male ferns *Dryopteris filix-mas*	no	90 × 90 cm	3 × 3′	5–9
3	Hart's tongue ferns *Asplenium scolopendrium*	yes	40 × 40 cm	16 × 16″	6–10
4	Cornish ferns *Polypodium vulgare* 'Cornubiense'	yes	30 × 30 cm	1 × 1′	7–11
4	Soft shield ferns *Polystichum setiferum*	yes	120 × 90 cm	4 × 3′	5–11
		Flower			
5	Turk's cap lilies *Lilium martagon*	maroon	1.5 m	5′	7
30	*Wood anemones *Anemone nemorosa*	white	15 cm	6″	3–4

SITE
A shady border, which might be backed by a wall or a fence with honeysuckle trailing over it.

SCALE
4 m (13′) wide and 2 m (6½′) deep, although this is easily adaptable.

PLAN
Back: Plant three male ferns to the left and centre and one soft shield fern to the right.
Middle: Plant the three remaining soft shield ferns to the left and centre with the Victorian lady fern to the right.
Front: Plant the three hart's tongue ferns in a group to the left, and the two lady ferns and four Cornish ferns in a group to the right.
Plant wood anemones and Turk's cap lilies amongst them all.

WHEN TO PLANT
An April planting suits all the ferns. The anemones should be planted in the following September or October, 3–5 cm (1¼–2″) deep, 15 cm (6″) apart. The lilies should be planted when they are available, between October and March, 10 cm (4″) deep and 25 cm (10″) apart. Avoid any dry, shrivelled bulbs.

Male ferns like the shadier end of the border, perhaps at the back beneath the fence or wall, while lady ferns prefer light shade and might be better suited to the front of the border. The rest of the ferns are all very adaptable. They will tolerate any loamy, neutral or alkaline soil.

AFTERCARE
Give the lady ferns a top dressing of bonemeal in early spring, then mulch the border with leaf mould or compost while the soil is damp. The lady ferns' rootstocks gradually rise up out of the ground, so it is best to lift and replant them every three or four years. The hart's tongue fern may look untidy by March, so cut away the tattered old fronds and enjoy the new growth. With the other ferns, it is best to let the leaves die down *in situ*, thus creating a natural mulch. The bulbs will fend for themselves and should gradually increase over the years.

male ferns

soft shield ferns

hart's tongue ferns   *Turk's cap lilies*

soft shield fern

Victorian lady fern

lady ferns & Cornish ferns

DESCRIPTION

By July the fern garden is at its best. Slowly, the new fronds unfurl to reveal the most exquisite shapes. The lady fern is deciduous, and in early summer it has very dainty fresh green growth. 'Victoriae' is a crested form which has a criss-cross pattern all the way up the stems. Its deep green fronds are most distinctive and make a delightful addition to the garden. The male ferns are deciduous as well, but much larger in scale and better placed near the back of the border where they can form bold clumps. They are well able to adapt to the shadiest of positions and are certainly easy to look after.

The remaining ferns are evergreen. The hart's tongue fern is glorious in June and July when its glossy bright green fronds are uncurling. Unlike the other ferns, they are broad and strap-shaped. They take centre stage near the front of the border and make a good contrast to the Cornish ferns nearby. These have fine lacy fronds which look good all year round, but are best in mid to late summer, when the fresh green growth appears particularly pleasing. The three soft shield ferns make a great impact. They are one of the most adaptable ferns in the garden and are suitable for many difficult sites, always presenting an impressive display. The new fronds are covered with pale brown and white scales, and as they mature they exhibit finely divided leaves.

Maroon Turk's cap lilies add both colour and elegance for several weeks in July, just when the ferns are at their best. They rise about 1.5 m (5′) high, with six or seven flowers to a stem. The petals fly backwards to reveal dark spots underneath.

April-flowering wood anemones can also be used to add variety. Their dainty white heads and delicate foliage bring a freshness which is otherwise lacking in the fern garden at this time of year. Both the bulbs and the ferns appear very much at home together.

43 A Summer Butterfly and Bee Border

INGREDIENTS

No req	Name	Description	Ht × Spr (cm/m)	Ht × Spr ("/')	Best
1	Butterfly bush *Buddleja davidii* 'Fascination'	lilac	2.4 × 2.4m	8 × 8'	7–8
2	Globe thistles *Echinops ritro* 'Veitch's Blue'	blue	120 × 60cm	4 × 2'	6–9
1	Shrubby mallow *Lavatera* 'Barnsley'	pink	1.8 × 1.8m	6 × 6'	6–10
2	Lavenders *Lavandula angustifolia* 'Hidcote'	violet-blue	60 × 60 cm	2 × 2'	7–9
3	Michaelmas daisies *Aster novae-angliae* 'Harrington's Pink'	pink	120 × 60cm	4 × 2'	8–9
1	Bergamot *Monarda fistulosa* 'Prairie Night'	purple	90 × 45cm	36 × 18"	6–8
4	Bellflowers *Campanula persicifolia*	blue	90 × 30 cm	3 × 1'	6–7, 8–9
2	Phlox *Phlox maculata* 'Alpha'	pink	90 × 45 cm	36 × 18"	7–9
2	Ice plants *Sedum spectabile*	pink	45 × 45 cm	18 × 18"	8–10
4	Valerian *Centranthus ruber*	pink	60 × 30 cm	2 × 1'	6–7, 9–10
2	*Thrift *Armeria maritima* 'Dusseldorf Pride'	pink	15 × 30 cm	6 × 12"	6–8
12	*Poached egg plants *Limnanthes douglasii*	yellow/ white	15 × 10 cm	6 × 4"	6–7
5	*Honesty *Lunaria annua*	purple	75 × 30 cm	30 × 12"	4–5
3	*Sweet rockets *Hesperis matronalis*	mixed	45 × 15 cm	18 × 6"	6

SITE
A sunny border backed by wall, hedge or fence.

SCALE
5 m (16½') wide and 2 m (6½') deep. Treat this as a separate border or join it to Recipe 44 to make a 10-m (33') border.

PLAN
Back: Plant the butterfly bush on left with shrubby mallow on right, both 75 cm (30") from the back of the border. Plant globe thistles in the middle with phlox in front. Plant three honesty and three sweet rockets along the sides and back of the border.
Front: Alternate thrifts, ice plants and poached egg plants along the path, on either side of the lavenders. In-fill on both sides with Michaelmas daisies, bellflowers, bergamot, valerian and the remaining honesty.

WHEN TO PLANT
October to November or March to April for the butterfly bush, shrubby mallow and bergamot. Poached egg plant seeds can be sown where they are to flower in September or March. Sow the sweet rockets elsewhere in April, plant them out in June, and put them in their final positions in autumn. Plant the rest of the ingredients from October to March.

AFTERCARE
Keep the butterfly bush to a manageable size by pruning it hard in March. Cut back all previous growth to within 5 cm (2") of the old wood. Cut the globe thistles to ground-level in October. Prune the shrubby mallow to shape in the spring. Trim the lavender in late summer. The Michaelmas daisies and phlox should be cut down to just above ground-level in October. Cut the bergamot down in late autumn. The bellflowers will flower again in late summer if the first flower spikes are cut down in mid-July. The ice plants are long-lived but from time to time need dividing in spring to prevent floppiness later in the year. Remove the ice plant flower heads in spring.

	butterfly bush		*globe thistles*			*shrubby mallow*
Michaelmas daisy	*bellflowers*		*phlox*		*bergamot*	*Michaelmas daisies*	*bellflowers*
ice plants		*valerian*		*lavenders*		*valerian*

Deadhead the valerian to prevent self-seeding and to encourage a second flowering in the autumn. Deadhead the thrift. Allow the poached egg plants, sweet rockets and honesty to set seed so that they produce new plants for the following year; remove the surplus in spring.

DESCRIPTION

From July to August the butterfly bush is in flower. 'Fascination' has lilac flowers with a strong scent, which act like a magnet to dozens of butterflies of varying types. The love affair will go on for many weeks. Look out for the magnificent peacock with its rich colouring and famous 'eyes'. At the same time, tall spiky blue heads of the globe thistle will be alive with bees. Watch them move from one head to another, eclipsed by the summer blue sky. The shrubby mallow, with its lovely soft pink flowers, provides a wonderful counterbalance to the butterfly bush, both in terms of colour and stature. It, too, is buzzing with bees and more than the occasional butterfly will pay its respects. Here even the white cabbage butterfly looks enchanting. The same is true of the lavender. It is a favourite with bees but the butterflies like it as well.

In late August and September, the Michaelmas daisies are in full flower, a lovely bright pink amongst the shaggy purple bergamot and the tall blue bell-flowers. 'Harrington's Pink' is not prone to rust like some of its relatives. The valerian is in its second flowering, and plays host to many visitors. Another great favourite is the pink phlox, lasting from July to September. By then the old ice plants are softly changing colour from a delicate green to pink. They are best seen near the front of the border, where it is easy to peer down on the outstretched wings of the peacock or the small tortoiseshell delicately poised drinking the nectar. Like the valerian and the butter-fly bush, it has masses of little flowers tightly clustered together, providing an easy source of food and a sturdy perch.

Winter arrives and all is quiet, then, the following June, the valerian will begin its first flowering. It is undoubtedly one of the key plants in this garden. Particularly in its pink form, it attracts a host of butterflies, including red admirals, peacocks, large and small white, tortoiseshell, wall and meadow brown.

At the same time, neat clumps of pink thrift and yellow poached egg plants line the path. The honesty is over in June, but the old-fashioned sweet rocket with its simple lilac flowers is blooming and playing host to the butterflies and bees before the powerful attraction of the butterfly bush lures them away again in July.

44 The Butterfly and Bee Border Continued

INGREDIENTS

No req	Name	Description	Ht × Spr (cm/m)	Ht × Spr ("/')	Best
1	Ceanothus *Ceanothus* 'Gloire de Versailles'	blue	2 × 2 m	6½ × 6½'	6–10
2	Hollyhocks *Althaea rugosa*	pale yellow	150 × 60 cm	5 × 2'	7–9
1	Lavender *Lavandula angustifolia* 'Royal Purple'	purple	80 × 80 cm	32 × 32"	7–8
1	Hyssop *Hyssopus officinalis*	blue	45 × 45 cm	18 × 18"	7–9
4	Valerian *Centranthus ruber*	pink	60 × 30 cm	2 × 1'	6–7, 9–10
2	Snapdragons *Antirrhinum majus* 'Yellow Monarch'	yellow	45 × 30 cm	18 × 12"	6, 8–9
3	Sneezeweeds *Helenium autumnale* 'Wyndley'	yellow, copper	60 × 60 cm	2 × 2'	6–8
1	Bronze fennel *Foeniculum vulgare* 'Purpureum'	yellow	180 × 60 cm	6 × 2'	8–9
3	Sunflowers *Helianthus annuus* 'Autumn Beauty'	gold	180 × 75 cm	72 × 30"	8–9
2	Evening primroses *Oenothera missouriensis*	yellow	25 × 60 cm	10 × 24"	6–9
3	Ice plants *Sedum spectabile*	pink	45 × 45 cm	18 × 18"	8–10
1	Caryopteris *Caryopteris* × *clandonensis* 'Heavenly Blue'	blue	90 × 90 cm	3 × 3'	8–9
6	*Honesty *Lunaria annua*	purple	75 × 30 cm	30 × 12"	4–5
12	*Poached egg plants *Limnanthes douglasii*	yellow/white	15 × 10 cm	6 × 4"	6–7

SITE
A sunny border backed by a wall, hedge or fence.

SCALE
5 m (16½') wide and 2 m (6½') deep. This recipe can be treated as a separate border or a continuation of Recipe 43.

PLAN
Back: Plant the honesty along the back and sides of the border, with three sunflowers on the right.
Middle: Plant hollyhocks on the left, then the ceanothus, with two sneezeweeds and two snapdragons in the centre middle and bronze fennel to the right.
Front: Plant the lavender on the left, then an evening primrose and the caryopteris in the middle, with a series of poached egg plants, ice plants and the second evening primrose to the right. In-fill behind with hyssop, valerian – they will spill forwards – and sneezeweeds.

WHEN TO PLANT
October to March for most of the ingredients. Plant the caryopteris either from September to October or from March to April. Poached egg plants and sunflowers are annuals. Sow them where they are to flower from September to March for poached egg plants, and March or April for the sunflowers. Use three sunflower seeds to each station, then reduce to the strongest seedling. Honesty is biennial and should be sown elsewhere in May or June, and planted out in September.

AFTERCARE
Apply a general rose fertiliser in early spring and then mulch while the ground is damp. Do not prune the ceanothus unless the front needs restricting. This hollyhock is not prone to rust and needs staking only if it is exposed. Its seeds are not reliably true, so eventually new stock will be needed. Trim the lavender after flowering, to within 5 cm (2") of the hard wood. Prune the hyssop in March. Deadhead the valerian to prevent self-seeding and to encourage a second flowering in the autumn. Treat the snapdragons as perennials. They will self-seed if that is wanted. Stake the sneezeweeds in early summer.

hollyhocks		ceanothus	sneezeweeds	sunflowers	bronze fennel
			hyssop	snapdragons	sneezeweeds
lavender	evening primrose	caryopteris	valerian	ice plants	evening primrose

Remove the seedheads of the bronze fennel early to prevent self-seeding. Save some sunflower seeds to sow the following spring.

Prune the caryopteris in March. Remove all weak stems, and cut others hard back to a strong healthy bud. Allow the honesty and poached egg plants to set seed so they produce new plants for next year; remove the surplus in the spring. Cut the stems of the hollyhocks, valerian, snapdragons, sneezeweeds, bronze fennel and evening primroses to ground-level in late autumn. Leave the old flower heads on the ice plant until spring.

DESCRIPTION

The ceanothus is in flower all summer and late into the autumn with its powdery blue flower spikes; it is very dainty and most attractive to both bees and butterflies. What a treat it is to see a holly blue butterfly rest on the flowers. They are exactly the same colour. Another joy is to watch a big fat bumblebee investigating the delicate papery flower of the tall yellow hollyhock. In he goes, round and round the stamen, getting ever more covered with pollen. No wonder each flower produces so many seeds! By August the lavender is buzzing, and nearby the hyssop is too. The rich blues are fine bedfellows for one another, vying for company amidst the summer throng. Valerian sits close by them both, producing masses of pink flowers to attract the butterflies all summer long. Snapdragons are old cottage garden favourites; here, two yellow ones give colour both in June and from August to September, if the early flowers are cut back. Just watch the bees weight down the lower lips and put their tongues inside.

A golden picture emerges in late summer to the right of the border with the sneezeweeds and bronze fennel in full flower. The fennel, now nearly 2 m (6½') high, is alive with insects of all kinds. Ladybirds gobble up the aphids while hoverflies and bees work the tiny yellow flowers which perfume the air with their distinctive aniseed-like smell. Forming a framework behind are the three giant sunflowers. Bees love to feed on the nectar. Later, birds will feast on the seeds.

Right at the front of the border, the evening primroses are still flowering; they have a clear yellow open flower with a lovely scent at dusk. The ice plants attract butterflies and bees alike – indeed their flat heads act like a magnet. The scene would not be complete without them. Right at the heart of the autumn border is the caryopteris with its fragrant grey-green foliage and fuzzy blue flowers. The bees adore it and on a sunny afternoon it will be teeming with activity.

The border lies dormant throughout the winter but comes alive in spring when the purple honesty is in flower. Both bees and butterflies love it. Bees simply can't resist the poached egg plants, also known as bee plants, which line the early summer path with their yellow and white faces.

45   The Cottage Fruit Garden

INGREDIENTS

No req	Name	Distance between plants/rows (cm/m)	Distance between plants/rows ("/')	Plant	Harvest/ In Flower
30	Sweet peas mixed *Lathyrus odoratus* 'Antique Fantasy'	20 cm/45 cm	8"/18"	9–10, 3	6–9
3	Rhubarb 'The Sutton'	1 m	3¼'	2–3	3–7
14	Raspberries 'Malling Jewel'	40 cm/1.8 m	16"/6'	11–3	7
2	Gooseberries 'Lancer'	1.2 m	4'	10–3	6–7
2	Blackcurrants 'Wellington XXX'	1.2 m	4'	10–3	6–7
2	Redcurrants 'Red Lake'	1.2 m	4'	10–3	6–7
14	Nasturtiums mixed *Tropaeolum majus* 'Tom Thumb'	45 cm	18"	4	7–10

SITE

All of these plants prefer an open sunny position. Although redcurrants, blackcurrants, gooseberries and raspberries will tolerate a little shade, a frost hollow will impair their crops.

SCALE

7 m (23') wide and 3.6 m (12') deep, with a path on one side.

PLAN

See the ingredients list for the spacing between plants and rows. The raspberries could be closer if space is short.

From back to front: Plant the gooseberries, redcurrants and blackcurrants in pairs, followed by two rows of raspberries, one row of rhubarb and a double row of sweet peas. Sow the nasturtium seeds all along the edge of the path.

As an alternative plan, include four rows of strawberries instead of the currants and gooseberries. Or grow them as an extra crop and allow for an additional 3 m (10') so that the plot measures 10 m (33') wide and 3.6 m (12') deep.

WHEN TO PLANT

See the ingredients list. Prepare the soil well before planting by mixing in generous supplies of compost and well-rotted manure. Ideally, protect all of the soft fruit with a cage and netting.

AFTERCARE AND DESCRIPTION

Sweet peas benefit from well-prepared ground with lots of compost added. Sow the seeds in autumn or March, and thin the plants in April. Pinch out the growing tips when the young plants are 10 cm (4") high. Encourage the plants to scramble up canes or netting. Spray for blackfly. Deadhead regularly. Do not allow the sweet peas to go to seed or flowering will cease. Give them a weekly liquid feed throughout the summer. Remove the plants at the end of autumn. Sow fresh seed for the following season. They provide plenty of scent, and the more you pick, the more they flower.

Rhubarb: 'The Sutton' is a main crop which rarely runs to seed. Prepare the ground well with plenty of manure mixed in at the base of the hole and in the top soil. Mulch in early spring, and feed the plants with a liquid fertiliser regularly throughout the summer. Apply a general fertiliser in July, 120 g per m² (4 oz per sq yd). Avoid cropping in the first season, and pick only a few stems in the second and third years. Do not eat the poisonous leaves.

Raspberries: 'Malling Jewel' is an early to mid-season heavy cropper. Provide a 2.5 m (8') post at either end of the rows, sunk 60 cm (2') into the ground, and then arrange three wires, 75 cm (30"), 1.1 m (3½') and 1.7 m (5½') high, to stretch between them and tie in the canes.

Feed the raspberries 30 g per m² (1 oz per sq yd) sulphate of potash in January and 15 g per m² (½ oz per sq yd) sulphate of ammonia in March. Mulch in April, and water well during the summer. Prune the raspberries after planting, reducing each cane to 35 cm (14"). They will bear no fruit the following

gooseberries   redcurrants   blackcurrants   nasturtiums   raspberries   rhubarb   sweet peas

summer, but the canes will become much stronger. In the second summer, after fruiting, cut all the canes that have borne raspberries down to ground-level and tie in the strongest new canes 7.5–10 cm (3–4″) apart. Remove the rest. Pull out the suckers. In February cut the soft unripe tips of the new canes to within a few inches of the top of the wire. The yield from fourteen mature canes should be approximately 7.5 kg (15 lb).

Gooseberries: 'Lancer' is a green mid-season fruit which can be used for desserts or cooking. Buy two- or three-year-old bushes. In January feed the gooseberries 22 g per m² (¾ oz per sq yd) sulphate of potash. Mulch in the spring while the ground is damp, and water in dry spells. Protect the buds from birds by stringing black cotton between the shoots in November, or cage them in. Prune the plants in February. Cut off half of the new wood growing from the eight best shoots of the two-year-old bushes. Remove all the other shoots, cutting them off just above the bottom bud. In the following winters, prune the leading shoots by half and the laterals to two buds. From about the fifth winter trim all the current season's growth by 3 cm (1¼″). Remove any congested old wood from the centre. Thin the fruits from late May onwards, aiming at 8 cm (3″) intervals between those remaining. The yield from two mature bushes should be about 8–10 kg (16–20 lb) of fruit.

Blackcurrants: 'Wellington XXX' is a mid-season heavy cropper with sweet fruits. Feed the plants in January with 30 g per m² (1 oz per sq yd) sulphate of potash and in March with 30 g per m² (1 oz per sq yd) sulphate of ammonia. Every third year feed them 60 g per m² (2 oz per sq yd) superphosphates. Mulch

generously after the autumn pruning and again in the spring while the ground is damp; water in dry spells.

Prune the blackcurrants hard immediately after planting them. There will be no crop in the first year. In the first autumn, cut the weakest shoots to 2.5 cm (1″) above ground-level, just above a bud. In succeeding autumns, cut down about one-third of the branches to promote strong growth. The anticipated yield from two mature bushes is 10–14 kg (20–30 lb) of fruit.

Redcurrants: 'Redlake' is a mid-season cropper. Feed the bushes in winter with 30 g per m² (1 oz per sq yd) sulphate of potash. In spring give them a further 30 g per m² (1 oz per sq yd) sulphate of ammonia. Every third year apply 60 g per m² (2 oz per sq yd) superphosphates. Mulch generously in winter. Water in dry spells in spring and summer.

Prune them in February. If you are planting young bushes, cut all the branches back to four buds above the base of the stems; the top bud should point out. During the second winter, shorten each branch by half, cutting back to an outward-facing bud. In the following winters, cut back the leading shoots by half and cut the laterals to two buds. Aim to promote a bush with an open centre. From the fifth winter onwards, cut back the season's growth by 2.5 cm (1″). Remove any congested growth. The anticipated yield from two mature bushes is 8–10 kg (16–20 lb) of fruit.

Nasturtiums need little attention, but guard against blackfly. Pick growing tips, young leaves and flowers to use in salads. Sow new seeds each spring, although you may find they will self-seed. Do not feed them. They flower better on poor soils, and will create a blaze of fiery colour.

46 The Cottage Vegetable Garden

INGREDIENTS

Rotation Group	Name	Distance between plants/rows (cm)	Distance between plants/rows (")	No of rows*	Harvest
1	Carrots (main crop)	15 cm/25 cm	6"/10"	2	7–10
	Parsnips	15 cm/40 cm	6"/16"	2	9–2
2	Runner beans	30 cm/45 cm	12"/18"	2	7–9
	French beans	25 cm/45 cm	10"/18"	2	7–9
	Broad beans	15 cm/25 cm	6"/10"	2	6–7
	Peas (main crop)	6 cm/45 cm 3 peas sown across a 10-cm (4") drill	2½"/18"	1	7–9
3	Tomatoes (bush)	45 cm	18"	1	8–10
	Marrows	60 cm	24"	3 plants	8–10
	Giant pumpkin			1 plant	10
	Potatoes (1st early)	35 cm/50 cm	14"/20"	4	6–7
4	Cauliflowers	60 cm/60 cm	24"/24"	2	7–10
	Brussels sprouts	45 cm/45 cm	18"/18"	2	11–3
	Cabbages (autumn and winter)	45 cm/60 cm	18"/24"	2	10–2
	Cabbages (spring)	30 cm/45 cm	12"/18"	2	4–5
5	Leeks	25 cm/40 cm	10"/16"	2	11–3
	Beetroots	10 cm	4"	1	9–10
	Onions (main crop)	10 cm/30 cm	4"/12"	3	9

* For sowing instructions, see pages 180–2.

SITE AND SCALE
An open and sunny plot 3 m (10') wide and 10 m (33') deep with a path along one side. Don't forget to allow a permanent space for a compost area.

PLAN
Plant the vegetables in the order listed in the ingredients, starting with onions at the front and working backwards.

CROP ROTATION/PREPARATION
Vegetables benefit from being moved round the plot on a yearly basis, as it helps to prevent the build-up of soil-living pests and diseases which favour particular crops. Apply a general fertiliser to the plot two weeks before sowing except for where the potatoes are to be planted.

The rotation crops are as follows:
1. The umbelliferous family: carrots and parsnips. Do not add manure or lime before sowing.
2. Legumes: beans and peas. Add compost or well-rotted manure and lime if the soil is acidic.
3. The potato family: potatoes and tomatoes. The marrows and giant pumpkin have been included here so that they can take advantage of the empty plot once the early potatoes have been removed. Don't add manure or lime before planting the potatoes.

runner beans   tomatoes   cauliflower
        pumpkin   Brussels sprouts   leeks   beetroot   onions

4. Brassicas: Brussels sprouts, cauliflowers and cabbages. Dig in lots of compost or well-rotted manure and add lime if the soil is acidic.

5. The onion family: onions and leeks; the beetroot is included here for convenience. Add lots of compost or well-rotted manure, and lime if the soil is acidic.

Intercrop lettuces between the runner bean rows, to mature before the beans grow very high, or on the early potato patch.

COMPANION PLANTING SCHEMES
Incorporate herbs amongst the vegetables to repel aphids and other troublesome insects. Plant chives alongside the carrots, and thyme and sage plants on either side of the brassica plot with a row of dill in the middle. Plant basil and tagetes around the bush tomatoes, with summer savory beside the broad beans.

These herbs will greatly enhance the garden: chive flowers are a beautiful sight and basil and dill are wonderfully fragrant. One packet of tagetes can transform a summer vegetable patch into a colourful patchwork. Tomatoes need not be the only vegetables to benefit; plant tagetes all around the plot.

DESCRIPTION
The vegetable patch was once the hub of the cottage garden. The size of this plot is based on one that has provided enough fresh vegetables over a period of twenty-five years to feed a family of five throughout the year. The only exception was the potatoes. Early varieties only were grown. Space for main-crop varieties has been sacrificed to other summer crops.

But you don't have to plant everything! Try some early potatoes, red and green lettuces, peas, runner beans and tomatoes. Mix the vegetables with the herbs and you will soon derive enormous pleasure from them all, however large or small the plot. You could also try growing some vegetables in the other borders.

Even without the companion herbs, the vegetable garden is a delight to the eye in many seasons. Brussels sprout rosettes in mid-winter, when they are laden with snow or dusted with frost, are a marvellous sight. To see scarlet runner beans in flower or the rich red veins on the beetroot leaves and the crinkly leaves of the Savoy cabbage, the bed of onions drying in the sun, or the huge golden ball of the giant pumpkin are great pleasures as well. There is so much to enjoy in the growing of the crop, let alone in the harvesting and eating of it!

47   The Cottage Orchard

No req	Name	Description	Ht × Spr (m)	Ht × Spr (')	Needs pollinator	Best
1	Apple tree 'Worcester Permain'	crimson	3.5 × 3.5 m	11½ × 11½'	yes	8–9
1	*Apple tree 'Sunset'	yellow/red	3.5 × 3.5 m	11½ × 11½'	yes	10–12
1	*Pear tree 'Williams Bon Chrétien'	golden	3.5 × 3.5 m	11½ × 11½'	yes	8–9
1	*Pear tree 'Conference'	dark green	3.5 × 3.5 m	11½ × 11½'	yes	10–11
1	Damson 'Merryweather'	deep purple	3.5 × 3.5 m	11½ × 11½'	no	9
1	Plum 'Victoria'	red, yellow	3.5 × 3.5 m	11½ × 11½'	no	8-9

SITE

A sunny area, ideally with as much shelter as possible to reduce the effect of frost and wind. A good evergreen shelter belt, such as holly, to the north and east would be very desirable. A wall would also act as a windbreak.

SCALE

The sizes given here are for bush fruit trees; smaller ones, called dwarf bush, can be obtained or larger trees can be grown from half or full standards. The area of the orchard and numbers required will determine tree size. These trees require at least 150 m² (1650 sq ft) or a plot 10 m (33') wide and 15 m (50') deep. Ballerina fruit trees would take up considerably less space and still crop well, although the orchard effect would be lost.

PLAN

Front: Plant the damson and the 'Worcester Permain' apple.
Middle: Plant the 'Victoria' plum and the 'Sunset' apple.
Back: Plant the 'Williams Bon Chrétien' pear and the 'Conference' pear. Spring bulbs can be planted to naturalise beneath the trees once the latter are established.

WHEN TO PLANT

November. Prepare the soil well, adding a general fertiliser, 90 g per m² (3 oz per sq yd). Provide stakes for all the new trees.

AFTERCARE

Pollination: Although the apple and pear trees listed here require pollinators, the second one named in each case is ideal for pollinating the first.

Pruning: Once established and bearing fruit, the 'Sunset' apple and both pear trees need pruning regularly. Complete the winter pruning by February, shortening lateral growths to the third or fourth bud from the base of the previous season's wood and shortening leaders by one third of their length. Summer pruning involves cutting the current season's growth back above the sixth leaf from the base (not counting the cluster of leaves at the base of a shoot).

Feed: Apples and pears: In January apply 30 g per m² (1 oz per sq yd) sulphate of potash. Add 60 g per m² (2 oz per sq yd) superphosphates every third year. In March add 60 g per m² (2 oz per sq yd) sulphate of ammonia. Damson and plums: Also in March, apply 15 g per m² (½ oz per sq yd) sulphate of ammonia and 15 g per m² (½ oz per sq yd) sulphate of potash to improve fruit quality. Every third year apply 60 g per m² (2 oz per sq yd) superphosphates. Sprinkle them thinly over an area a little larger than the spread of the branches.

Support: Plum and damson trees need help with heavily laden branches to stop them from splitting away from the main trunk. Remove suckers from the base.

Water: Until the trees are established, they should be watered, particularly in dry summers when the fruit is forming and swelling. Keep the grass short in summer so it does not compete for moisture.

damson   plum   apple

DESCRIPTION

The cottage orchard in autumn is one of the most glorious sights in the whole year – bountiful in its crop, rich in colour and evocative in smell. Ripe red apples hang on the 'Worcester Permain', one of the first apples to ripen just when the schoolchildren return for the autumn term. Brilliant in colour, they are the most delicious of fruits, and are ready for eating immediately. It is October before the 'Sunset' apples are ready, but they will feed the family right through to Christmas and beyond. They are crisp dessert apples with an excellent flavour.

'Williams Bon Chrétien' is a marvellous golden pear with white juicy flesh. It should be picked in late August and ripened off the tree for eating in September. The 'Conference' pear has dark green tapering fruits which should be picked in September and eaten in October and November.

Damsons make one of the best jams in the world; the fruit is deep purple in colour and rich in flavour. Try them as a jelly on their own, or mix them with crab apples or cooking apples to create a delicious substitute for redcurrant jelly. Add rosemary and other herbs when eating them with pâtés and roast meats. They will transform many simple meals. The fruit makes lovely pies and crumbles. Plums are a cottage favourite too. The old 'Victoria' plum crops heavily and makes excellent fruit pies, crumbles and jam.

A delightful picture can emerge in late winter and early spring with drifts of snowdrops, aconites, crocuses, and anemones. Daffodils and later bluebells will also make a colourful carpet just when the fruit blossoms are out. The pears, plums and damson all bear white flowers, but the apple blossoms are a delicate combination of pinks and whites. They transform the orchard into one of the prettiest sights in the garden.

48   Open Grassland

INGREDIENTS

No req	Name	Description	Ht × Spr (cm/m)	Ht × Spr ("/')	Best
150	Wild daffodils *Narcissus pseudonarcissus lobularis*	pale yellow	15 cm	6"	3–4
75	Snake's head fritillaries *Fritillaria meleagris*	pink, white	25 cm	10"	4–5
24	Cowslips *Primula veris*	yellow	15 × 15 cm	6 × 6"	4–5
6	*Common bird's foot trefoils *Lotus corniculatus*	yellow	25 × 25 cm	10 × 10"	5–8
6	*Ox-eye daisies *Leucanthemum vulgare*	white	60 × 30 cm	2 × 1'	6–8
6	*Meadow cranesbills *Geranium pratense*	purple-blue	60 × 60 cm	2 × 2'	6–8
6	*Devil's bit scabious *Succisa pratensis*	pink-purple	90 × 60 cm	3 × 2'	7–9
6	*Greater knapweeds *Centaurea scabiosa*	reddish-purple	90 × 45 cm	36 × 18"	7–9

SITE
A sunny grassland area. It could be one part of the lawn or a patch beyond the garden gate. Alternatively, it might be close to the orchard or in a small field.

SCALE
Approximately 10 m² (108 sq ft). Scale the ingredients down by one-third for an area of 3 m² (32 sq ft).

PLAN
Central area: Space the daffodils, snake's head fritillaries and cowslips in a wide group.
Sides: Interplant the daisies and devil's bit scabious on one side of the patch, and the cranesbills and knapweeds on the other.
Front: Plant the bird's foot trefoils near the front or against the path if there is one. The bulbs and plants should all multiply well over the years.

WHEN TO PLANT
Mow the grass closely before planting. The bulbs should be planted in September. Plant the daffodils 10 cm (4") deep and 20 cm (8") apart. Plant the snake's head fritillaries 5 cm (2") deep and 15–20 cm (6–8") apart. Plant the cowslips in between, at the same time. The rest of the plants can be planted either in autumn or in early spring. Remove a large turf of grass where each plant is to go, so the plants have a chance to become established before the grass grows back. The bird's foot trefoils prefer poor, dry soil, so plant them with extra sand mixed into the soil.

AFTERCARE
Very little attention is necessary except to make sure newly planted specimens are kept moist, until they are established, and free from weeds. The cowslip and bulb area may be mown in late July, but the outer area should not be mown until September or October, when the scabious and knapweeds have set seed.

cowslips   *daffodils* *snake's head fritillaries*   *cowslips*

DESCRIPTION

The spring scene of wild daffodils, snake's head fritillaries and cowslips growing in grassland is most evocative. These daffodils are quite short, unlike some of their relatives, but they are sturdy and naturalise well. They soon make a lovely drift of pale yellow trumpets. The graceful flowers on the fritillaries hang down to reveal small chequered markings on the petals, hence the common names snake's head fritillary and guinea-hen flower. Soon the cowslips begin to show colour, as the rich yellow flowers hang in clusters from a central stem. They are quite short at first but grow much taller as the flowers mature. These are sweetly scented and very pretty.

Throughout May and June the bird's foot trefoils are in bloom. They are low spreading plants which have small heads of yellow flowers. The buds are tinged with crimson. They make a lovely bright show and are much sought after by bees and the common blue butterfly. By June the ox-eye daisies are open.

White daisy heads with yellow centres add a brightness to the early summer scene. They are joined by the purple-blue flowers of the meadow cranesbills, which appear from June to August and are valuable for their rich colouring and attractive foliage.

By July the devil's bit scabious are beginning to bloom. They are rather tall, but naturalise well and are good weed suppressors. They have lots of small deep pink-purple flowers, which are highly attractive to the late summer butterflies, including tortoiseshells, commas and red admirals. They are also an important food for caterpillars, and popular with seed-eating birds in autumn. Greater knapweeds attract the bees and butterflies with their dense thistle-like heads of reddish-purple flowers which are produced from July to September. They can grow from 30 to 150 cm (12–60″) depending on conditions. Together the scabious and knapweeds make a fine late summer show, bringing with them lots of insects and birdlife.

49 *Beside the Cottage Stream*

No req	Name	Description	Ht × Spr (cm/m)	Ht × Spr ("/')	Best
1	Sweet briar *Rosa rubiginosa*	pink	2.5 × 2.5 m	8 × 8'	6–7, 8–11
3	Ragged robins *Lychnis flos-cuculi*	pink	45 × 45 cm	18 × 18"	5–8
2	Meadowsweet *Filipendula ulmaria*	creamy white	90 × 45 cm	36 × 18"	6–9
2	Hemp agrimony *Eupatorium cannabinum*	pink	60 × 60 cm	2 × 2'	7–9
2	Tufted vetch *Vicia cracca*	blue	75 cm	30"	7–9
3	Teasels *Dipsacus fullonum*	mauve	200 × 30 cm	6½ × 1'	7–8
5	*Primroses *Primula vulgaris*	pale yellow	15 × 20 cm	6 × 8"	3–4
5	*Lady's smocks *Cardamine pratensis*	pale lilac	15 × 10 cm	6 × 4"	4–5

SITE
A partly sunny, partly shady area by a stream or ditch, or a flat damp meadow.

SCALE
A 3 or 4 m² (32 or 43 sq ft) stretch.

PLAN
By a stream or ditch: Plant the lady's smocks, sweet briar and teasels on top of the bank, with the hemp agrimony and meadowsweet below and the ragged robins in the marshy area near the water's edge. Let the vetch clamber up on the shady side of the rose, with primroses forming a cascade down the bank below.

In a meadow: Plant the vetch, primroses and lady's smocks in the shade of the sweet briar, with the ragged robins nearby, and hemp agrimonies and meadowsweet together. The teasels should stand in a group on their own. All these plants grow in sun or semi-shade.

WHEN TO PLANT
Plant any time between November and March.

AFTERCARE
The hemp agrimony self-seeds profusely, so dead-head it to prevent this happening. Cut them down to ground-level after flowering. Cut down the meadow-sweet at the same time. The teasels are biennial but they will self-seed. They can be left as silhouettes all winter, then removed. The ragged robins, vetch, primroses and lady's smocks need no attention. If necessary, prune the rose in February.

sweet briar *tufted vetch* *teasels*
hemp agrimony *ragged robins* *meadowsweet*

DESCRIPTION

By early July the sweet briar, with its familiar pale pink flowers, delicately scented and so well loved, is in full array. Long arms of growth reach up into the sky or gently arch to the ground, each one adorned with many beautiful blooms. Down below, a mass of ragged robins enjoys the damper spot near the water. The pink petals are deeply divided, hence the descriptive name. They have been in flower since May. They naturalise well in sun or shade so long as the ground is damp. Meadowsweet is their taller bedfellow. It has creamy white flowers which are light and feathery. They are so strongly scented that the plant was used as a strewing herb in Elizabethan times. Even the dark green leaves are fragrant.

The hemp agrimony is also tall and makes a very pretty clump for any damp spot. It can tolerate very deep shade, so it often makes a useful contribution where little else can grow, but it thrives in sun as well. Here it will be festooned with butterflies which love to gather on its broad fluffy pink heads.

By July the tufted vetch is creating a lovely patch of purple-blue flowers as it scrambles up the sweet briar.

It is an eye-catching display which goes on for many weeks as the vetch grows taller and taller. In contrast, the teasels support themselves on thick spiny stems which can grow up to 2 m (6½'). The flower heads are spiny too, bearing rings of rose-purple blooms which are a great attraction to bees and butterflies. Even two or three plants make a marvellous sight silhouetted against the sky. They are both majestic and architectural. In time they will create a large colony and there will be plenty of heads to cut for winter arrangements. The birds love to eat the seeds in autumn and will tug persistently until all have gone. They enjoy the scarlet hips on the sweet briar too. The beautiful sprays are a fine sight from August or early September onwards, but as the days shorten, they disappear quickly.

In early spring the wild primroses form a lovely cascade of soft yellow flowers down the bank beneath the sweet briar. Soon the pretty lady's smocks will be in flower with their pale lilac petals. It is not showy at all, but .where a group establish themselves they provide a gentle carpet of late spring colour. Watch out for the orange tip butterfly which feeds on them.

50 The Cottage Pond

INGREDIENTS

No req	Name	Description	Water Depth (cm)	Water Depth (")	Ht × Spr (cm/m)	Ht × Spr ("/')	Best
1	Water lily *Nymphaea alba*	white	45 × 80 cm	18 × 32"	floating 1 m	3¼"	7–8
3	Yellow flag irises *Iris pseudacorus*	yellow	45 cm	18"	75 × 60 cm	30 × 24"	5–7
3	Water forget-me-nots *Myosotis palustris*	blue	8 cm	3"	25 × 25 cm	10 × 10"	6–9
1	Water mint *Mentha aquatica*	lilac	8 cm	3"	30 × 45 cm	12 × 18"	7–10
3	Purple loosestrifes *Lythrum salicaria*	purple			90 × 45 cm	36 × 18"	6–8
12 bunches	*Water starworts *Callitriche stagnalis*	green	floating				5–9
2	Marsh marigolds *Caltha palustris*	yellow	15 cm	6"	30 × 25 cm	12 × 10"	3–5

SITE

In sun, away from large trees.

SCALE

The depth of the pond should be over 80 cm (32") so that it remains unfrozen and can sustain wildlife in winter. A shallow area at the side will allow bog and wetland plants to grow and wildlife to move in and out. The size can vary considerably. This planting scheme would suit an area of 6 m² (64 sq ft).

PLAN

Plant the water lily near the centre. Plant the flag irises and water forget-me-nots in the shallows at one side. Plant the marsh marigolds in the shallows or on land and the loosestrifes on land at the other side. Plant the water mint somewhere near the edge of the pond, with the water starwort in the deeper parts. Other wild flowers may be introduced around the banks.

WHEN TO PLANT

For those plants which need to be submerged, use perforated containers and a specially prepared compost called Aquasoil, which has been sterilised and contains no additional food elements which would otherwise seep into the pond water and upset the natural balance.

The oxygenator, water starwort, is worth establishing early on so that it can begin work immediately. Allow two bunches of oxygenator to every 1 m² (11 sq ft) of water. They should be planted in perforated containers. Plant the purple loosestrifes from February to April. Plant the marsh marigolds from March to September using a perforated basket at a depth of 15 cm (6"). It will also thrive close to the water's edge on land. From March to April, plant the yellow flag irises near the edge of the pond. In April or May, plant the water lily in a perforated basket and cover it with 25 cm (10") of good, rich, saturated soil, then sand or gravel to anchor it. Set the basket in the water at a minimum depth of 45 cm (18"). The water forget-me-nots and water mint – the latter imprisoned in a container – can also be planted in April or May, at water-level or 8 cm (3") below the surface.

AFTERCARE

The water lily is rampant and needs controlling, hence the use of the basket. After three or four years, thin it in April or May by severing 20 cm (8") from the strongest tubers and replanting them. Discard the rest. Divide and replant the irises every three years. Water forget-me-nots may become too rampant, so remove the excess. Water mint should be contained. Cut the loosestrifes back in autumn. The marsh marigolds should be left undisturbed.

flag irises
water forget-me-nots

water lily

purple loosestrife
marsh marigolds
water mint

DESCRIPTION

The cottage pond is full of many native plants which are colourful and beautiful and very attractive to wildlife. The white water lily is particularly notable in July and August for its beautiful wax-like flowers and their conspicuous yellow stamens. The blooms rest just on top of the water, surrounded by large, rounded leaves. These afford useful shade to the wildlife below. The water lily can become rather too prolific, but trapped in a special perforated container, and attended to every three or four years, it can easily be kept under control. What a contrast in shape there is between the lily and the tall flag irises with their long sword-like foliage. The irises have distinctive bright yellow flowers which are produced from May to July, and are followed by large seed pods. They make a handsome grouping at the edge of the pond with the water forget-me-nots growing at their feet. As the summer progresses, the forget-me-nots grow taller and their tiny blue flowers make a lovely sight from June to September. In early summer, they combine beautifully with the yellow flags above.

Water mint grows nearby and gives off a lovely scent when it is touched. The bees love it. Purple loosestrife creates a dazzling clump at the edge of the pool; its tall heads are a mass of purple from June to August. Water starworts have rosettes of small leaves which float on the surface of the pond; below there are long trails of growth mingling with other leaves and roots. It is not a showy plant but it gives off valuable oxygen which helps to support underwater insect and fish life and to reduce algae.

Early spring sees the marsh marigolds bloom. They are often known as king cups for their bright yellow cup-shaped flowers. From March through to May, they look lovely set against glossy bright green leaves.

Cottage Containers
INTRODUCTION

Container gardening is very much part of the cottage scene, particularly where no borders exist in front of the house or by the front door. Indeed, you don't have to have garden soil at all to create the cottage effect. Flat dwellers and householders alike can grow cottage containers.

Grow lavender in a pot right by your door and enjoy the scent every time you come home. Why not grow a wildlife border in a barrel? Plant a butterfly bush with ice plants and evening primroses and watch the bees and butterflies fizz and flutter in the late summer sunshine. Why not have a herb garden hanging by your kitchen window? Stretch out for the variegated mints and parsley, the golden marjoram and lemon balm, the thymes and edible flowers. With their colourful leaves and delicious fragrance they will be enchanting.

Cottage containers can also be used very effectively in the garden itself. Sometimes they draw attention to the surrounding plants, adding colour and height, yet blending in well. Look at the foxglove trough. You can hardly see where the container begins and ends. But in winter the picture is different. The elephant's ears provide a bold clump of foliage which rises well above the border so that they can be enjoyed from inside the house as well. Its position also serves another purpose in hiding a man-hole cover!

A wide range of plants can be bought or raised to fill the containers, including bulbs and bedding plants, herbs, colourful summer annuals, tender geraniums and fuchsias, and a host of others besides. They can be planted singly or grouped together to create a profusion of colour and interest. Let them blend with their surroundings or stand out like a glorious tapestry. With a little bit of planning, you can have colour and scent nearly all year round.

Many different types of containers can be used, as long as they have drainage holes in the base. Wooden troughs and barrels, clay pots and window boxes, lead and stone troughs, hanging baskets, hay racks and wicker baskets are all appropriate, and add charm and colour to the cottage. More unusual objects of interest, such as an old wooden wheelbarrow, a seakale or rhubarb forcing pot turned upside-down, patterned chimney pots and painted buckets can also be planted to great effect. With regular care and attention they can all look as pretty as a picture.

In order to make this chapter easier to follow and to make planning easier, the schemes have been divided into three groups: autumn through to spring, summer and long-term.

AUTUMN THROUGH TO SPRING
These containers fall into two sections depending on their planting time. First are those which include bulbs and must be planted in autumn. With careful planning, you can plant a series of containers using early flowering and later flowering bulbs which will be in their full glory from March to May. Extend this period by planting winter-flowering pansies, violas and daisies on top of the bulbs. They will bloom, during mild spells, from the time of planting onwards. Other items of winter interest are evergreens such as ivy, stonecrop and thymes. Or use old cottage favourites such as forget-me-nots and wallflowers to add further colour in late spring. It is a simple matter to fill containers so that they provide colour and interest from September to May, a period of nine months which is often neglected.

In severe weather, all these containers need to be protected. If possible, move them into a frost-free garage or barn or bring them close to a house wall sheltered from the cold winds. If they are too heavy to move, cover them with sacking or bracken. They are all hardy plants, but in a container they are far more exposed than when they are tucked in the ground.

The second section refers to those containers which exclude bulbs. Planted in March, they will look their best in April and May. They are a useful group because they give a quick reward. They also avoid the possible failure of winter schemes when arctic conditions prevail. Moreover, they fill the gap between the main bulb display and the time when the summer bedding containers can be put out at the end of May. This is often a lean time for containers, especially if spring comes early. Included here are primroses, cowslips and polyanthus, violas, daisies and lots of herbs, mainly used for their foliage and scent. These plants will grow quickly with the warmer weather in spring and are sure to produce a good display of colour. They might flower a little later than their counterparts planted in autumn, but the results will be reliably good without the long wait.

SUMMER
Summer containers often housed tender plants introduced from other countries. Geraniums are probably the best known. Cottagers liked them for their strong leaf colourings, the horseshoe markings or their bright flowers. Singles were used at first until the

doubles became more widespread. Tender fuchsias were also common. Graceful and colourful, with a wide range of colours, they had to be over-wintered at a temperature of 7–10°C (45–50°F). Indoor window-sills were often used.

Many of the cottage favourites were annuals. They included alyssum, ageratum, clarkia, candytuft, cosmos, pot marigolds, nemesia, stocks, tobacco plants, phlox and larkspur, as well as many others. They would be grown each year from seed and used to fill lots of containers at very little expense. The same can be done today.

In this category, we also find old-fashioned mignonette which was so well loved for its sweet fragrance. The flowers are insignificant in comparison with most other summer annuals but that did not stop it from being one of the most common annuals grown. It was also used as a winter-flowering pot plant indoors. Now, sadly, hardly anyone seems to grow it, although seed is still readily available. Grow it with 'Cherry Pie' heliotrope, another great scented old favourite. It combines a lovely sweet scent – just like a freshly baked cherry pie – with pretty blue flowers. Now, at last, it is seen more widely in the garden centres.

Containers made a wonderful home for fragrant plants, where their scents could be fully appreciated. Rose-scented geraniums and lemon verbena make a lovely combination, specially placed near a path or doorway where the foliage is frequently brushed against. Their foliage was often used to flavour cakes and jellies. Planted with fuchsias, they can be left in the same pot for two or three years and allowed to become bigger specimens. Treat them as short- or long-term schemes.

LONG-TERM

These are the containers which house plants on a more permanent basis. They still need care and attention, but they do not need to be replanted each season. Most can be left for two or three years in the same pot or trough before they need dividing or potting on into larger containers with fresh soil. Most but not all of them are hardy. Many of them won't look very special during the first season, but as the plants develop and mature the display will get better and better.

Some of the long-term schemes are lovely in mid-summer; some peak later in the year; others are at their best in the depths of winter. Just look at the barrel of winter jasmine, viburnum and ivy echoed in the hanging basket. With the minimum of care and attention, you can have a display which will last from November to March, and even beyond. Once the winter-flowering jasmine is in leaf, it can be used to create a backcloth for the seasonal containers. It will look good the whole summer through, providing a solid green wall to show off some brighter spring and summer flowers.

These long-term schemes include some of the tender cottage plants which need over-wintering in frost-free conditions. One lovely example is *Francoa ramosa*, the old bridal wreath, which was once a universal favourite. Now it is hardly ever seen, despite its pretty pink and white flowers; fortunately a few nurseries still stock it. Grown as a long-term container plant, it will grow bigger and more sumptuous, giving a fine display year after year.

FIVE GOLDEN RULES

1. DRAINAGE: Make sure your container has adequate drainage, whether you are using a window box or a lined wicker basket. Water-logged soil is a great killer of plants, especially in cold weather.

2. SOIL: Always use fresh soil in your containers. It is expensive in time and effort, but the rewards will certainly justify the cost. I usually recommend John Innes No 2 (or 3 for long-term containers) for pots and troughs, window boxes and barrels. It dries out less quickly than the usual soil-less compost and is kinder on the environment. However, with densely planted spring and summer hanging baskets and wicker baskets, I often like to use lighter composts with water-retaining crystals added. This way, the containers seem to get off to a fast start and last much better in hot weather. They may be based either on cocoa nut fibre – an old idea which has been revived – or peat, though environmentalists will not be happy with the latter. The manufacturers and garden centres are still trying to solve the problem. Peat-based composts far outnumber those based on cocoa nut fibres, although more alternatives are coming on the market.

The amount of soil needed will depend on the inside measurements of the container and the amount of soil attached to the various rootballs. Summer plants generally do not have large root systems, but those on shrubs will be significant. As a rough guide to measure an oblong container, such as a trough or window box, take the length, width and depth in centimetres and multiply them to arrive at the volume required.

For example, a deep trough 87.5 cm long, 20 cm deep and 12.5 cm wide would need:
$87.5 \times 20 \times 12.5 = 21,875$ cu cm $= 21.9$ litres.

If you have a round barrel or pot, measure the radius (i.e. half the diameter) and the depth. The formula is $3.14 \times$ radius squared $\times$ depth.

For example a large wooden half-barrel with a 30 cm radius, 37.5 cm deep would need:
$3.14 \times 30 \times 30 \times 37.5 = 105,975$ cu cm $= 106$ litres.

In both cases these are generous estimates, as they do not allow for 5–8 cm (2–3″) of drainage at the base of the container, or the normal 2.5 cm (1″) allowance at the top. But it is far better to have too much soil than too little. What is more, it will settle considerably.

3. WATERING: Check that the soil is moist. Touch it with your finger to feel whether it is dry or not. If the soil sticks, it is damp. If your finger comes away clean, the soil is dry. Be prepared to water the containers daily in hot weather, if not twice a day. Avoid watering when the sun is shining on the foliage, as ugly burn marks will soon appear. It is better to water at soil-level so as not to spoil the flowers. Autumn, winter and, particularly, spring containers need water, especially where they are close to the house wall, but never water them in frosty weather.

4. FEEDING: We often expect great things of our containers, yet the growing space is so small. Results will depend very much on the application of a general fertiliser on the long-term pots and a weekly liquid feed to the spring and summer pots and baskets. There are many excellent brands on the market, although I still use Tomorite. New soil already contains a four-week reservoir of nutrients to get the plants started. Therefore, in general, seasonal containers have a four-week growing life before you need to apply the extra zip.

5. PEST CONTROL: Slugs and snails can do terrible damage to plants, especially when the conditions are damp and plants are wet after rain or the evening watering session. Keep a constant watch and act accordingly. Night-time prowling with a torch can be very rewarding. If you decide to use a chemical method, be sure to choose one which is as friendly as possible to other garden life, and do collect all the dead slugs and snails so that they can be disposed of safely.

Greenfly and whitefly are the other main problem. There are several so-called 'safe' brands of insecticide available now, but some of these contain natural pyretheum, which is in fact harmful to bees. Apparently those based on fatty soaps and pirimicarb do not kill bees. But what about the ladybirds? So often the small print only reveals part of the story.

Keep your plants well fed and watered so they will be far more healthy and less likely to be attacked. But if you do see a problem starting, act quickly. Don't wait for the population to build up: aphids have no notion of birth control.

Each container photographed here has been planned and planted especially for this book, so they are tried and tested. The recipe formula has again been applied, with a detailed list of all the plant ingredients used to create each scheme. Where strips are mentioned, assume that there are eight small plants in each one. Otherwise, adjust the numbers accordingly. The size of the pot, basket, box or barrel is given so that you can copy or adapt the recipe to your own containers. Each specifies the site, whether in sun or shade, the type of soil, drainage material, moss – where relevant – and any other details which may be helpful, including hints on aftercare. Try out the recipes, experiment with alternative colours and varieties and create your own favourite combinations.

If you would like further ideas for cottage garden containers, many of the recipes in my other container gardening books are directly relevant. Particularly noteworthy in *Creative Container Gardening* are Recipes: 43, including hydrangea, summer jasmine and periwinkle; 83 and 84, wallflowers with tulips; 90, tulips and forget-me-nots; 94, cowslips and forget-me-nots; 96, wallflowers and bellis daisies; 104, a hanging basket with old-fashioned scented geraniums, verbena and mother of thousands; and 112, dwarf sweet peas and alyssum.

There are many more containers in *Seasonal Container Gardening*. Indeed, this book devotes an entire section to old planting schemes (*see* Recipes 107–28 inclusive), with a brief container history of each one used. Elsewhere, 2 and 3 use holly and mahonia; 10 illustrates the full glory of bleeding heart; 11 shows hostas and lily of the valley together; 13 has pink foxgloves; 15 has beautiful pink roses. Many of the bulb recipes are appropriate, including 44, 45 and 47 with polyanthus, daisies and wallflowers. There is a section on herbs mixed with edible flowers (*see* 91 and 92), and a hanging basket of mints and lemon balm (*see* 96) and another of strawberries, marjoram and parsley (*see* 97). It pictures so many lovely ideas. These are just some of them.

51 The Primrose Basket

Primroses and anemones make pretty partners in this spring wicker basket.

SITE
Sunny or shady.

CONTAINER
Varnished wicker basket: 37.5 cm (15″) in diameter, 15 cm (6″) deep. Preserve it with three coats of yacht varnish so that it can sit outside all winter.

WHEN TO PLANT
September to October.

BEST
March to April.

INGREDIENTS
2 Large primroses *Primula vulgaris*.
20 *Anemone blanda* 'Mixed', which will include blue, white and mauve-pink.
6 Litres of John Innes No 2 soil or a multi-purpose compost.
Drainage: Small pieces of polystyrene or horticultural grit.
Black plastic sheeting to fit inside the basket. Cut out a bin liner or a soil sack.

METHOD
1. Line the basket with plastic sheeting so that it fits snugly round the bottom and comes right up to the top of the basket (the excess can always be tucked in later). Cut six 2.5-cm (1″) slits in the bottom to allow excess moisture to escape.
2. Cover the liner with 2.5 cm (1″) of drainage material and add 8 cm (3″) of soil.
3. Plant the primroses on either side of the basket.
4. Space the anemones round the edge of the basket and in the centre.
5. Fill in the gaps with soil, bringing the level to within 2.5 cm (1″) of the rim of the basket.
6. Water well. Firm in the plants. Add more soil if necessary.

AFTERCARE
Place the basket in a sheltered spot for the winter: the sunnier the aspect the earlier the primroses will come into flower. In severe winter weather take the basket into an outbuilding or cover it with a protective sack. Keep the soil moist by watering it as necessary, but never water it in frosty conditions. Give liquid feeds in early and late March. After the anemones and primroses have finished flowering, plant them out along a garden path in sun or shade.

52 'Rip Van Winkle' in a Hanging Basket

Golden stonecrop creates a living green lining which dispenses with the need for moss and unsightly bare bottoms. The old-fashioned 'Rip Van Winkle' daffodils and rosemary have the same spiky quality.

SITE
Sunny and sheltered.

CONTAINER
A wire hanging basket: 35 cm (14″) in diameter, with a 27.5 cm (11″) bracket.

EARLY PREPARATION
The stonecrop lining is easy to produce by 'home' propagation. Trim the ends from one large stonecrop plant in early summer on to some damp compost. Keep it moist and allow it to spread until autumn when it will have become a dense mat. You need a large expanse. I used the upturned top of an old dustbin lid (with a drainage hole). Alternatively, allow six large plants to develop in the garden.

WHEN TO PLANT
September to October.

BEST
The violas should flower on and off all winter, during mild spells. The daffodils will flower in March or early April. The rosemary and stonecrop will look good in autumn, winter and spring.

INGREDIENTS
 1 Circle (50–60 cm/20–24″ diameter) of stonecrop *Sedum acre* 'Aureum', or use several established plants.
 1 Rosemary *Rosmarinus officinalis*, at least 30 cm (12″) high.
10 Daffodils *Narcissus* 'Rip Van Winkle', an old dwarf variety, or try 'February Gold' or 'Tête-à-tête'.
 3 Purple violas *Viola tricolor* 'Prince Harry', or try 'Johnny Jump Up' which is purple and yellow.
10 Scilla or squills *Scilla siberica* 'Spring Beauty'.
10 Litres of John Innes No 3 soil.

METHOD
 1. Line the basket with stonecrop so that it comes right up above the rim. If it falls short, leave gaps at the back and plug them with moss.
 2. Add 8 cm (3″) of soil.
 3. Plant the rosemary towards the centre back.
 4. Plant the daffodils in the middle and around the

sides. Push the bulbs down into the soil.
 5. Cover the bulbs with soil.
 6. Plant the three violas around the centre front and sides.
 7. Plant the scillas in any available spaces in the middle or front and at either side.
 8. Top up with soil bringing the level to within 2.5 cm (1″) of the rim of the basket.
 9. Water well. Firm in the plants. Add more soil if necessary.

AFTERCARE
Keep the basket moist throughout the winter and spring, but never water it in frosty weather. Apply a liquid feed in mid-March to boost the violas. After flowering, plant the rosemary and bulbs in a sunny spot in the garden and keep the bulbs well watered until the leaves die down naturally. Take cuttings from the lining of stonecrop for the following autumn, then divide the old plant and plant it out.

53 Tulips in a Basket

This is a delightful combination of 'Peach Blossom' tulips, pink bellis daisies and purple violas. The old favourites make a memorable planting scheme.

SITE
Sunny.

CONTAINER
A varnished rustic wicker basket: 27.5 cm (11″) in diameter, 12.5 cm (5″) deep. Preserve it with three coats of yacht varnish so that it can sit outside all winter. Alternatively, use a window box or pot.

WHEN TO PLANT
September to October.

BEST
Late March or early April, although the violas and daisies should flower from autumn onwards during mild spells.

INGREDIENTS
10 Dwarf pink 'Peach Blossom' tulips. All double early varieties are excellent for containers.
2 Violas *Viola cornuta* 'Prince Harry'.
2 Pink bellis daisies *Bellis perennis* 'Tasso Rose', or one very similar.
4 Litres of John Innes No 2 soil or a multi-purpose compost.
Drainage: Small pieces of polystyrene or horticultural grit.
Black plastic sheeting to fit inside the basket. Cut out a bin liner or a soil sack.

METHOD
1. Line the basket with plastic sheeting so that it fits snugly round the bottom and comes right up to the top of the basket (the surplus can always be tucked in later). Cut six 2.5-cm (1″) slits in the bottom to allow excess moisture to escape.
2. Cover the liner with 2.5 cm (1″) of drainage material and add 8 cm (3″) of soil.
3. Plant the violas and the daisies around the handles of the basket, on opposite sides.
4. Plant the tulips in the centre of the basket and between the plants around the edge. Push them well down in the soil.
5. Water well. Firm in the plants. Add more soil if necessary.

AFTERCARE
Place the basket in a sunny position for autumn and winter, but in severe weather take it into the shelter of a garage with a window or put it right beside the house wall. Keep the soil moist, but never water it in frosty conditions. Give a liquid feed in early and late March. Discard the plants and bulbs after flowering. Wash, dry and revarnish the basket for summer.

54 A Rustic Trough

Thymes and stonecrop are both very hardy and make good winter greenery for a window box or trough. Add lovely blue scillas and colourful polyanthus for a long-lasting spring display.

SITE
Sunny or partially shady.

CONTAINER
A wooden trough or window box: 90 cm (36″) long, 15 cm (6″) wide and 20 cm (8″) deep (inside measurements).

WHEN TO PLANT
September to October. Replace the polyanthus if they do not fare well in the winter.

BEST
Late March to May.

INGREDIENTS
2 Thymes. *Thymus vulgaris* is bushy and has a good flavour.
1 Biting stonecrop. *Sedum acre* 'Aureum' is very hardy and easy.
1 Lemon thyme. *Thymus* × *citriodorus* 'Aureus' is a low-growing thyme with a strong lemon scent.
2 Golden feverfew *Tanacetum parthenium* 'Aureum'.
2 Polyanthus *Primula* × *polyantha*. Any yellow or red ones would fit in well here.
10 Scillas or squills *Scilla siberica* 'Spring Beauty', or add some dwarf daffodils.
25 Litres of John Innes No 2 soil.
Drainage: Small pieces of polystyrene.

METHOD
1. Cover the base of the container with 2.5 cm (1″) of drainage material and add 10 cm (4″) of soil.
2. Plant the bushy thymes at either end.
3. Plant the lemon thyme in the middle, with the feverfew on the front left and the stonecrop on the right.
4. Plant the two polyanthus towards the back, on either side of the lemon thyme.
5. Plant the scillas in any remaining gaps.
6. Bring the soil-level to within 2.5 cm (1″) of the rim of the container.
7. Water well. Firm in the plants. Add more soil if necessary.

AFTERCARE
Maintain the soil moisture throughout the autumn, winter and spring. Apply a liquid feed around the polyanthus in early March. After the polyanthus have finished flowering, remove and replant them in the garden, and replace them in the trough with orange pot marigolds.

55 A Barrel of Tulips and Forget-me-nots

Forget-me-not blue looks wonderful with the pink tulips. They make a popular combination which has been well tried over the decades.

SITE
Sunny.

CONTAINER
A wooden half-barrel or large pot: 60 cm (24″) in diameter, 40 cm (16″) deep.

WHEN TO PLANT
September to mid-November.

BEST
Late April to May.

INGREDIENTS
12 Pink late-flowering tulips *Tulipa* 'Douglas Bader'.
 6 Forget-me-nots *Myosotis alpestris* 'Blue Ball'. These can be bought in pots or in a strip, which is cheaper. Sometimes white and pink ones are available in the garden centres. A mixture would be lovely. If you already have seedlings in the garden, dig them up and use them.
100 Litres of John Innes No 2 soil.
Drainage: Pieces of polystyrene or old crocks.

METHOD
1. Cover the base of the container with 8 cm (3″) of drainage material and add 20 cm (8″) of soil.
2. Space tulips around the centre of the barrel.
3. Cover the bulbs with soil, bringing the level to within 2.5 cm (1″) of the rim of the container.
4. Plant the forget-me-nots near the edge of the barrel.
5. Water well. Firm in the plants. Add more soil if necessary.

AFTERCARE
Keep the soil moist throughout the autumn, winter

and spring, but never water it in frosty weather. The forget-me-nots will look limp in freezing conditions, but should soon pick up when the milder weather returns. Allow the tulips to die down naturally after flowering and then plant them out in a sunny spot in the garden. Alternatively, remove them while their leaves are still intact and replant them, but keep them watered. Discard the forget-me-nots after flowering.

56 Black and White Tulips

The delicate frill of sweet woodruff has a lovely softening effect on the contrasting black and white tulips.

SITE
Sunny.

CONTAINER
A terracotta pot: 35 cm (14″) in diameter, 18 cm (7″) deep. Use any medium-sized pot or barrel.

WHEN TO PLANT
September to mid-November.

BEST
Late April to May.

INGREDIENTS
10 Black or dark purple tulips *Tulipa* 'Queen of Night'.
10 White tulips *Tulipa* 'White Virgin'.
 4 White sweet woodruffs *Asperula odorata*. Once this is established in the garden you will have plenty to use in containers each year.
20 Litres of John Innes No 2 soil.
Drainage: Pieces of polystyrene or old crocks.

METHOD
1. Cover the base of the container with 5 cm (2″) of drainage material and add 5 cm (2″) of soil.
2. Space the tall black tulips in an inner circle, surrounded by the slightly shorter white tulips.
3. Cover the bulbs with soil, bringing the level to within 2.5 cm (1″) of the rim of the container.
4. Plant the sweet woodruffs around the edge of the pot.
5. Water well. Firm in the plants. Add more soil if necessary.

AFTERCARE
Keep the soil moist throughout the autumn, winter and spring, but be sure never to water it in frosty

weather. The sweet woodruffs will grow new leaves in early spring and form a pretty frill around the tulips. Allow the tulips to die down naturally after flowering and then plant them out in a sunny spot in the garden. Alternatively, remove and replant them while their leaves are still intact, but keep them watered. Plant the woodruffs out in the garden where they will grow in sun or complete shade. They will soon spread and can be used again next season.

57 A Polyanthus and Parsley Basket

The parsley acts as a beautiful green foliage plant, peeping out amongst the polyanthus. Pick the parsley for the kitchen and use the polyanthus flowers to decorate cakes and salads.

SITE
Sunny or partially shady. On a porch or table.

CONTAINER
A wicker basket: 35 cm (14″) in diameter, 15 cm (6″) deep. Preserve it with three coats of yacht varnish.

WHEN TO PLANT
Early March.

BEST
April to May.

INGREDIENTS
5 Polyanthus *Primula × polyantha*, any colour mixture will be lovely, although deep reds show up well with the rich green of the parsley.
4 Parsley plants or half a strip *Petroselinum crispum*.
9 Litres of John Innes No 2 soil or a multi-purpose compost.
Drainage: Small pieces of polystyrene or horticultural grit.

Black plastic sheeting to fit inside the basket. Cut out a bin liner or a soil sack.

METHOD
1. Line the basket with plastic sheeting so that it fits snugly round the bottom and comes right up to the top of the basket (the excess can always be tucked in later). Cut six 2.5-cm (1″) slits in the bottom to allow excess moisture to escape.
2. Cover the liner with 2.5 cm (1″) of drainage material and add 8 cm (3″) of soil.
3. Plant four polyanthus around the edge of the basket and one in the middle.
4. Space the parsley plants between the polyanthus around the edge of the basket.
5. Fill in the gaps with soil bringing the level to within 2.5 cm (1″) of the rim of the basket.
6. Water well. Firm in the plants. Add more soil if necessary.

AFTERCARE
Keep the soil moist by watering the container as necessary, but never water it in frosty conditions. Give liquid feeds in early and late April. At the end of May, plant the polyanthus out along a garden path in sun or shade. Plant the parsley near the front of a border where you can continue to enjoy the foliage. Wash and revarnish the basket for summer use.

58 Violas and Daisies in a Hanging Basket

Cheap and cheery, this is a colourful spring basket. Its red daisies and yellow violas look lovely together. As an alternative, try pink and white daisies mixed with blue violas for a pretty wedding or christening basket.

SITE
Sunny or partially shady.

CONTAINER
A wire hanging basket: 35 cm (14″) in diameter, with a 27.5 cm (11″) bracket.

WHEN TO PLANT
Late March to mid-April. These plants are all hardy.

BEST
April to early June.

INGREDIENTS
3 Strips of yellow violas *Viola cornuta* 'Prince John'.
3 Strips of red daisies *Bellis perennis* 'Tasso Rose'.
1 Strip of parsley *Petroselinum crispum*.
10 Litres of John Innes No 2 soil or a hanging basket compost with water-retaining crystals.
A basket of sphagnum moss or florist's wreath moss.
A circle of plastic about the size of a saucer.

METHOD
1. Line the basket with a generous thickness of moss; start at the base and work one-third of the way up the sides.
2. Cut four 2.5-cm (1″) slits in the circle of plastic, then place it over the moss lining in the bottom of the basket. Add soil to the level of the moss.
3. Alternate the violas and daisies, planting them in a circle about one-third of the way up the sides of the basket. Make sure the roots have good contact with the soil. You will probably use one strip each of both plants.
4. Tuck the moss between each plant, then add another ring on top to bring it level two-thirds of the way up the sides of the basket. Add more soil to this level.
5. Repeat another circle of violas and daisies, adding three clumps of parsley around the centre front and sides. Where possible, try to stagger the layers so that a viola plant in the top layer is placed over a daisy in the bottom.
6. Tuck more moss between each plant, then another layer so that it forms a collar 2.5 cm (1″)

above the rim of the basket. This is to avoid gaps when it settles.
7. Bring the soil to just beneath the rim of the basket.
8. Plant more violas, daisies and parsley in the top of the basket, saving a good strong parsley for the centre. Plant any remaining parsley plants in the garden.
9. Water well. Firm in the top plants. Add more soil and moss if necessary.

AFTERCARE
Keep the basket moist at all times. Give it liquid feeds at the end of April and in mid-May. Deadhead the flowers to prolong the flowering period. After flowering, discard the violas and daisies, but plant the parsley in a sunny spot in the garden. Water it well until it becomes established.

59 A Herb Hanging Basket

Scented herbs and edible flowers create an intricate tapestry of colour from April to June.

SITE
Sunny or partially shady.

CONTAINER
A wire hanging basket: 35 cm (14″) in diameter, with a 27.5 cm (11″) bracket.

WHEN TO PLANT
Late March to mid-April. These plants are all hardy.

BEST
April to May and into June.

INGREDIENTS
2 Variegated apple mints *Mentha × rotundifolia* 'Variegata'.
2 Eau de Cologne mints *Mentha × piperita* 'Citrata'.
1 Lemon balm *Melissa officinalis* 'Aurea'.
3 Red daisies *Bellis perennis* 'Tasso Rose'.
2 Golden marjoram *Origanum vulgare* 'Aureum'.
4 Parsley *Petroselinum crispum*.
3 Heartsease *Viola tricolor*.
1 Rosemary *Rosmarinus officinalis*.
2 Cowslips *Primula veris*.
1 Yellow viola *Viola cornuta* 'Prince John'.
2 Pink daisies *Bellis perennis* 'Tasso Rose'.
10 Litres of John Innes No 2 soil or a hanging basket compost with water-retaining crystals.
A basket of sphagnum moss or florist's wreath moss.
A circle of plastic about the size of a saucer.

METHOD
1. Line the basket with a generous thickness of moss; start at the base and work one-third of the way up the sides.
2. Cut four 2.5-cm (1″) slits in the circle of plastic, then place it over the moss lining in the bottom of the basket. Add soil to the level of the moss.
3. Alternate apple mints and eau de Cologne mints around the sides of the basket, with the lemon balm and a red daisy at the centre.
4. Ensure the roots have good contact with the soil.
5. Tuck the moss between each plant, then add another layer to bring it level two-thirds of the way up the sides of the basket. Add more soil.
6. Plant a red daisy and heartsease in the centre, with two golden marjoram and two parsley plants on either side.

7. Tuck more moss between each plant, then add another layer, so that it forms a collar 2.5 cm (1″) above the rim of the basket. This is to avoid gaps when it settles.
8. In the top, plant the rosemary at the centre back, with cowslips on either side just in front. Plant the yellow viola, pink daisies and the remaining heartsease, red daisy and parsley plants all round the sides and front of the basket. Fill in the gaps with soil.
9. Water well. Firm in the top plants. Add more soil and moss if necessary.

AFTERCARE
Keep the basket moist at all times. Give it liquid feeds at the end of April and in mid-May. Crop the herbs as needed. Use the violas and daisies in salads, otherwise deadhead them to prolong the flowering period. Dismantle the basket in June. Discard the violas and daisies. Site the rest of the plants in a sunny part of the garden. Water them until they are established. The cowslips, marjoram, balm, mints and rosemary can be used again next year.

60 A Basket of Herbs

A moveable feast of herbs and edible flowers, this can be used as an alternative to the herb hanging basket, or try them both together.

SITE
Sunny or partially shady. On a porch, step or table.

CONTAINER
A wicker basket: 35 cm (14″) in diameter, 15 cm (6″) deep. Preserve it with three coats of yacht varnish. This one has decorative gaps in the sides through which to plant. An old broken basket with holes could be used. If the one you use has no gaps, adapt the recipe accordingly; it will still look attractive.

WHEN TO PLANT
Late March to early April.

BEST
April to May.

INGREDIENTS
 1 Strip of heartsease or little violas *Viola tricolor*.
 1 Strip of pink daisies *Bellis perennis* 'Tasso Rose'.
 1 Clump of chives *Allium schoenoprasum*.
 2 Variegated apple mints *Mentha × rotundifolia* 'Variegata' (there are many alternatives).
 1 Lemon thyme *Thymus × citriodorus* 'Aureus'.
 1 Lemon balm *Melissa officinalis* 'Aurea'.
 1 Golden marjoram *Origanum vulgare* 'Aureum'.
 1 Parsley *Petroselinum crispum*.
11 Litres of John Innes No 2 soil or a hanging basket compost with water-retaining crystals.
Drainage: Horticultural grit.
Black plastic bin sheeting to fit inside the basket. Cut out a bin liner or a soil sack.

METHOD
1. Line the basket with the plastic sheeting so that it fits snugly round the bottom and comes right up to the top of the basket (the excess can always be tucked in later). Cut six 2.5-cm (1″) slits in the bottom to allow excess moisture to escape.
2. Cover the liner with 1 cm (½″) of horticultural grit and add 8 cm (3″) of soil.
3. Cut slits through the plastic sheeting where holes appear in the sides of the basket.
4. Alternate violas and daisies at the sides. Garden seedlings are ideal, as their roots are still small.
5. Bring the soil level to within 2.5 cm (1″) of the rim of the basket.
6. Now plant the chives and one mint on either side of one handle with the lemon thyme around the other at the top.
7. Plant the lemon balm and the golden marjoram at the ends, with the parsley in the centre.
8. Plant more violas and daisies along the sides, with the second mint near the thyme.
9. Water well. Firm in the plants. Add more soil if necessary.

AFTERCARE
Keep the soil moist by watering it as necessary. Give the container liquid feeds in early and late April. Crop the herbs, especially the lemon balm to keep it neat and to retain its golden colouring. Cut the chives once or twice before allowing them to flower. Use the daisies and violas in salads, otherwise deadhead them to prolong their flowering period. Dismantle the basket in June. Plant the violas, daisies and chives in the garden in sun or partial shade. Mint, thyme, lemon balm, marjoram and parsley prefer a sunny spot. Wash and revarnish the basket.

61 A Basket of Summer Delights

The little pink diascia and pretty blue Swan River daisy make a charming combination in this rustic wicker basket. It is easy to plant and simple to look after; the display will go on for months.

SITE
Sunny. On an old bench, a sunny porch or the top of a well.

CONTAINER
A rustic wicker basket: 27.5 cm (11″) in diameter, 12.5 cm (5″) deep. Preserve it with three coats of yacht varnish. Alternatively, use a window box or pot.

WHEN TO PLANT
Mid to late May.

BEST
June to September.

INGREDIENTS
  3 Swan River daisies *Brachycome iberidifolia* has thread-like foliage and small purple-blue flowers.
  3 *Diascia* 'Ruby Field'. This is a low-growing hardy perennial which flowers all summer.
  6 Litres of John Innes No 2 soil or a hanging basket compost with water-retaining crystals.
Drainage: Small pieces of polystyrene or horticultural grit.
Black plastic sheeting to fit inside the basket. Cut out a bin liner or a soil sack.

METHOD
1. Line the basket with the plastic sheeting so that it fits snugly round the bottom and comes right up to the rim of the basket. Cut six 2.5-cm (1″) slits in the bottom to allow excess moisture to escape.
2. Cover the liner with 2.5 cm (1″) of drainage material and add 8 cm (3″) of soil.
3. Alternate the Swan River daisy and diascias around the basket.
4. Water well. Firm in the plants. Add more soil if necessary.

AFTERCARE
Keep the soil moist by watering it daily if necessary. Give the basket a weekly liquid feed throughout the flowering period. There is little need to deadhead or spray for greenfly. In the autumn, dismantle the plants. Discard the Swan River daisies, but plant the diascias in a sunny, sheltered spot in the garden so that they may be used again for another year.

62 A Scented Window Box

Old-fashioned mignonette and heliotrope 'Cherry Pie' make a delightfully scented combination in a window box or trough by the back door. The rich pink geranium adds extra colour in the centre.

SITE
Sunny.

CONTAINER
A small window box: 40 cm (16″) long, 15 cm (6″) wide and deep. For a larger box, adjust the number of plants. This was kept in the greenhouse until mid-June. As a result, the mignonette grew more upright than I have normally experienced.

WHEN TO PLANT
Sow the mignonette in March, following the instructions on the seed packet. It is easy to germinate. Prick it out as soon as it is large enough to handle, and pot it into 8-cm (3″) pots. Plant the window box out from mid May to early June.

BEST
July to August.

INGREDIENTS
1 Geranium *Pelargonium* 'Ailsa Craig'. This is compact and a better scale here than a larger variety. Vary the geranium according to the size of the container.
2 *Heliotropium* × *hybridum* 'Cherry Pie'. Pale blue varieties have the best scent.
4 Mignonette *Reseda odorata*.
10 Litres of John Innes No 2 soil or a hanging basket compost with water-retaining crystals.
Drainage: Pieces of polystyrene.

METHOD
1. Cover the base of the container with 5 cm (2″) of drainage material and add 5 cm (2″) of soil.
2. Plant the geranium in the centre, with the 'Cherry Pie' heliotropes on either side.
3. Plant the mignonette along the sides, front and back, depending on the final position of the box or trough.
4. Water well. Firm in the plants. Add more soil to bring the level to within 2.5 cm (1″) of the rim of the container.

AFTERCARE
'Cherry Pie' heliotrope is susceptible to cold weather. Plant up the container in May but place it outside only in warm weather. Protect it if the nights are still cold. Otherwise, keep it in a greenhouse until mid-June. Keep it well watered, and water it daily in hot weather. Give it a weekly liquid feed from the end of June onwards. Deadhead the flowers. At the end of September, discard the mignonette. Pot up and overwinter the geranium and the 'Cherry Pie' heliotropes at 7–10°C (45–50°F).

63 The Ageratum Window Box

A simple row of pink geraniums, blue ageratum and white lobelia make an effective, well-used combination, with grey helichrysum trailing down the front of the window box.

SITE
Sunny.

CONTAINER
This window box looks like old-fashioned lead but is made of fibreglass, which is much cheaper and lighter: 90 cm (36″) long, 17.5 cm (7″) wide and deep.

WHEN TO PLANT
Mid to late May.

BEST
Late June to September.

INGREDIENTS
4 Upright pink geraniums *Pelargonium* 'Pink Glow'.
1 Strip of ageratum *Ageratum houstonianum* F_1 Hybrid. Its powdery blue flowers are loved by butterflies and bees.
1 Strip of white lobelia *Lobelia erinus* 'White Lady'.
2 Helichrysum *Plecostachys serpyllifolium* has a trailing habit with tiny grey leaves.

25 Litres of John Innes No 2 soil.
Drainage: Pieces of polystyrene.

METHOD
1. Cover the base of the container with 2.5 cm (1″) of drainage material and add 10 cm (4″) of soil.
2. Plant four geraniums along the length of the box.
3. Divide the bedding strips. Plant five ageratums along the front of the box, in-between and either side of geraniums. Plant three at the back.
4. Plant the lobelia in clumps along the front and ends of the box with the two helichrysum at either side of the centre.
5. Bring the soil to within 2.5 cm (1″) of the rim.
6. Water well. Firm in the plants. Add more soil if necessary.

AFTERCARE
Water regularly throughout the summer, and daily in hot weather. Deadhead the geraniums and ageratum. Apply a weekly liquid feed from the end of June. Discard the ageratums and lobelia at the end of the summer. Pot up geraniums and helichrysum and overwinter them at 7–10°C (45–50°F). Use the helichrysum for cuttings early next spring. The geraniums can be used for two or three years. Take cuttings and multiply them.

64 A Summer Hanging Basket

A colourful mixture of summer favourites, including geraniums, fuchsias, petunias and lobelia, make this a delightful cottage basket.

SITE
Sunny or partially shady.

CONTAINER
A wire hanging basket: 35 cm (14″) in diameter, with a 27.5 cm (11″) bracket.

WHEN TO PLANT
Mid to late May.

BEST
Late June to September.

INGREDIENTS
There are many other varieties and colours to choose from. Use these as a guide only.
- 2 Strips of trailing lobelia *Lobelia erinus* 'String of Pearls', a mixture of lilac, white and blue flowers, or try self-coloured groups such as 'White Lady'.
- 3 Trailing geraniums *Pelargonium* 'Flamingo'.
- 2 Fuchsias. *Fuchsia* 'Winston Churchill' is a pretty pink and lilac double which hangs well.
- 1 Upright geranium *Pelargonium* 'Scarlet', a strong-growing modern Century hybrid.
- 2 Petunias *Petunia* F1 Hybrid; choose cerise or try a deep blue.
- 10 Litres of hanging basket compost with water-retaining crystals.
- A basket of sphagnum moss or florist's wreath moss.
- A circle of plastic about the size of a saucer.

METHOD
1. Line the bottom of the basket with a generous thickness of moss, bringing it half-way up the sides.
2. Cut four 2.5-cm (1″) slits in the circle of plastic, then place it over the moss lining in the bottom of the basket. Add 8 cm (3″) of soil.
3. Carefully divide the first strip of lobelia and plant it in a circle half-way up the sides of the basket.
4. Add more moss so that it forms a collar just above the basket rim. Add 5 cm (2″) of soil.
5. Plant three trailing geraniums around the front of the basket with two fuchsias in-between.
6. Plant the upright geranium at the centre back of the basket with petunias in front on either side.
7. Plant the remaining lobelia around the rim of the basket or in any available gaps.
8. Water well. Firm in the plants. Add more soil and moss where necessary.

AFTERCARE
Water the basket daily in hot weather, at soil-level. Apply a weekly liquid feed from the end of June. Spray for aphids on the fuchsias and petunias particularly, but use one acceptable to bees and other garden friends. Bees love lobelia and will be constant visitors in sunny weather. Deadhead the geraniums, fuchsias and petunias regularly. Dismantle the basket in September. Discard the lobelia and petunias. Pot up the geraniums and fuchsias, and overwinter them at 7–10°C (45–50°F).

65 Summer Scents in a Pot

Lemon verbena is not a showy plant, but its leaves exude a powerful lemony aroma when they are touched. The rose-scented geranium is not very colourful, but it is memorable for the perfume of its foliage. Here, both are surrounded by an exuberant fuchsia and two beautiful variegated geraniums.

SITE
Sunny.

CONTAINER
A medium to large pot, depending on the age of the plants. All of the plants here are two or three years old. This pot is 47.5 cm (19″) in diameter, 32.5 cm (13″) deep.

WHEN TO PLANT
Mid to late May.

BEST
June to September.

INGREDIENTS
1 Lemon verbena *Aloysia triphylla*.
1 Rose-scented geranium. *Pelargonium* 'Attar of Roses' has a hairy leaf and stem and pale pink petals.
1 *Fuchsia* 'Lye's Unique', a fast-growing upright with pretty white/salmon flowers. Try 'Thalia' as an alternative, or a modern bush variety.
2 Variegated leaf geraniums *Pelargonium* 'Hills of Snow'. The bright light pink flower is pretty with the leaf colouring. 'Mrs Parker' makes a good alternative, or use a modern pink one.
35 Litres of John Innes No 2 soil, depending on the age of the plants and the size of rootballs.
Drainage: Pieces of polystyrene.

METHOD
1. Cover the base of the container with 8 cm (3″) of drainage material and add 15 cm (6″) of soil.
2. Plant the lemon verbena in the centre of the pot, with the rose-scented geranium at the front and the fuchsia behind.
3. Plant the two 'Hills of Snow' on either side.

4. Fill in the gaps with soil, bringing it level to within 2.5 cm (1″) of the rim of the pot.
5. Water well. Firm in the plants.

AFTERCARE
Water the container regularly, at soil-level; it may need to be watered daily in hot weather. Apply a liquid feed weekly from the end of June, particularly to the fuchsia. Deadhead all the flowers. At the end of the summer, bring the pot into a frost-free greenhouse and overwinter it with the plants *in situ*. Pot on into a larger pot the following March, or dismantle it in early autumn and pot up the plants individually.

66 The Hay Manger

Hay mangers are popular with today's cottagers. Plant something which will tumble luxuriantly right over the front. Nasturtiums provide an easy answer if the spot is warm and sunny.

SITE
Sunny. At eye level where you can fully enjoy it and easily look after it.

CONTAINER
This hay manger is of the original proportions: 75 cm (30″) long, 30 cm (12″) wide and 45 cm (18″) deep. Modern hay racks are smaller, so adjust plant numbers accordingly.

WHEN TO PLANT
Sow the nasturtiums in March following the instructions on the seed packet, planting six seeds each in two 20-cm (8″) pots. After germination, allow only three plants to grow in each. Plant the hay manger at the end of May.

BEST
Late June to early October.

INGREDIENTS
6 Nasturtiums *Tropaeolum nanum* 'Dwarf Cherry Rose'. There are many dwarf ones to choose from which should trail at least 45 cm (18″). Avoid the climbing or trailing varieties as they will have no support.
1 *Geranium pelargonium* 'Dolly Varden'.
2 *Fuchsia* 'Thalia', upright with bronze foliage.
2 *Fuchsia* 'Coralle', upright orange flowers.
2 *Bidens* 'Golden Goddess', small yellow flowers.
50 Litres of John Innes No 1 soil.
Black plastic sheeting to fit inside the manger. Cut out a bin liner or a soil sack.
Black netting.
A basket of sphagnum moss or florist's wreath moss.

METHOD
1. Spread the netting over the front of the manger and tie it around the bottom, sides and top.
2. Create a generous wall of moss right up the front of the manger, behind the netting.
3. Place the plastic sheeting down the wall – to keep the wall dry – and across the bottom.
4. Carefully add the soil, bringing it to within 8 cm (3″) of the rim of the container.

5. Plant the nasturtiums in two groups on either side of the front.
6. Plant the geranium in the centre, with two *Fuchsia* 'Thalia' behind, one 'Coralle' on either side and the bidens in both corners.
7. Water well. Firm in the plants. Add more soil and moss as necessary.

AFTERCARE
Water the manger regularly, as it will dry out quickly. Give the fuchsias a liquid feed every two weeks from the end of June. Spray for aphids, and particularly for blackfly on the nasturtiums, but use a spray that is friendly to bees and ladybirds. Deadhead the flowers regularly. At the end of the summer, discard the bidens and nasturtiums. Overwinter the fuchsias and geraniums at 7–10°C (45–50°F).

67 Sunflowers and Bronze Fennel

Sunflowers are an old cottage favourite. These velvety red ones look charming amongst the thread-like foliage of the dusky bronze fennel. Bees love to feed on the nectar. Later, birds will feast on the seeds.

SITE
Sunny and sheltered.

CONTAINER
A wooden half-barrel or large pot: 60 cm (24″) in diameter, 40 cm (16″) deep.

WHEN TO PLANT
This is a mixture of perennials and annuals and can be treated as a long-term planting scheme with the sunflowers added each year. Sow the sunflowers in March following instructions on the packet. Allow double the number of seeds, i.e. eight, and keep only the strongest four plants. Either sow the seeds *in situ* in the container or transfer the plants after germination.

BEST
July to September, although the bronze fennel will be pretty from late spring onwards.

INGREDIENTS
1 Bronze fennel *Foeniculum vulgare* 'Purpureum'. A mature specimen will look best. Dig one up from the garden in early spring. Or use four young plants with a shorter variety of sunflower.
4 Sunflowers *Helianthus annuus* 'Velvet Queen'. This has a dark red flower which is particularly good with the bronze fennel. Alternatively, try yellow sunflowers with green fennel.
100 Litres of John Innes No 3 soil.
Drainage: Pieces of polystyrene.

METHOD
1. Cover the base of the container with 5 cm (2″) of drainage material and add 25 cm (10″) of soil.
2. Plant the bronze fennel in the centre of the container and bring the soil-level to within 2.5 cm (1″) of the rim of the container.
3. Plant the sunflowers towards the edge of the container.
4. Water well. Firm in the plants. Add more soil if necessary.

AFTERCARE
Keep the soil moist by watering it as necessary. If the bronze fennel has been transferred from the garden it will require lots of extra water to begin with. Watch out for slugs and snails on the sunflowers; they will soon eat the leaves. Support the sunflowers with bamboo canes or use the bronze fennel stalks as supports. Give a liquid feed every week once the sunflowers come into bud. Leave the seedheads intact so that finches can enjoy the autumn feast. Cut the bronze fennel down to ground-level in late autumn and leave it in the container throughout the winter. Replace the sunflowers with new plants in the following spring.

68 A Barrel for Winter and Spring

These familiar cottage shrubs produce colour from November to April. First, with pretty yellow stars on the winter-flowering jasmine and second, with the scented white flowers of the viburnum. Recipes 68 and 69 together create a wonderful winter column of flowers and greenery.

SITE
Any aspect, preferably sheltered.

CONTAINER
A wooden half-barrel or a large pot: 60 cm (24″) in diameter, 40 cm (16″) deep.

WHEN TO PLANT
Plant either in spring or autumn. With a spring planting, the plants have time to mature for a good winter display the following winter and will be even better in the years to follow.

BEST
November to April, depending on the aspect. If the barrel is south-facing, it will be in flower several weeks earlier than if it faces north. The viburnum will normally be at its best when the jasmine is over.

INGREDIENTS
1 Winter-flowering jasmine *Jasminum nudiflorum*. Choose a large plant.
1 Viburnum. *Viburnum tinus* is evergreen and produces scented white flowers.
1 Variegated ivy *Hedera helix*. 'Goldchild' has good creamy gold edges to the leaves. 'Heise' has silver variegated leaves and would be better in a northerly aspect.
100 Litres of John Innes No 3 soil.
Drainage: Pieces of polystyrene or old crocks.

METHOD
1. Cover the base of the container with 5 cm (2″) of drainage material and add 25 cm (10″) of soil.
2. Plant the winter-flowering jasmine towards the back of the container.
3. Plant the viburnum in the centre, with the ivy trailing over the front.
4. Fill in the gaps with soil bringing the level to within 2.5 cm (1″) of the rim of the container.
5. Water well. Firm in the plants. Add more soil if necessary.

AFTERCARE
Water the barrel throughout the year. Take particular care in summer that the plants have moisture to grow and mature for the following season. Never water the container in frosty weather. Give it a general slow-release fertiliser in the autumn. Cut back old flower shoots on the jasmine, immediately after flowering, to within 8 cm (3″) of old wood. This will encourage new bushy growth and the formation of next season's flower buds. Aim to build up a strong framework of growth, eventually allowing the jasmine to flow through the viburnum which will act as its support. Use small bent wires to peg one or two ivy trails in the soil around the sides of the container to establish it there as well as in the front. Replant it into a larger container using fresh soil after the third season. Prune the viburnum in early May if necessary.

69 A Winter Hanging Basket

This cheery basket is studded with yellow stars on the winter-flowering jasmine, bringing welcome colour to the door in the very depths of winter.

SITE
Any aspect, preferably sheltered.

CONTAINER
A wire hanging basket: 35 cm (14″) in diameter, with a 27.5 cm (11″) bracket.

WHEN TO PLANT
Plant in the spring, using snowdrops 'in the green' with leaves intact, or in late August to early September using dry bulbs. With the spring planting, the plants have time to mature for a good display the following winter and will be even better thereafter.

BEST
November to March, depending on the aspect and weather. If the basket is south-facing, it will be in flower several weeks earlier than if it is facing north. The snowdrops follow after the winter-flowering jasmine is virtually over.

INGREDIENTS
 1 Winter-flowering jasmine *Jasminum nudiflorum*. Choose a large plant.
 1 Variegated ivy *Hedera helix*. 'Goldchild' has good creamy gold edges to the leaves. 'Heise' has silver variegated leaves and would be better in a northerly aspect.
15 Snowdrops *Galanthus nivalis*.
10 Litres of John Innes No 3 soil.
A basket of sphagnum moss or florist's wreath moss.
A circle of plastic about the size of a saucer.

METHOD
 1. Line the basket with a generous thickness of moss; start at the base and work up the sides, so that you eventually form a collar above the rim.
 2. Cut four 2.5-cm (1″) slits in the circle of plastic, then place it over the moss lining in the bottom of the basket. Add 8 cm (3″) of soil.
 3. Plant the winter-flowering jasmine towards the centre back of the basket.
 4. Plant the ivy at the centre front.
 5. Plant the snowdrops in any available spaces in the middle and at either side.
 6. Fill in the gaps with soil.

 7. Water well. Firm in the plants. Add more soil and moss if necessary.

AFTERCARE
Water the container throughout the year. Take particular care in summer that the plants have moisture to grow and mature for the following season. Never water the basket in frosty weather. Apply a liquid feed during a mild spell in November and early January. Also give an occasional feed in summer. Cut back old flower shoots on the jasmine, immediately after flowering, to within 8 cm (3″) of old wood. This will encourage new bushy growth, and the formation of next season's flower buds. Allow the snowdrops to die down naturally. Use small bent wires to peg in some ivy trails to form a ball of growth around the sides and underneath the basket. Also peg in a few jasmine stems and allow the new growth to break out from these points. Replant the container after the third season.

70 The Foxglove Trough

In summer, the container almost disappears amongst the profusion of shade-loving plants which surround it. This is carefully orchestrated, as the trough stands on a man-hole cover which would otherwise create a gap in the border scheme. The winter picture is very different. Then the bold foliage of the elephant's ears contrasts with the delicate tracery of the evergreen fern and the whole container stands out, raised up above all hints of other greenery around.

SITE
Shady or partially shady.

CONTAINER
A 'stone trough' created from a butler's sink (by adding a mixture of sand and cement): 75 cm (30″) long, 37.5 cm (15″) wide, 25 cm (10″) deep.

WHEN TO PLANT
September to November; or March to April, adding crocuses in the autumn.

BEST
June to July; February to early April.

INGREDIENTS
1 Male fern. *Dryopteris filix-mas* is evergreen in sheltered spots.
1 Granny's pin cushion *Astrantia maxima*.
1 Lady's mantle *Alchemilla mollis*.
1 Elephant's ears *Bergenia cordifolia* 'Purpurea'.
1 Foxglove *Digitalis purpurea* 'Alba'.
1 *Hosta fortunei* 'Marginato-alba' or 'Thomas Hogg'; both have white edges to the leaves.
20 Dutch crocuses *Crocus vernus* 'Purpureus Grandiflorus'.
50 Litres of John Innes No 3 soil.
Drainage: Pieces of polystyrene.

METHOD
1. Cover the base of the container with 5 cm (2″) of drainage material, and add 15 cm (6″) of soil.
2. *Back, left to right*: Plant the fern, the granny's pin cushion and the lady's mantle.
3. *Front, left to right*: Plant the elephant's ears, the foxglove and the hosta.
4. Plant the crocuses 5 cm (2″) deep to the middle and right.
5. Fill in the gaps with soil.
6. Water well. Add more soil if necessary to bring it level to within 2.5 cm (1″) of the rim of the container.

AFTERCARE
Never water in frosty weather, but maintain the soil moisture throughout the year, especially in spring and summer. Give the container a slow-release fertiliser in early spring each year. Apply a liquid feed in early June. Remove any untidy leaves on the fern and elephant's ears in early spring. The foxgloves may need staking if the winds are strong. Keep slugs and snails off the hostas. Allow the crocuses to die down, then remove any dry leaves. Cut off the old flower stems of the elephant's ears immediately after flowering. Treat the lady's mantle, foxglove, and hosta in same way. Tidy the plants in autumn, removing foliage debris. Replace the foxglove each spring.

71 Creeping Jenny and Hostas in a Hanging Basket

This is a very useful combination for a shady corner where the bright yellow foliage of the creeping Jenny provides a carpet of gold for the musk and hostas above. It is planted as a hanging basket, but it is seen here resting on a water barrel.

SITE
Shady or partially shady.

CONTAINER
A wire hanging basket: 35 cm (14″) in diameter, with a 27.5 cm (11″) bracket. Try a medium pot as an alternative.

WHEN TO PLANT
March to April.

BEST
June to September.

INGREDIENTS
3 *Hosta* 'Gold Edger'. This is a small-leaved hybrid which produces good lilac flowers.
4 Musk *Mimulus* 'Calypso' F_1 Hybrids.
1 Creeping Jenny. *Lysimachia nummularia* 'Aurea' is the golden form.
10 Litres of John Innes No 3 soil or hanging basket compost with water-retaining crystals.
A basket of sphagnum moss or florist's wreath moss.
A circle of plastic about the size of a saucer.

METHOD
1. Line the basket with a generous thickness of moss; start at the base and work up the sides so that you eventually form a collar above the rim.
2. Cut four 2.5-cm (1″) slits in the circle of plastic, then place it over the moss lining in the bottom of the basket. Add 8 cm (3″) of soil.
3. Space the three hostas in the centre.
4. Plant the musk around the edge with the creeping Jenny at the centre front.
5. Fill in the gaps with soil.
6. Water well. Firm in the plants. Add more soil and moss if necessary.

AFTERCARE
Maintain damp soil throughout year, taking particular care in summer when the plants must have plenty of moisture to flourish. Apply a liquid feed in early June and then every two weeks until late summer. Remove the hosta spikes after flowering. The leaves will become more golden as the season progresses and will match the creeping Jenny. The creeping Jenny will form long trails, perhaps 60 cm (24″) long. Cut them off at the end of September. Remove dead hosta leaves. Place the basket at ground-level, in a sheltered spot for the winter. Replace musk in the spring and hang it up again, away from early slugs. You may need to divide hostas and repot them after two years using fresh soil.

72 Bridal Wreath in a Basket

Bridal wreath is an old favourite, and is grown outside in summer pots or trained round a wire hoop in the cottage window. Its flowers are a delicate mixture of pink and white. Sadly, it is rarely seen today.

SITE
Sunny.

CONTAINER
Wire baskets are now becoming more readily available. This one has been painted with a black metal paint and is 25 cm (10″) in diameter, 15 cm (6″) deep. The recipe is also suitable for a small to medium pot.

WHEN TO PLANT
April to May, or whenever available.

BEST
June to July.

INGREDIENTS
1 Bridal wreath *Francoa ramosa*. Even a small plant will give an excellent result within a year. It is perennial but not fully hardy.
1 Strip of white alyssum. *Lobularia maritima* is very sweet smelling and is loved by bees.
10 Litres of John Innes No 2 soil.
Drainage: Pieces of polystyrene.
Black plastic sheeting to fit inside the basket. Cut out a bin liner or a soil-sack.
A basket of sphagnum moss or florist's wreath moss.

METHOD
1. Line the basket with a generous thickness of moss; start at the bottom and bring it right up the sides.
2. Cover the base and sides with black plastic sheeting. Cut six 2.5-cm (1″) slits in the bottom to allow for drainage.
3. Cover the base with 2.5 cm (1″) of drainage material.
4. Add enough soil to bring it level within 2.5 cm (1″) of the rim of the basket.
5. Plant the bridal wreath in the centre of the basket.
6. Divide the alyssum and plant it around the sides.
7. Water well. Firm in the plants. Add more soil or moss if necessary.

AFTERCARE
The bridal wreath needs moisture during the spring and summer, but keep the soil on the dry side. Overwinter the container in a greenhouse or indoors, and keep it fairly dry. Repot it in early May. Give it a liquid feed every two weeks during the flowering period. Remove the flower spikes after flowering. Discard the alyssum in September and renew it in May.

73 Lavender Pot-pourri

Lavender creates a wonderful scene with its beautiful soft blue flower spikes and heavenly scent. Bees and butterflies love it too!

SITE
Sunny. Try it by the front door so that you can enjoy it every time you come home.

CONTAINER
A medium pot: 37.5 cm (15") in diameter, 27.5 cm (11") deep. It could be larger, depending on the variety of lavender used.

WHEN TO PLANT
Plant the lavender from March to April or September to October, and the dianthus in April or May.

BEST
July to August.

INGREDIENTS
3 Lavenders. *Lavandula angustifolia* 'Hidcote' is a compact variety suitable for a medium-sized container. 'Grappenhall' is taller and lighter in colour with more scent; 'Royal Purple' is also taller, has good scent and rich colouring. Both would suit a larger pot.

3 *Dianthus* 'Strawberry Parfait', a modern hybrid which flowers all summer. Alternatively, use scented garden pinks, such as 'Dad's Favourite'.
25 Litres of John Innes No 2 soil.
Drainage: Pieces of polystyrene.

METHOD
1. Cover the base of the container with 5 cm (2") of drainage material and add 15 cm (6") of soil.
2. Plant the lavenders towards the edge of the pot, leaving space for the dianthus in-between.
3. Fill in the gaps with soil, bringing it level to within 2.5 cm (1") of the rim of the pot.
4. Water well. Firm in the plants.

AFTERCARE
Keep the soil moist throughout the spring and summer. Apply a slow-release fertiliser in early spring, and give the container a liquid feed at the end of June. Deadhead and trim the lavender after flowering to within 5 cm (2") of the old growth. During the winter months, keep on the dry side and give the soil extra protection in severe weather. Replace the dianthus in April or May. Repot all the plants into a larger container after two years. Take lavender cuttings in August and be prepared to start again with young plants after four years.

74 The Butterfly Barrel

This is a planting scheme dominated by the tall butterfly bush which acts as a magnet to colourful peacocks, small tortoiseshells, and red admirals.

SITE
Sunny and sheltered.

CONTAINER
A large container. This is a painted galvanised container: 85 cm (34″) long, 60 cm (24″) wide and 30 cm (12″) deep. It has been drilled to provide drainage.

WHEN TO PLANT
October or March.

BEST
July to September.

INGREDIENTS
2 Evening primroses *Oenothera biennis*.
1 Butterfly bush *Buddleja davidii* 'Fascination'; there are several lilac alternatives.
3 Valerian *Centranthus ruber*.
3 Ice plants *Sedum spectabile*.
1 Thrift *Armeria maritima* 'Dusseldorf Pride'.
1 *Aubrieta deltoidea* 'Dr Mules'.
150 Litres of John Innes No 3 soil.
Drainage: Pieces of polystyrene or old crocks.

METHOD
1. Cover the base of the container with 5 cm (2″) of drainage material and add 15 cm (6″) of soil.
2. *Back*: Plant one evening primrose on the left and the butterfly bush to the right.
3. *Middle*: Plant two valerian on the left and another in the centre.
4. *Front*: Plant two ice plants to the left, the thrift, the second evening primrose, the aubrieta and then another ice plant.
5. Fill in the gaps with soil, bringing it level to within 2.5 cm (1″) of the rim.
6. Water well. Firm in the plants. Add more soil if necessary.

AFTERCARE
Keep the container well watered especially in spring and summer. Watch for unwanted slugs and snails.

Give the evening primroses support; either tie them to a strong cane as with the back one, or prop them up at ground-level as has been done with the front one shown here. Remove the evening primroses in the autumn and replace them in the spring. Deadhead the valerian after it flowers in June to encourage flowers later. Leave the seedheads on the ice plants through the winter, then remove the stems in spring. Give the container extra protection in severe winter weather. Prune the butterfly bush in March each year, to within 8 cm (3″) of the old wood. Give the container a slow-release general fertiliser in spring. Replant everything in new soil after three years. The ice plants should then be divided.

Plant Lists

INTRODUCTION

The names in this list refer only to those plants which have been used in the garden and container recipes in this book. It is not, therefore, a complete list of cottage garden plants.

The plants have been grouped under fourteen headings. Four refer to the time of flowering: spring, early summer, late summer to autumn and winter. Others refer to the nature of the plant: whether they are bulbs or climbers, or trees and shrubs. Some plants have different characteristics. They might be richly fragrant, capable of being dried easily or used as herbs. There is a heading for wild flowers, and another for the butterfly and bee nectar plants. There is also a list of all the fruit and vegetables grown.

Often the plants naturally fall under two or more headings. Should lavender be put among the late summer flowers, dried, scented or butterfly and bee nectar plants? A decision has to be made one way or the other. But where other lists are relevant, a cross reference is always given.

Details in the plant lists often give a clue as to why some of these plants were chosen. The date of introduction, where given, will be an indicator that this particular plant has been grown in cottage gardens for decades or centuries, and has stood the test of time. In other words, it is a 'good doer'. Many of the old-fashioned varieties are still available and have strong constitutions. Unlike many of their younger relatives, they are often scented too. Other plants may be chosen for health reasons. Certain varieties of phlox will get mildew; certain hollyhocks will get rust. By choosing the right varieties, many disasters can be avoided.

Use the lists to get an idea of alternative plants. There are a multitude of roses, many garden pinks, lots of honeysuckles, lavenders and hostas, as well as a host of daffodils. Where possible, old varieties are used, but this is not always the case. For instance, where modern hybrids retain the scent and extend the flowering period, then both old and modern are used: garden pinks are just one example.

Details are often given of how to propagate many of the herbaceous plants, either by seed or by cuttings or division. Those that seed themselves will be mentioned. Some are so prolific that it is sometimes recommended that the seedheads are removed before they have the chance to disperse. Many of the cottage favourites were self-propagating. It is one of their many charms. It also might explain why cottage gardens sometimes look so unplanned!

Dimensions refer to the height and spread of mature plants in the garden. Container plant sizes have been omitted, as much depends on available root space, and the amount of food and water given.

The plant lists indicate in which garden or container recipe each plant was used. Some species or individual cultivars are employed several times. This is partly because these plants are justifiably good in the cottage garden setting. Cross reference the other family names and see where and how they are used. It may help you to understand their value so that you can think of other possible homes for them.

1 Spring Bulbs

Spring bulbs are so bright and cheery, there will always be room for lots of them in the cottage garden. Many good old-fashioned varieties are still available. You will find them at many of the thousand or so garden centres stocked by O. A. Taylor and Sons Bulbs Ltd, who specialise in a wonderful range of old favourites. Of course, they are also available in many of the bulb catalogues. These bulbs have stood the test of time and many fit in beautifully with the cottage borders and grassland areas.

Choose hyacinths, the glory of the snow, grape hyacinths, many of the daffodils and all the tulips named below for planting in the mixed borders. The wild daffodils, anemones, crocuses and bluebells will also be at home in the orchard or in the grass verges.

Many of the bulbs are beautifully scented. Hyacinths are justly renowned; so are the pheasant's eye daffodils. Crocuses and grape hyacinths have a sweet fragrance as well.

On the whole, they much prefer to be left undisturbed so that they can spread quietly by themselves. They should all be long lasting if the ground is well prepared, free draining and mulched regularly with compost or leaf mould. This will create a moisture-retentive soil with plenty of food value to help good growth. The strength of next year's bulb relies on the goodness from the current season's leaves going back into it and building it up. Therefore, it is important that this process goes on uninterrupted, that the leaves are not allowed to die through lack of water, that they are not tied up and that they are not prematurely cut off. If the bulbs are grown in grass, allow at least six weeks after flowering before mowing. Deadheading is recommended where seeding is not wanted, as it will prevent a loss of vigour.

ANEMONE: *Anemone blanda* is neat in habit and stands only 10 cm (4″) high; it has an attractive leaf and is long lasting. It flowers from February through to April. The flowers open wide in sunshine, 5 cm (2″) in diameter, and are mid-blue, mauve-pink or white. They can be obtained in mixed selections or individual colours. They tolerate sun or shade but are happiest under deciduous shrubs or trees, where they will receive dappled shade in spring and more shade in the hot summer months that follow. *See* Recipes 10, 24 and 51. Top dress the bulbs with leaf mould in autumn. They will seed themselves to form large groupings, or they may be propagated simply by dividing the tubers in early autumn or after flowering in late spring.

Anemone nemorosa (wood anemone) is a British native which is at home in a cool shady spot or beneath the canopy of shrubs or trees. A small clump will soon form a neat mat of attractive ferny leaves, 15 cm (6″) high. Throughout March and April, its dainty nodding flower heads are held clear above the foliage, but in sunlight they turn upwards and open wide, 3–5 cm (1¼–2″). White is the most common form available, although lavender-blue tints also exist. *See* Recipes 25 and 42. Top dress the bulbs with leaf mould in autumn. They spread quickly by creeping rhizomes. Propagate the anemones by division in late spring after they have flowered.

BLUEBELL: This is an old favourite. Its pretty 30-cm (1') spikes of rich blue flowers appear in April and May. It prefers shady conditions beneath trees or shrubs but will tolerate many sunny spots and will naturalise in grass. Two types are often seen in gardens and both may appear with blue, white or pink flowers. Both will seed very freely. The first is our native British bluebell, *Hyacinthoides non-scripta*, which has nodding racemes of little bells on one side of its flower spike. *See* Recipe 18. The second is the Spanish bluebell, *Hyacinthoides hispanica*, a more robust plant with wider strap-like leaves and little bells held all around the flower spike. It does not bend over at the apex. All the bluebells will intermarry and seed, so deadhead them to retain a white or pink colour scheme if it is desired. *See* Recipes 2, 11 and 25.

CROCUS: The early crocuses bridge the gap between late winter and spring. *Crocus chrysanthus* 'Blue Pearl' is only 8 cm (3") high, and flowers in February and March. It has exquisite pale silvery-blue petals on the outside which are white within, and showy orange stamens. It can cope with being planted in short grass – give it an extra mow in late autumn – as well as in border positions. It looks beautiful grouped beside snowdrops. *See* Recipe 23. The later Dutch crocus is much larger, growing to 10 cm (4") or more. Try mixing the purple and white together in short grass – give it an extra mow in late autumn – so that seeding will eventually give the full range of tints and create a beautiful carpet in March and April. *See* Recipes 16, 19 and 70. Plant the bulbs in a sunny, well-drained position, although the Dutch crocuses can tolerate a little shade. They will self-seed and can also be propagated by dividing established clumps in early autumn.

CROWN IMPERIAL: This is an old favourite which has been grown since the sixteenth century. It is a stately plant which reaches a height of 75 cm (30") and carries a number of large pendant bells in April. *Fritillaria imperialis* 'Aurora' has coppery-orange flowers and is fairly close to the original brick orange type grown in Iran. A red and yellow

may also be grown. Cottagers often grew them in a row amongst their vegetables, or in a line in the front garden. They have a foxy smell when they first appear. *See* Recipe 31. Apply a tomato fertiliser in early spring before any new shoots are seen. Crown Imperials will tolerate partial shade or full sun, but thrive best where the soil dries out in summer.

DAFFODIL: Many of the old cottage garden daffodils are easy to naturalise, especially the wild forms. For a verge or grassland area, try *Narcissus pseudonarcissus lobularis*. It is  an early dwarf daffodil with a pale primrose trumpet which flowers at the end of March and early April. *See* Recipes 16 and 48. The Tenby daffodil, *Narcissus pseudonarcissus obvallaris*, is another native, all-yellow daffodil which flowers in March and April. It is quite short at only 25 cm (10") high. *See* Recipes 4 and 11. *Narcissus* 'Van Sion' is another reliable wild form, introduced from Florence in about 1620. It is a double which grows 35 cm (14") high and flowers in March and April. It is larger and showier than the two mentioned above and is at home in grass or the border. *See* Recipes 18, 22 and 30. Probably not a wild form, but known and grown for at least 300 years, 'Rip Van Winkle', 15 cm (6") high, is even more double. Indeed, the shape of its flower in April is dandelion-like! It is happy in grass (*see* Recipe 24) or in a spring hanging basket where its unusual form can easily be admired. *See* Recipe 52.

Breeding has now created a whole range of new daffodils, but we still have firm favourites from amongst the early ones that are highly suitable for the cottage garden. For a short 15-cm (6") all-yellow daffodil, 'February Gold' is recommended. It was introduced in 1923. It flowers in some seasons at the end of February but may last until early April. Strong and sturdy, it associates well with the early anemones and Dutch crocuses and is particularly good for cottage containers. *See* Recipes 8, 25 and 27. For a much bigger variety which grows to about 45 cm (18"), 'King Alfred' is one of the best. Introduced in about 1890, it is a single yellow April daffodil, tall and showy, and good for any border situation. *See* Recipe 19. Another tall old cottage garden daffodil is the pheasant's eye, *Narcissus poeticus recurvus*. It has flat, pure white glistening petals with a small orange cup. It is well scented, 40 cm (16″) tall and very late to flower: it waits until the honesty and tulips are out in May. *See* Recipes 2, 4, 6 and 23.

Daffodils will grow well in sun or partial shade, and will even tolerate full shade, although they probably won't multiply as quickly. Plant the bulbs three times as deep as the size of the bulb.

GLORY OF THE SNOW: *Chionodoxa luciliae* has short slender flower spikes 10 cm (4″) high, with several light blue flowers, each with a white centre. The flowering season lasts from February and throughout March, creating a lovely carpet of colour. *See* Recipe 36. The bulbs are easily grown in sun or partial shade. Once they are established, they will seed themselves readily.

GRAPE HYACINTH: From the middle or end of March to April, the flower spikes of *Muscari armeniacum* 'Heavenly Blue', 15 cm (6″) high, will be surrounded by a dense covering of tiny bell-shaped flowers of the most lovely and intense blue. The bulbs should be planted in full sun, although they will tolerate partial shade. They are ideal planted at the foot of a sunny wall. *See* Recipe 21. They are also a familiar sight along many cottage paths. The leaves can sometimes be untidy but these may be hidden by growing *Alyssum saxatile* over them. The bulbs multiply easily and seed themselves too. *Muscari botryoides* is the nineteenth-century version, neater and not as big in flower. 'Album' is white and was once a great favourite known as the 'Pearls of Spain'. All can still be found.

HYACINTH: *Hyacinthus orientalis* 'Lady Derby', 20 cm (8″) high, is an old bedding hyacinth dating back to 1875. It is strongly perfumed and has a rich pink colour, making it an attractive specimen. *See* Recipe 21. *Hyacinthus orientalis albulus* 'Snow White', 15 cm (6″) high, is a multi-flowered Roman hyacinth, which makes a dainty and much-loved alternative to the heavier flower spikes of the ordinary bedding hyacinths. It is more difficult to find these days, but well worth the search. *See* Recipe 2. Both types of hyacinth flower in April and will grow in sun or partial shade.

SCILLA OR SQUILL: *Scilla siberica* 'Spring Beauty', 15 cm (6″) high, has three or four stems per bulb which carry three to five bell-shaped flowers in March and early April. They are a beautiful blue. *See* Recipes 52 and 54.

SNAKE'S HEAD FRITILLARY: *Fritillaria meleagris*, 25 cm (10″) high, is one of our wild meadow bulbs, much loved for its chequered markings and nodding habit. It occurs naturally in pink, purple or white and flowers from April to May. It prefers well-drained soils which do not dry out in summer and full sun or dappled shade. It is easily grown in grass with cowslips and wild daffodils. *See* Recipe 48. *See also* Recipe 23, where it appears under an old apple tree.

TULIPS: These have long been regarded as the queen of all the spring flowers. Plant the bulbs extra deeply where the soil is light, and leave them undisturbed. The short double early Murillo tulips became very popular towards the end of the nineteenth century. Flowering in early to mid-April, they make excellent bedfellows with anemones, hyacinths and grape hyacinths in the border, in wicker baskets or in other containers. 'Peach Blossom' is a particularly beautiful pink example dating back to 1890. *See* Recipe 53. Red, crimson, yellow and white forms can also be obtained.

Many tulips are taller than the Murillos. The red or yellow Apeldoorns are Darwin hybrids which were introduced in 1951, but they are of such a strong constitution that they are highly recommended as reliable growers. Flowering towards the end of April and into early May, they look particularly good bedded out with wallflowers. *See* Recipe 1, which uses 'Beauty of Apeldoorn', a mixture of yellow and rose, 45 cm (18″) high. From the May-flowering tulips, choose the old-fashioned 'Clara Butt', introduced in 1889, which is a pretty salmon-pink Darwin variety, 60 cm (24″) high (*see* Recipe 32), the rich pink 'Douglas Bader' (*see* Recipe 55) or 'White Virgin' (*see* Recipe 56). All are lovely with forget-me-nots.

The cottage variety of tulip also flowers in May. 'Halcro' is 75 cm (30″) tall, but very sturdy and good in exposed places. It is brilliant red and looks beautiful on its own, but put it beside golden feverfew or yellow-green spurge and the results are wonderful. *See* Recipes 7 and 9. 'Palestrina' 45 cm (18″) high, salmon-pink, and 'Mrs John T. Scheepers', 65 cm (26″) high, yellow, are two others of this kind which would make good alternatives in any border plan. 'Queen of Night', 65 cm (26″) high, is one of the darkest tulips grown. It looks lovely beside white, pink or blue forget-me-nots. *See* Recipe 26. It is sturdy and long lasting, and a good subject for pots and barrels. Try it with sweet woodruff. *See* Recipe 56.

See also lists:
3 Turk's cap lily.
4 colchicum and Guernsey lily.
7 Madonna lily.
14 cyclamen, snowdrop and winter aconite.

2 Spring Flowers

March to April

After the winter darkness, the spring border plants bring a breath of freshness to the cottage borders. Primroses, violets, auriculas, polyanthus, daisies and soldiers and sailors are amongst some of the prettiest and most welcome of flowers. They are such dependable sorts, and come into bloom year after year, despite the vagaries of the weather. Many are tolerant of sun and shade, although alyssum and aubrieta like to bask in the spring sunshine where their friends the butterflies and bees are sure to find them.

ALYSSUM: *Alyssum saxatile*, 25 × 45 cm (10 × 18″), also known as gold dust, is one of the most familiar plants growing on low cottage walls or spreading out over the paths. Its bright yellow flowers last from April to June. *See* Recipe 19. Propagate it from cuttings taken in June. This is an evergreen shrubby perennial which should be cut back hard after flowering. It prefers well-drained soil and sun.

AUBRIETA: *Aubrieta deltoidea* 'Dr Mules', 15 × 45 cm (6 × 18″), is one of the old favourites, with its violet-purple flowers from April to June. *See* Recipes 19 and 74. It is an evergreen perennial. Aubrietas thrive where the soil contains lime, which is why they do so well hanging on dry limestone walls. Remove the old flowering stems after flowering. Take basal cuttings in August or September.

AURICULA: The most common was *Primula auricula* 'Old Yellow Dusty Miller', 15 × 15 cm (6 × 6″), which flowers from April through to May. It is a charming plant with soft yellow flowers and white powdered leaves. *See* Recipe 31. This is an evergreen perennial which can be propagated from little rooted sections removed from the main plant. It likes full sun but can tolerate partial shade.

BITING STONECROP: *Sedum acre*, 3 × 15 cm (1¼ × 6″), also known as wall pepper, is a European and British native plant often seen growing on old walls. The golden form 'Aureum' is particularly attractive in spring and early summer and is excellent for winter and spring containers. *See* Recipes 52 and 54. The flowers are small and yellow, and appear in June. *See* Recipe 20. Propagate the biting stonecrop from cuttings taken in early summer.

COMFREY: *Symphytum × uplandicum* 'Variegatum', 30 × 60 cm (1 × 2′), is an evergreen perennial which flowers in April and May in sun or shade. The little hanging flowers are pink but change to bright blue. *See* Recipe 20. This variegated kind will not be as rampant as its greener relatives. Propagate it by division in October or March.

CORYDALIS: *Corydalis lutea*, 15 × 30 cm (6 × 12″), is a native plant often seen growing on old walls, where it seeds itself happily and produces ferny leaves and yellow flowers from April to November. It likes any well-drained garden soil in sun or shade. *See* Recipe 34.

DAISY: *Bellis perennis* 'Dresden China', 5 × 12 cm (2 × 5″), has the prettiest pink flowers and has been well loved since Victorian times. The flowers last from March to mid-summer or longer. It is excellent beside the path and in containers. *See* Recipes 31, 53, 59 and 60. A red variety called 'Lilliput' is used in Recipes 58 and 59. Divide it in March each year when the ground is damp. Otherwise, if left unattended, too many crowns will develop from one root and the plant will fail to get enough water.

ELEPHANT'S EARS: *Bergenias* are familiar plants in the cottage garden, for their bold rounded evergreen foliage looks good all year round and acts as an anchor plant in the border. They are sometimes used as a continuous edging like small box. The flower spikes emerge in April and vary from white, pink and salmon-pink to purple. They thrive in sun or shade and will tolerate dry conditions. *Bergenia stracheyi* 'Silberlicht', 30 × 45 cm (12 × 18″), was introduced in 1950. It has good white flowers. *See* Recipes 4, 5, 10 and 22. *Bergenia* 'Eric Smith', 45 × 45 cm (18 × 18″), has large crinkly foliage which colours in winter and produces salmon-pink flowers in spring. *See* Recipe 14. *Bergenia cordifolia* 'Purpurea', introduced in 1879, was one of Gertrude Jekyll's favourites. Large rounded leaves 60 cm (2′) high, with a plant spread of 75 cm (30″), become tinged with purple in winter. It produces magenta flowers on red stalks. *See* Recipes 25 and 70.

FORGET-ME-NOT: *Myosotis alpestris*, 15 × 15 cm (6 × 6″), is useful amongst all the spring flowers, particularly tulips. From April to May or perhaps early June, it provides a delicate carpet of scented tiny bright blue flowers. Pink and white can also be found. *See* Recipes 26, 32 and 55. It self-seeds.

HEARTSEASE: *Viola tricolor*, 8 × 25 cm (3 × 10″), a native of Britain and Europe, is a welcome, if uninvited guest in the cottage garden, seeding itself where it chooses without being asked! It flowers from April to September. Its bright little purple and yellow faces make a lovely association with the pink bellis daisy, and are perfect for paths and containers in sun or partial shade. *See* Recipes 31, 59 and 60.

HEPATICA: *Hepatica nobilis*, 10 × 25 cm (4 × 10″), is an old-fashioned little woodland plant that used to be so common in all cottage gardens. Its starry blue flowers form lovely clumps throughout February, March and early April. It is also available in white and pink, although the common blue is the most vigorous. *See* Recipes 5 and 12. It thrives in limey soil with added leaf mould. It will tolerate a sunny spot, although it prefers partial shade. It is described as a semi-evergreen herbaceous plant. Propagate it by division in August or September.

MOSS PHLOX: *Phlox subulata* 'Alexander's Surprise', 8 × 45 cm (3 × 18″), creates a pink cushion at the front of the border which flowers throughout April and May. *See* Recipe 32. Moss phlox is also available in red, white, lavender-blue and pale pink. It is a hardy evergreen sub-shrub which thrives in full sun. Propagate it from basal cuttings in July.

PERIWINKLE: *Vinca major* 'Variegata', 20 × 90 cm (8 × 36″), is the larger form of variegated periwinkle. It has light green and white-edged leaves and pale blue flowers from late March to May. It is a spreading evergreen sub-shrub which is good where colour is wanted in difficult dry or shady positions. *See* Recipe 25. Propagate it by division any time between September and April.

Vinca minor 'Aureo-variegata', 8 × 90 cm (3 × 36″), is a lower growing plant with smaller leaves than its cousin. The variegation here is creamy yellow; the flowers are still a lovely pale blue but appear slightly earlier, from early March to May. This variety is ideal for a shady or partially shaded bank or beneath a hedge. *See* Recipe 18. Propagate it in the same way as *Vinca major*. It is good for winter and spring containers.

POLYANTHUS: *Primula* × *polyantha*, 10 × 20 cm (4 × 8″), are garden hybrids which flower during April and May in a whole range of colours, from white, yellow and red to maroon and blue. Developed a hundred years ago, they are familiar plants which are excellent for sunny or shady spots in the cottage border or beside a path, although they prefer not to dry out in spring or summer. *See* Recipe 3. They are also useful in spring containers. *See* Recipes 54 and 57. Polyanthus is easily grown from seed. Propagate it by division in autumn.

PRIMROSE: *Primula vulgaris*, 15 × 20 cm (6 × 8″), our common hedgerow plant, is so welcome in the cottage garden despite its familiarity. Scented pale yellow flowers are produced throughout March and April. It can be grown in sun, partial shade or full shade, but it prefers a moist home throughout the year. It is equally at home in the border, under a hedge or in grass. *See Recipes 11, 18, 35 and 49. It is also useful in spring containers. See Recipe 51.* Propagate it by division in autumn. Beautiful double forms also exist.

Primula × *pruhonicensis* 'Wanda', 8 × 25 cm (3 × 10″), produces rich claret flowers from March to May. It thrives in sun or shade, and is hardy and neat. *See Recipe 31.* Propagate it by division in autumn.

SOLDIERS AND SAILORS: *Pulmonaria officinalis*, 25 × 45 cm (10 × 18″), also known as lungwort or spotted dog, has evergreen spotty leaves. Its flowers open pink and then turn blue with age. They last from March to May. It is loved by bees and is excellent for the shady wildlife garden. *See Recipes 12 and 35.*

Pulmonaria saccharata, 30 × 60 cm (1 × 2′), 'Margery Fish' was named in 1974 in honour of the famous cottage garden writer. It is a later flowering plant than the *officinalis* above, with more handsome leaves and flowers. It blooms from March to May. *See Recipe 27.* Divide both varieties in October or March. They thrive in shade.

STINKING HELLEBORE: *Helleborus foetidus* 'Wester Fliske', 60 × 60 cm (2 × 2′), is an evergreen herbaceous perennial with dark green, deeply divided leaves. It flowers from March to May; its wide yellow-green flowers edged with reddish-purple are borne on purple-red stems. It associates well with bold hosta leaves, and the orange and purple shading of the honeysuckle 'Goldflame'. *See Recipe 27.*

VIOLA: *Viola labradorica* 'Purpurea', 10 × 20 cm (4 × 8″), has small scentless mauve-blue flowers from late April to June and green leaves which are tinged with purple. A hardy perennial from Greenland and North America, it is useful for underplanting roses or other shrubs, as it is tolerant of sun or shade. *See Recipe 36.* Propagate it using basal cuttings taken in July.

Viola 'Mollie Sanderson', 15 × 25 cm (6 × 10″), is the type of viola so well loved in the old gardens, where it was planted close to the path to flower from April to October. Its deep purple or blue-black face makes a strong contrast to the more brightly coloured spring flowers. *See Recipe 32.* It thrives in sun or shade. A short-lived herbaceous perennial, it should be propagated by using basal cuttings taken in July. There are many others to choose from, including 'Maggie Mott', a delightful scented pale blue viola which flowers from May to September. *See Recipe 3.* Other old-fashioned violas include 'Bowles Black', 'Irish Mollie', 'Jackanapes' and 'Lorna'.

VIOLET: *Viola odorata*, 8 × 25 cm (3 × 10″), is our native violet, so well loved for its pretty face and delicate scent. Purple and white forms exist. They spread  quickly by runners and also by seed. They flower from February to April. *See Recipes 12 (white), 18 (white and purple) and 34 (purple).*

See also lists:
1 spring bulbs.
3 spurge.
6 clematis.
7 scented wallflowers.
11 honesty.
12 fruit blossoms of apple, damson, pear and plum.
13 Japanese quince and forsythia.

3 Early Summer

May to Mid-July

This is one of the most exciting times in the cottage garden, when so many of the herbaceous plants are in full growth and are coming into bloom: lovely tall irises, beautiful delphinium spires, foxgloves, bell-flowers and cranesbills. There is so much variety in height and colour and foliage. All the plants inter-mingle, and are supportive and friendly, setting one another off in the most delightful way. By now the cottage roses are in bloom, clothing the walls and gracing the borders. It is a sumptuous picture to be enjoyed to the full.

AGERATUM: *Ageratum houstonianum* F$_1$ Hybrid, 15 × 15 cm (6 × 6"), is a dwarf compact half-hardy annual which produces powdery blue flowers all summer long. It prefers a sunny sheltered site where it will be attractive to butterflies. Deadhead the plants to prolong the flowering period. *See* Recipe 63.

BELLFLOWER OR CAMPANULA: *Campanula cochleariifolia*, 8 × 25 cm (3 × 10"), is a dwarf peren-nial species with white bell-shaped flowers which appear from June to August. It is easily grown and good for the front of the border. *See* Recipe 32. Propagate it by division in October.

Campanula lactiflora 'Loddon Anna' may reach 1.2 m (4') with a spread of 1.5 m (5'). It thrives anywhere, even in grass. The branching heads are full of soft lilac-pink flowers from June to August. It is a good perennial to use with shrub roses. *See* Recipe 41. Propagate it by division in October, March or April.

Campanula latiloba 'Highcliffe', 90 × 45 cm (36 × 18"), is a tall evergreen perennial with deep violet-blue bowl-shaped flowers from June to August. It is an old favourite, which is useful for ground cover in difficult places in sun or shade. *See* Recipe 25. Propagate it by division in October, March or April.

Campanula persicifolia, 90 × 30 cm (3 × 1'), is sometimes known as the peach-leaved campanula. It is an excellent evergreen perennial. Its wiry stems produce beautiful blue flowers (*see* Recipes 3 and 43), or white ones as in the 'Alba' variety (*see* Recipe 38),

from June to July, although if it is cut down after the first flowering it will flower again in August and September. Both varieties are lovely with roses. Propagate them by division in October, March or April.

Campanula poscharskyana, 30 × 60 cm (1 × 2′), is rampant in a border, but is most effective growing beside a wall either in sun or shade, smothering itself in lavender-blue star-like flowers throughout June and July. *See* Recipes 20 and 34. Propagate it by division in October, March or April.

BIDENS: *Bidens* 'Golden Goddess' is a trailing half-hardy perennial which has small yellow starry flowers from June to September. Deadhead it to encourage further flower production. It prefers a sunny position. *See* Recipe 66.

BLEEDING HEART: *Dicentra spectabilis*, 60 × 45 cm (24 × 18″), is a tall herbaceous plant with pink heart-shaped flowers which dangle gracefully from arching stems throughout late April, May and June. It also has a beautiful white form. It thrives in sun or shade but needs to be sheltered from late spring frosts and strong winds. The foliage will die down completely by mid-summer. *See* Recipe 11. It is also excellent in pots and tubs. Propagate it by division from October to March.

CATMINT: *Nepeta* × *faassenii*, 45 × 45 cm (18 × 18″), is a delightful companion to pink roses. It is useful at the edge of the border where it can spill out over the path. Throughout June it produces soft lavender-blue sprays of flowers. If it is cut back, after flowering, it will produce another show again in the early autumn. *See* Recipe 9.

Nepeta 'Six Hills Giant', 90 × 90 cm (3 × 3′), is a much larger version, otherwise it has a similar life pattern but it is slightly hardier. Use it in larger scale cottage borders fronting shrub roses. *See* Recipe 38.

Both plants tolerate full sun or partial shade and are much loved by bees. Propagate the catmints by division in March or April.

CRANESBILL: These are all hardy perennial geraniums which can be propagated by division any time between September and March. They tolerate sun or shade.

Geranium clarkei 'Kashmir White', 30 × 30 cm (1 × 1′), flowers over a long period from June to September. It has lilac veining to its white flowers, and handsome deeply dissected leaves. *See* Recipe 10. *Geranium renardii* is a less rampant alternative. It has beautifully lobed leaves and white flowers.

Geranium endressii 'Wargrave Pink', 60 × 90 cm (2 × 3′), is a useful evergreen coloniser, dating back to 1930. It can be planted in sun or partial shade. Its succession of salmon-pink flowers

last from June onwards. The leaves are light green and well divided. *See* Recipe 37.

Geranium himalayense 'Grandiflorum', 30 × 60 cm (1 × 2'), produces violet-blue flowers in June and July and then its leaves take on rich autumn tints in October. *See* Recipe 37.

Geranium 'Johnson's Blue', 30 × 60 cm (1 × 2'), was introduced in 1950 and has been a favourite ever since. Its delightful lavender-blue flowers appear in June and July. *See* Recipe 11.

Geranium macrorrhizum 'Walter Ingwersen', 30 × 60 cm (1 × 2'), has soft rose-pink flowers from May to August. It is a strong grower and a good weed suppressor. It has rich autumn tints to the leaves, which are semi-evergreen. It is a good variety to use in a difficult place beneath a shady wall. *See* Recipe 20.

Geranium sanguineum striatum 'Splendens', 12 × 30 cm (5 × 12″), was cultivated prior to 1732. It produces light pink flowers with crimson veins from June to September. It grows wild on the Isle of Walney, Lancs. *See* Recipe 3.

Geranium wallichianum 'Buxton's Variety', 30 × 90 cm (1 × 3'), was introduced in about 1900. From July until the autumn, it produces masses of spode-blue flowers, each with a white centre accentuated by dark stamens. It is a lovely plant which likes well-drained soil and is so good beside paving. It is happy in sun or shade, and associates beautifully with yellow. *See* Recipes 6 and 34.

CREEPING JENNY: *Lysimachia nummularia* is an easy low perennial for a shady spot – the damper the better – where it can spread its long 60-cm (2') trails. Bright yellow cup-shaped flowers appear along its stems in June and July. Also known as moneywort, it was a familiar plant in the old cottage gardens. *See* Recipe 34. A golden form known as 'Aurea' is available. *See* Recipe 71. Propagate both forms by taking stem cuttings in April or September.

DAY LILY: These are easy hardy perennials which thrive in sun or shade, but not in deep shade. Propagate them by division between October and April.

Hemerocallis fulva, 90 × 90 cm (3 × 3'), is the old orange-red form, dating back to Japan in the sixteenth century. It flowers from June to August. It has a strong constitution and increases freely below ground. It is happy in grass or in a border, and is useful because its strappy foliage grows very early in spring and is a good light green. This plant has been described as almost indestructible! *See* Recipe 30.

Hemerocallis fulva 'Kwanso Flore Pleno', 90 × 90 cm (3 × 3'), has the same constitution, but it produces a double orange flower from June to August. It was introduced from Japan in 1860. The orange flower looks good set against greenery. *See* Recipe 14.

Hemerocallis lilio-asphodelus, 75 × 45 cm (30 × 18″), has been grown since the late sixteenth century. It is a great favourite in May and June with its lemon-yellow flowers and lovely fragrance. *See* Recipe 14.

Hemerocallis 'Stella D'Oro', 55 × 60 cm (22 × 24″), is rather smaller than the others here. It is a recent dwarf, introduced in 1975, which flowers in mid-season in June and July and then again from September to October. It has fragrant yellow flowers. *See* Recipe 34.

DELPHINIUMS: These are hardy perennials with colours ranging from dark or light blue, lilac and pink to white and cream. They flower from the end of June through to mid-July. Some varieties are taller, up to 2 m (6½'), while others are shorter. The taller ones need to be staked and they will all need protecting from slugs, particularly in spring. But if the plants are grown well, in a rich well-drained soil, in a sunny position, the display will be magnificent. Propagate them by division in March and April.

Delphinium 'Blue Dawn', 150 × 90 cm (5 × 3'), has tall spikes of pretty pale blue flowers with brown eyes. *See* Recipe 38.

Delphinium 'Blue Tit', 120 × 60 cm (4 × 2'), has medium tall spikes of magnificent rich dark blue flowers with black eyes. It was raised in 1960. *See* Recipe 8.

ERIGERON: *Erigeron*, 60 × 40 cm (24 × 16″), is a useful spreading hardy perennial with daisy-like flowers which last from June to August. It needs twiggy support. Propagate it by division from October to March. There is a wide choice of varieties. 'Darkest of All' has violet-blue flowers. *See* Recipe 26. 'Quakeress' has lilac flowers and was the favourite for many years. *See* Recipes 26 and 32.

FLAG IRIS: *Iris pallida*, 90 × 30 cm (3 × 1'), is an easy hardy perennial for a sunny, well-drained spot. It is of ancient origin, and a great favourite. It produces silky lavender-blue flowers in May and June, and is well scented. Unlike many of its relatives, its pointed grey sword-like leaves remain attractive until autumn: it is an architectural plant. *See* Recipes 8, 19 and 37.

Propagate it after flowering by dividing the rhizomes, otherwise leave the clumps alone.

FOAM FLOWER: *Tiarella cordifolia*, 15 × 30 cm (6 × 12″), creates a good low-growing clump of pale green leaves in a shady spot beneath shrubs, trees or walls. Creamy white flowers are held aloft on erect flower spikes in May and June. *See Recipe 20*. It is a hardy perennial. Propagate it by division in October or April.

FOXGLOVE: *Digitalis purpurea*, 90 × 45 cm (36 × 18″), is our well-known wild foxglove which has tall spikes of pink and purple flowers, or white as in 'Alba', throughout June and July. *See Recipes 5, 11, 15, 18, 23, 35, 41 and 70*. It is a hardy biennial but may be treated as perennial where it is happiest. It is easily grown from seed to flower the following year and is good in sun or shade. It fits in perfectly with the cottage garden scene, as it is lovely with roses and forms a focal point by a tree or pillar. It is also good beneath a hedge. Hybridisation has created a colourful mixture of tones, *see* 'Excelsior Hybrids Mixed', as in Recipe 38. It will self-seed, although cross-pollination with wild foxgloves will eventually dilute the hybrid strain and produce pink and purple forms.

GRANNY'S BONNET: Aquilegias are hardy herbaceous perennials, native throughout most of Europe, which flower in May and June, producing graceful tall spurred flowers above attractive foliage. They are also known as columbines. They are short-lived, but are easily grown from seed, or they can be propagated by division from October to March.

Aquilegia vulgaris, 45 × 30 cm (18 × 12″), produces blue, pink or white short spurred flowers. This variety is easy to grow in sun or partial shade and will self-seed easily. *See Recipe 10*.

Aquilegia vulgaris 'Snow Queen', 75 × 45 cm (30 × 18″), has pure white short spurred flowers, and it too is happy in sun or partial shade. *See Recipe 35*.

The 'McKana Hybrids', 75 × 45 cm (30 × 18″), prefer a sunny spot. They will produce a wide and lovely range of pink, yellow, crimson or blue flowers, many bi-coloured – all are very elegant, with long spurs. *See Recipe 7*.

GRANNY'S PIN CUSHION: *Astrantia maxima*, 60 × 45 cm (24 × 18″), also known as masterwort, has star-like shell-pink flowers in June and July. It prefers a damp shady spot and associates well with all the woodland plants. *See Recipe 12 and 35*. It is also useful for shady containers. *See Recipe 70*. It is easily grown as a hardy perennial. Propagate it by division between October and March.

HOSTA: These are easily grown hardy perennials which produce a striking array of large leaves in May,

with lilac, mauve or white flowers in July. They are useful for sun or shade, but beware of slugs. They also make excellent specimen plants for containers. Divide and propagate them in March.

Hosta fortunei 'Marginato-alba', 75 × 60 cm (30 × 24″), also known as 'Shogun', has large sage-green leaves attractively edged with a broad band of white and lilac flowers. *See Recipe 24*, where it is planted in grass, or Recipe 70, where it is planted in a container.

Hosta fortunei 'Obscura Marginata', 75 × 60 cm (30 × 24″), is also known as 'Yellow Edge' due to the creamy yellow band around its broad green leaves. Its flowers are mauve. *See Recipe 27*.

Hosta 'Gold Edger', 10 × 15 cm (4 × 6″), is a small-leaved hybrid which produces good lilac flowers. The foliage becomes much more golden as the season progresses. *See Recipe 71*.

Hosta sieboldiana 'Elegans', 75 × 60 cm (30 × 24″), has large crinkled blue-grey leaves which are deeply veined, and lilac-white flowers in July. *See Recipes 11 and 41*.

Hosta 'Thomas Hogg', 30 × 50 cm (12 × 20″), has dark green pointed leaves with a creamy white margin and pale lilac flowers. It is a smaller hosta than most of those described above. *See Recipes 6 and 12*.

HOUSELEEKS: This is a large family which is commonly found on walls, roofs, well heads, and so on. Evergreen, neat and shapely, these plants are good in containers as well. They are easy to grow and will propagate from offsets. *Sempervivum tectorum*, 10 × 20 cm (4 × 8″), is the common houseleek with bright green rosettes 5–12 cm (2–5″) wide, which are sometimes maroon-tipped. Flowers appear in July. *See Recipe 19*.

IVY-LEAVED TOADFLAX: *Cymbalaria muralis*, 5 × 45 cm (2 × 18″), is a hardy perennial often seen growing on old walls. It has tiny pink flowers from May to September. It thrives in sun or partial shade. *See Recipe 20*. It is an old favourite for hanging baskets.

LONDON PRIDE: *Saxifraga × urbium*, 30 × 30 cm (1 × 1′), was often used to edge shady cottage paths. The dark green rosettes produce dainty flower sprays in May, creating a soft pink cloud. *See Recipes 12 and 34*. It is a very easy hardy perennial. Propagate it by division after flowering.

LUPIN: *Lupinus* 'Tom Reeves', 75 × 75 cm (30 × 30″), has fragrant yellow flower spikes in June. It comes in a wide range of colours: blue, pink and white, russet, red, crimson and bi-colours are available. *See Recipe 9*. Propagate it from seed or take cuttings in March or April. It is a hardy perennial, but is not long-lived.

MEADOW RUE: *Thalictrum aquilegifolium* 'Thundercloud', 100 × 60 cm (3¼ × 2'), produces tall dainty blue-grey foliage, above which rise fluffy lilac flowers in June and July. *See* Recipe 41. This hardy perennial will need staking and is best in sun or light shade. Propagate it from seed.

MEXICAN DAISY: *Erigeron karvinskianus*, 10 × 30 cm (4 × 12"), is an avid seeder and will quickly colonise steps and paving. It is a hardy perennial with daisy-like flowers which open white and then turn pink from June to October. It is pretty and very easy to grow. *See* Recipe 33.

ROCK ROSE: *Helianthemum nummularium* 'Wisley Pink', 25 × 60 cm (10 × 24"), is one of the many different colours of rock rose available. All varieties love to be in full sun. Masses of flowers are produced from June to August. *See* Recipe 33. This is a hardy evergreen sub-shrub which should be propagated by heel cuttings in June and August.

SOLOMON'S SEAL: *Polygonatum × hybridum*, 60 × 30 cm (2 × 1'), produces arching stems from which clusters of small white flowers dangle in May and June. It is extremely hardy and will grow in sun or shade, so long as its roots are in shade. *See* Recipes 11, 23 and 35. Propagate it by division in October or March.

SPURGE: *Euphorbia characias* is a hardy perennial which grows 1.2 m (4') high, with a spread of 1 m (3¼'), and produces narrow spikes of green flowers with dark brown centres on large terminal heads in April and May. *See* Recipe 7.

Euphorbia characias 'Lambrook Gold' is a similar plant but the flowers are yellow-green. *See* Recipe 1.

Both plants thrive in sun or shade. Propagate them using basal cuttings taken in April and May. They are architectural plants which make bold specimens.

TURK'S CAP LILY: *Lilium martagon*, 1.5 m (5') high, produces tall stems with maroon flowers in July. The petals are recurved and have dark spots on them. It is a lime-tolerant lily which associates well with ferns. *See* Recipe 42.

WALLFLOWER: *Cheiranthus* 'Bowles Mauve', 50 × 30 cm (20 × 12"), is a short-lived perennial wall-flower which likes the sunshine. Its tall mauve flower spikes last for many weeks from May through to July. *See* Recipe 36. Take heel cuttings in June and July, as it needs propagating regularly. Butterflies and bees love it.

See also lists:
4 bridal wreath, fuchsia and geranium.
5 cottage roses.
6 clematis, hop and Japanese wisteria.
7 scented garden pinks, honeysuckle, lilac, lily of the valley, Madonna lily, mock orange, peony, sweet pea and sweet rocket.
8 chives, rosemary and other herbs.
9 marsh marigold, meadowsweet, ragged robin, water forget-me-not and yellow flag iris.
10 bergamot, poached egg plant, thrift and valerian.
11 baby's breath, globe thistle, love-in-a-mist, Oriental poppy and sea holly.
12 soft fruits and vegetables.
13 laburnum.

4 Late Summer to Autumn

Late July to October

From the end of July to October, the borders are still rich in colour as the late perennials come into flower. Graceful Japanese anemones, towering hollyhocks, giant sunflowers, crocosmias and perennial peas, all a blaze of glorious colour, are joined by a host of fuchsias, hydrangeas, the butterfly bush and others. The lavender and many roses are still in bloom and the late clematis are at their best.

By now the containers are full of colour from the tender fuchsias and geraniums, as well as the many other bedding plants which have been used. They will continue to bloom until September.

As autumn approaches, changes are taking place all round the border perimeters, which help to transform the cottage garden into an even richer tapestry of colours. The orchard is laden with ripening apples, pears, plums and purple damsons. In the hedge there is a mixture of orange haws, long sprays of red hips, black-fruited dogwood, and white snowberries. On the shady arch the honeysuckle is a mass of fleshy orange berries; the firethorn is smothered with orange berries too. The pergola is draped in hops, and the cottage walls are clothed in fiery Virginia creeper. It is an exciting time, full of autumnal scents and colour.

BRIDAL WREATH: *Francoa ramosa*, 90 cm (3') high, is a clump-forming evergreen perennial which is not fully hardy and requires winter protection. It has long been a great favourite of cottagers. It is also known as maiden's wreath and was grown either in containers outdoors or as a pot plant on the windowsill. The flower stems are branched with loosely arranged white flowers, the petals of which are sometimes spotted. It has a long flowering period from summer to early autumn. *See* Recipe 72. It is not easily available, but Rushfields of Ledbury stock it (*see* page 190). Propagate it by division in early spring.

CARYOPTERIS: *Caryopteris* × *clandonensis* 'Heavenly Blue', 90 × 90 cm (3 × 3'), is a small upright deciduous shrub which produces clusters of deep blue flowers in August and September. *See* Recipes 1, 9 and 44. It likes a sunny position. Propagate it using lateral cuttings of half-ripened wood in August or September. The foliage is aromatic and grey-green, which makes it very attractive for the autumn border and a great favourite with bees.

COLCHICUM: *Colchicum speciosum* 'Album', 15 cm (6") high, flowers in September and October, but its leaves appear later. Try these white blooms beside the weeping birch tree, where they will flower amongst the falling leaves. They grow happily in long grass. *See* Recipe 24.

CROCOSMIA: Crocosmias thrive in a sunny position but need plenty of moisture in summer. Divide the corms every three years, either just after flowering or just before the growth starts in the spring.

Crocosmia 'Emily MacKenzie', 70 cm (28") high, has orange flowers with crimson mahogany throats on arching stems from August to September. Its leaves are strap-like. *See* Recipe 9.

Crocosmia masonorum 'Firebird', 80 cm (32") high, has flame orange flowers on arching stems from July to September. It too has strap-like leaves. *See* Recipe 37.

DIASCIA: *Diascia* 'Ruby Field' is a mat-forming perennial which produces dainty, tubular, wide-lipped pink flowers all summer long. It is lovely at the front of a border or mixed with Swan River daisies in a basket. *See* Recipe 61. Overwinter it, then cut back the old stems in spring.

FUCHSIAS: Hardy fuchsias have long since been cottage favourites. In flower from June to October, they give one of the best and most long-lasting displays in the garden. *Fuchsia magellanica* came from South America in 1788 and many of the garden forms we know today are derived from it. They are all happy in sun or shade, but like moisture during the summer months. They may need added protection during very cold winters, such as an extra thick mulch or sacking, otherwise they can be left in the garden for many years without much attention. Many old hybrids exist and are still available. 'Gracilis' dates back to 1823, 'Madame Cornelison' to 1860 and 'Lena' to 1862. Still more have been introduced over the last hundred years. The ones below all grow 90 cm (3') high in each season, so they show up well in the garden.

Fuchsia 'Chequerboard', 90 × 60 cm (3 × 2'), was introduced in 1948. It has an erect habit, long narrow drooping flowers with white sepals and a cerise-red skirt. *See* Recipes 6 and 31.

Fuchsia 'Hawkshead', 100 × 90 cm (3¼ × 3'), was introduced in the 1960s. Its narrow white flowers are tipped with green and make a lovely combination with white- or cream-edged hostas. *See* Recipe 12.

Fuchsia 'Mrs Popple', 90 × 90 cm (3 × 3'), was introduced in about 1930. Her crimson sepals surround a purple skirt. *See* Recipe 15.

Fuchsia 'Sealand Prince', 90 × 90 cm (3 × 3'), has dark pink sepals and a lovely skirt of pale violet. *See* Recipe 1, where it is planted next to the caryopteris.

There is a second type of fuchsia which includes those tender varieties which have been favourites for pots and other containers. They will flower from June until the first frosts, becoming more and more floriferous. There are a great many to choose from, depending on your personal likes and dislikes. Quite a few of the older varieties are still readily available in the garden centres or from specialist nurseries. However, don't worry if you can't find them, the fuchsia effect is still as good with the modern ones.

'Coralle' was introduced in 1905. It is similar to 'Thalia', below, with tubular orange flowers and upright growth, but the leaves are dark green. The flowers become longer and longer as the season advances. *See* Recipe 66.

'Lye's Unique' was introduced in 1886. The flowers are very pretty. The sepals are white, flushed with pink, and the corolla is pinky salmon-orange. It is a quick-growing upright fuchsia and makes a good standard shape if over-wintered. *See* Recipe 65.

'Thalia' was introduced in 1855 and was liked for its attractive bronze-green foliage and strongly contrasting clusters of orange-scarlet tubular flowers. It has an upright growth. It is still readily available. *See* Recipe 66.

'Winston Churchill' was introduced in 1942. The flowers are much fatter than those mentioned above, and are either double or semi-double. The coralla is lavender-blue, then magenta, with wavy petals. The sepals are bright rose-red. They make an attractive colour combination, especially with mixed lobelia. Because of the weight of the flowers, this is a good choice for a hanging basket. *See* Recipe 64.

GERANIUM: These are favourite container plants which need overwintering indoors or in a greenhouse. Most of them are available in garden centres, otherwise try geranium specialist nurseries. If the varieties listed here are difficult to find, just substitute a similar one: there are so many to choose from.

The old scented geraniums have long been popular. Rose-scented varieties were much used in cooking to flavour cakes and jellies. *Pelargonium radula* and 'Attar of Roses' both have a lovely rose fragrance. *See* Recipe 65.

Coloured and variegated leaf uprights quickly became popular in the second half of the nineteenth century. 'Hills of Snow' has creamy-edged variegated leaves which become pink-tinged when they are dried. The flowers are single and are a lovely rose-pink. It is a strikingly beautiful plant. *See* Recipe 65.

'Dolly Varden' is another old favourite. Again, the leaves are creamy-edged, but they also have bronze zoning, often with a hint of pinky-red. The flowers are single and rich orange-red. *See* Recipe 66.

Ivy-leaved trailing geraniums were popularised slightly later, although the white 'L'Elegante' and 'Madame Crousse' were widely used in hanging baskets and window boxes by the end of the nineteenth century. Both are available today. The cottage hanging basket which appears in this book uses more modern trailers known as 'Flamingo'. *See* Recipe 64. They are the same as 'Mexicana' which became popular in the 1960s. The 'Scarlet' upright in the same recipe is a Century hybrid which can be grown from seed and is ready to plant out in early summer. 'Pink Glow' in Recipe 63 is another Century hybrid. 'Ailsa Craig' in Recipe 62 is a small trailer of compact growth. For a larger window box 'Madame Crousse' would be more suitable.

GUERNSEY LILY: *Nerine bowdenii*, 60 cm (2') high, produces wonderful pink frilly flowers for the autumn border from September to November. The bulbs thrive in a sheltered, sunny position and are best planted beside a south-facing wall. *See* Recipe 21.

HELICHRYSUM: *Plecostachys serpyllifolium* is a useful shrubby evergreen for trailing over the edge of containers. Treat it as half-hardy and overwinter it at 7–10°C (45–50°F). *See* Recipe 63.

HOLLYHOCK: These are one of the most evocative plants of the cottage garden. Their beautiful spires, sometimes growing as high as 2 m (6½'), are an integral part of the late summer border. They are tolerant of sun or partial shade, and they self-seed actively all round the garden, so you may find relatives in the most unexpected places.

Althaea rosea 'Pinafore Mixed', 90 × 45 cm (36 × 18″), produces a lovely range of pink flowers all the way up the stem, often with six flower stems per plant. Semi-double or single flowers – the bees will prefer the single flowers – are produced continually from July through to late August and into early September. *See* Recipe 3. This is a hardy perennial but it is often susceptible to rust, so treat it as an annual and sow fresh seed each year.

Althaea rugosa, 150 × 60 cm (5 × 2'), produces lovely satiny primrose flowers which open wide like saucers. It flowers from July to September. *See* Recipes 7, 9, 26 and 44. This is a hardy perennial, easy to grow and not prone to rust. It is probably difficult to obtain as a plant, so it is best grown from seed initially. Source: Thompson and Morgan Catalogue. *See* the list of suppliers on page 190.

JAPANESE ANEMONE: These are graceful and extremely useful hardy perennials which produce flowers over many weeks and are easy to grow in sun or shade. They are deep-rooted and will tolerate quite dry conditions once they are established. They like being left alone so that they can spread into large colonies.

Anemone hupehensis 'September Charm', 75 × 45 cm (30 × 18″), was raised in 1932. It is a single pink, more salmon and paler than 'Queen Charlotte'. It flowers from August to September. *See* Recipe 10.

Anemone × hybrida 'Honorine Jobert', 150 × 60 cm (5 × 2'), dates back to *circa* 1858. It produces dark green foliage and tall white single flowers with lovely yellow stamens at the centre from July through to September. It is very graceful and worthy. *See* Recipe 12.

Anemone × hybrida 'Queen Charlotte', 80 × 45 cm (32 × 18″), dates back to 1898 and is a pink form slightly shorter than other varieties. Its flowers are semi-double and appear from August through to October. *See* Recipe 4.

Anemone × hybrida 'White Giant', 100 × 60 cm (3¼ × 2'), is a large-flowered strong-growing variety. It flowers between August and October. *See* Recipe 4.

MUSK OR MONKEY FLOWER: *Mimulus* 'Calypso' F₁ Hybrid produces open-throated flowers from June to September. It thrives in damp conditions. *See* Recipe 71, where it is very pretty in a container. It is useful by a pond or at the front of a damp border. Treat it as an annual.

PERENNIAL PEA: *Lathyrus latifolius*, 1.8 m (6') high, is the old-fashioned perennial pea which is smothered in magenta-pink flowers from June to September. It is a climber which needs the support of other plants to climb, otherwise it will sprawl quite happily over a bank. It is good against a wall with a deep pink climbing rose. *See* Recipe 3. It thrives on little attention and will come up year after year. It is not scented. Propagate it from seed.

Lathyrus latifolius 'Pink Pearl', 2 m (6½') high, produces lovely soft pink flowers from June to September, and is a charming plant for the border, where it can scramble over sturdy foliage of earlier flowering herbaceous plants like delphiniums. *See* Recipe 8.

Lathyrus latifolius 'White Pearl', 2 m (6½') high, is a pure white form which is lovely climbing beneath a pergola. It too flowers from June to September. *See* Recipe 39.

SUNFLOWER: *Helianthus annuus* were one of the favourites for the back of the cottage border. They are easily grown from seed. They make spectacular growth in a single season, up to 1.8 m (6′), no doubt the cause of frequent competition between neighbouring cottagers! They are a wonderful bright yellow which adds colour to the late summer border. In winter they provide plenty of food for the birds. *See* Recipe 44. The red, multi-flowered form called 'Velvet Queen', sold by Thompson and Morgan, looks lovely with bronze fennel. *See* Recipe 67.

SWAN RIVER DAISY: *Brachycome iberidifolia* was introduced from Australia in 1840. A half-hardy annual easily grown from seed, it was often used in bedding schemes and was valued for its pretty purple-blue daisy-type flowers. *See* Recipe 61.

FERNS

Ferns form a very important part of the cottage garden. The foliage offers great contrast to many other plants in the borders. The ones named here are all native. They are easy to grow and adaptable to many positions and soils, although the hard fern will not tolerate lime. They are particularly useful in shady spots under trees or hedges. They are also lovely massed together in a fernery. Most of them are at their best when the new fronds are unfurling in early summer. Then, when the new foliage is fully displayed, they make very elegant and handsome plants. The male fern and lady ferns take on autumn colourings as the days and nights get colder. The Cornish fern remains fresh until well into the autumn; only by late winter does it look tired.

Evergreen Ferns
CORNISH FERN: *Polypodium vulgare* 'Cornubiense', 30 × 30 cm (1 × 1′), is an attractive lacy fern with light green foliage. New growth emerges late in early summer, but it is at its best in late summer and the autumn. *See* Recipe 6, 22 and 42. It is a good coloniser and provides useful ground cover, especially in dry positions which it tolerates well. It can be grown in sun or shade.

HARD FERN: *Blechnum spicant*, 45 × 45 cm (18 × 18″), has dark green spreading fronds which are leathery and lance-shaped. It is good under shrubs and trees, or on banks and walls. It will tolerate drought or wet positions, but it likes lime-free soil. It is best from May to November. *See* Recipe 25.

HART'S TONGUE FERN: *Asplenium scolopendrium*, 40 × 40 cm (16 × 16″), produces strap-like leaves which are particularly lovely when the fronds first unfurl in June. It develops into a good clump which contrasts well with the lacy ferns elsewhere. It is hardy and easy to grow in any soil, but it dislikes drought. *See* Recipe 42.

SOFT SHIELD FERN: *Polystichum setiferum*, 120 × 90 cm (4 × 3′), is a beautiful fern which will thrive anywhere: in sun, shade or dry situations beneath a wall. It has lovely colouring when the fronds first unfurl, then great elegance and poise. The fronds become prostrate in winter. It is best from May to November. *See* Recipe 42.

Polystichum setiferum 'Acutilobum', 60 × 60 cm (2 × 2′), has long pointed dark green fronds which are arranged in a spiral fashion around the crown. Each is daintily divided and quite beautiful. It produces buds on the fronds which may be used for propagation. It is tolerant of a wide range of conditions. *See* Recipe 20.

Polystichum setiferum 'Plumoso-divisilobum', 50 × 90 cm (20 × 36″), is a tall dark green version of the soft shield fern which has very finely divided fronds. It makes a graceful plant beside the cottage. It is good in shade and dry positions. *See* Recipe 4.

Deciduous ferns
LADY FERN: *Athyrium filix-femina*, 70 × 70 cm (28 × 28″), dies down completely in the autumn but produces lacy fresh green fronds in late spring. It is best from May to September. It tolerates damp or dry sites in sun or shade. *See* Recipe 42.

'Victoriae' (Victorian lady fern), 80 × 80 cm (32 × 32″), is slightly larger than the lady fern. It is extremely graceful with fine lattice work all the way up the stem. Each frond is crested. It too is best from May to September. *See* Recipe 42.

MALE FERN: *Dryopteris filix-mas*, 90 × 90 cm (3 × 3′), is a long-suffering fern which will thrive in almost any shady dry or damp position. It is lovely in May when the fronds first unfurl. In sheltered districts it may stay evergreen. It is best from May to September. *See* Recipes 25, 34, 42 and 70.

Bellflower, catmint and lady's mantle from list 3 can all be coaxed into bloom again in September if the flowering stems are cut back immediately after the first flush is over. There are many others from that list which overlap.

See also lists:
  5 later flowering roses.
  6 *Clematis* 'Jackmanii', *tangutica* and *viticella*, grape vine and Virginia creeper.
  7 late honeysuckle and summer jasmine.
  8 bronze fennel and hyssop.
  9 purple loosestrife, tufted vetch and water lily.
 10 asters, butterfly bush, greater knapweed, ice plant and valerian.
 11 bear's breeches, Chinese lanterns, hydrangea and teasel.
 12 fruits and vegetables.
 13 firethorn and cottage hedgerow shrubs.

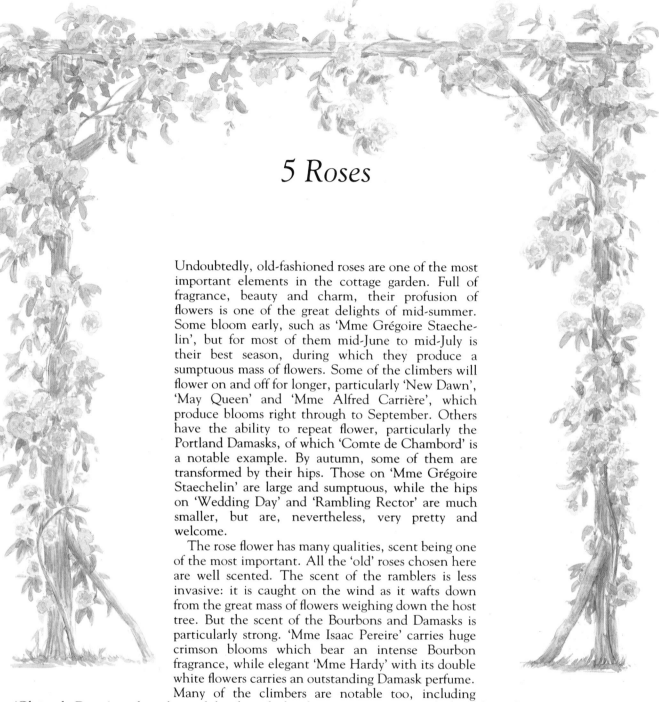

5 Roses

Undoubtedly, old-fashioned roses are one of the most important elements in the cottage garden. Full of fragrance, beauty and charm, their profusion of flowers is one of the great delights of mid-summer. Some bloom early, such as 'Mme Grégoire Staechelin', but for most of them mid-June to mid-July is their best season, during which they produce a sumptuous mass of flowers. Some of the climbers will flower on and off for longer, particularly 'New Dawn', 'May Queen' and 'Mme Alfred Carrière', which produce blooms right through to September. Others have the ability to repeat flower, particularly the Portland Damasks, of which 'Comte de Chambord' is a notable example. By autumn, some of them are transformed by their hips. Those on 'Mme Grégoire Staechelin' are large and sumptuous, while the hips on 'Wedding Day' and 'Rambling Rector' are much smaller, but are, nevertheless, very pretty and welcome.

The rose flower has many qualities, scent being one of the most important. All the 'old' roses chosen here are well scented. The scent of the ramblers is less invasive: it is caught on the wind as it wafts down from the great mass of flowers weighing down the host tree. But the scent of the Bourbons and Damasks is particularly strong. 'Mme Isaac Pereire' carries huge crimson blooms which bear an intense Bourbon fragrance, while elegant 'Mme Hardy' with its double white flowers carries an outstanding Damask perfume. Many of the climbers are notable too, including 'Gloire de Dijon', with its large globe-shaped, deeply perfumed blooms.

Other attributes are the shape and formation of the flower. Some create exquisite buds like 'Lady Hillingdon'; some are full and fat like 'Comte de Chambord'; some are small and petite but very shapely like 'Yvonne Rabier'. Others are velvety and heavily mossed like 'William Lobb'. Still others are delicately cupped, such as 'Louise Odier' when it first opens.

Roses can be used in so many different ways in the garden. The shrub roses can be used to create a summer rose border (*see* Recipe 41) or placed with herbaceous plants in a mixed border where smaller roses can grow side by side with summer favourites such as delphiniums and poppies. *See* Recipes 8 and 9. They can also be grown amongst the herbs in the herb garden, where they fit in so well with rosemary, sages and thymes. *See* Recipes 28 and 29.

The ramblers are better placed near tall trees or pergolas where they can meander as they please, transforming the host tree into a bubbling fountain of blooms. *See* Recipes 23 and 24. Or they can be used on large pergolas, which they will cover luxuriantly. *See* Recipes 38 and 39. For smaller arches, the climbers are a better choice. *See* Recipes 36 and 37. One of the most obvious sites for climbing roses is the cottage wall where they can enjoy the warmth and shelter and so delight the owner and passer-by alike. Most of them are suited to full sun (*see* Recipes 2, 3, 21 and 26), but there are those which will tolerate quite shady positions. *See* Recipes 6, 22, 27 and 35.

Together, the ramblers and climbers can completely change the garden, adding height to many parts, giving colour to bare walls and accentuating focal points such as arches. They can be used to make divisions within the garden, creating smaller intimate areas full of scent and colour.

The old-fashioned roses should be pruned each year to encourage new strong growth to form and bear flowers. It can be done in February, before the new growth starts, or left until after the summer flowering. With many roses the latter encourages the development of good flowering potential for the following year. It will also get rid of unsightly dead flowers. Pruning at this time will, in some cases, produce a second flush of flowers later the same summer.

There are few set rules. Look to the individual recipes for instructions. So often the site itself will determine how rigorous the pruning needs to be. The small bush roses, such as 'Yvonne Rabier', need hardly any attention and are probably best left to their own devices unless the shape is untoward. Others, such as 'Fantin-Latour' and 'Louise Odier', planted amongst other shrubs and herbaceous plants, need to be pruned very much with an overall shape in mind. Let 'Louise Odier' wander through the rosemary – that will add to the charm. With the climbers and ramblers, space is all-important. Where large walls exist, the roses can be fanned out, but where the rose is to be confined, prune it to establish flowering low down so that a column of colour will emerge and the flowers won't all be at the top. This is important on the pergolas and arches too. Aim for a wall of colour up the sides.

Offer climbing roses good support. If the roses are planted against a wall, fix wires to the wall in advance. It is best to tie the string to the wire before tying in the rose. Avoid nylon string and wire twists.

Beware of planting roses with vigorous climbing twiners, such as wisteria, honeysuckles, *Clematis montana* and 'Jackmanii'. They can be planted together, but be prepared to snip off the twiners before any harm is done.

BUSH/SHRUB

'Comte de Chambord': 90 × 60 cm (3 × 2'). Introduced in 1860. The blooms are a beautiful pink, quite large for the size of the plant, full and cupped. It has an excellent fragrance derived from the Portland Damask, yet it has a continuous flowering season throughout the summer and well into the autumn, from June to September. It enjoys a light open sunny position. Its foliage is grey-green. *See* Recipe 9.

'Fantin-Latour': 1.5 × 1.2 m (5 × 4'). Introduced in honour of the famous painter in about 1850. It is a Provence rose with double shell-pink flowers in June and July, which are shown off by its dark green leaves. The blooms are cupped at first, then reflex at the edges. If it is used as a pillar rose, it can climb to 3 m (10'). It is tolerant of poorer soils and likes full sun. *See* Recipe 38.

'The Herbalist': 90 × 90 cm (3 × 3'). Introduced in 1991 by David Austin. The semi-double blooms are fragrant and are a strongly coloured deep pink. They open flat, revealing a bunch of golden stamens, and last from June to September. This rose is very like the old *Rosa gallica officinalis*, known as the 'Apothecary's Rose', except that it has the ability to repeat flower, hence its inclusion in the herb garden. *See* Recipe 29.

'Louise Odier': 1.5 × 1.2 m (5 × 4'). Introduced in 1851. The blooms are a warm pink, double and cup-shaped like a camellia. They are produced in clusters, which sometimes create an arching effect on the vigorous but slender branches. It has a wonderful Bourbon perfume and flowers continuously throughout the summer from June to September. It enjoys full sun but is tolerant of shade. *See* Recipe 28.

'Mme Hardy': 1.5 × 1.5 m (5 × 5'). Introduced in 1832. It is a Damask rose, typically very well scented, with double white blooms in June and July. The centre petals fold inwards, accentuating a green eye. Its foliage is light green, and its growth is vigorous. It likes full sun but is tolerant of shade and can cope with poorer soils. It is one of the outstanding larger shrub roses. *See* Recipe 41.

Rosa gallica 'Versicolor' (Rosa Mundi): 90 × 90 cm (3 × 3'). It dates back probably to the sixteenth century. This is one of the oldest of all the striped roses: the petals are a various mixture of crimson, pink and white. The flowers bloom in June and July. The rose is tolerant of poor soil and likes full sun but it will grow in shade. It is suitable for hedging and containers, and its hips in autumn are attractive. It is a striking rose which should find a place somewhere in the cottage garden. *See* Recipe 41.

'William Lobb': known affectionately as Old Velvet Moss, 2 × 1.5 m (6½ × 5'). Introduced in 1855. This is a well-known and vigorous rose. It sends out long stems which carry large clusters of flowers in June and July, each distinctively mossed. The magenta-purple flowers are large, double and richly perfumed. It will tolerate poor soil. It likes full sun, but performs best at the back of a border with some support. *See* Recipe 41.

'Yvonne Rabier': 90 × 60 cm (3 × 2'). Introduced in 1910. This is one of the most attractive of all the old roses. It blooms from June to September in clusters of double white flowers, each with just a hint of yellow in its bud. Its spicy scent is at its best in the early autumn. What is more, it has attractive shiny light green foliage. It likes a sunny open position but

will tolerate shade and poorer soils. It is suitable for a container. It is lovely in a mixed border where its long flowering period can be enjoyed. *See* Recipe 8.

CLIMBERS

'Gloire de Dijon': 4.5 m (15′) high. Introduced in 1853. The flowers are large and globe-shaped. They hang down from the foliage and can be well appreciated from the ground. This makes it a good choice for a sunny rose arch. The pale buff yellow flowers are tinged with salmon and pink. They have a rich Bourbon scent and are produced continuously from June or July until October. It makes a striking combination with a purple grape vine, providing colour and contrast over a long period. *See* Recipe 36.

'Lady Hillingdon': 5 m (16½′) high. Introduced around 1917. It is justly renowned for its long elegant apricot-yellow buds set off by its glossy, bronze-tinted dark foliage. It has a rich Tea rose perfume. It flowers continuously from June to September and is a good choice for a sunny warm wall. *See* Recipe 26.

'Mme Alfred Carrière': 6 m (19½′) high. Introduced in 1879. This is a vigorous, trouble-free climber with loose, clear white, well-scented blooms which flower well throughout the summer from June to July, and again in September. It could be trained to climb through a tree. It is tolerant of poorer soils and is a good specimen for a pergola or a north wall. *See* Recipe 39.

'Mme Grégoire Staechelin': 5 m (16½′) high. Introduced from Spain in 1927, it is affectionately known as the 'Spanish Beauty'. The flowers are large and pale pink in colouring, with a deeper pink reverse. The display in June and July is memorable. It produces a magnificent show of hips in the autumn. It makes a lovely choice for a warm sunny wall, although it will tolerate a shady north wall. *See* Recipe 26.

'Mme Isaac Pereire': 1.5 m × 1.2 m (5 × 4′) as a bush or 3–4 m (10–13′) high as a climber. Introduced in 1881. It is the largest and most vigorous of all the Bourbons, and has deep pink flowers from July to September. Perhaps the most fragrant of all the cottage roses, it performs beautifully climbing up a sunny wall. It will also tolerate a shady position. *See* Recipe 3.

'Mrs Herbert Stevens': 3.5 m (11½′) high. Introduced in 1922. It flowers in July, with the chance of an autumn flush. It is one of the favourite white climbers for its elongated buds and shapely flowers. It has a lovely perfume typical of a Tea rose, and dark foliage. It likes sun, but is tolerant of a shady north wall. *See* Recipe 27.

'New Dawn': 4 m (13′) or more high. Introduced in 1930, this is a charming rose for the front of the cottage, whether to the north or south. The pale pink flowers have attractive buds and the flowers which follow are full and scented. They bloom in June and July. The foliage is healthy and glossy. It is an easy rose to place and mix with other summer favourites. *See* Recipe 2.

'Paul's Scarlet Climber': 3 m (10′) high. Introduced in 1916. It produces magnificent clusters of brilliant scarlet flowers in June and July with the occasional bloom in the autumn. The foliage is dark green. It will tolerate a north aspect, and even poor soils. It is almost thornless and so is a good subject for a shady arch. *See* Recipe 35.

'Pink Perpétue': 3.5 m (11½′) high. Introduced in 1965, this is one of the outstanding roses produced in more recent years. One of its parents is 'New Dawn'. It has rich pink, well-shaped flowers and dark green glossy foliage. It blooms continuously throughout the summer from June to September. It is happy in full sun, but it will also tolerate a shady north-facing wall. *See* Recipe 21.

'Zéphirine Drouhin': 3 m (10′) high. Introduced in 1868. It is well known as a thornless rose. The foliage is a rich bronze-red in early summer. Its semi-double blooms are a deep cerise pink. They have a strong Bourbon perfume, and flower from June to September. This rose is ideal for a north wall, although it can be grown as a shrub. *See* Recipes 6 and 22.

RAMBLERS

'Albertine': 5 m (16½′) high. Introduced by Barbier in France in 1921, this has become a great favourite for its wonderful full display of copper-pink flowers in June and July. Its leaves and stems are tinged red in early summer. The fragrance is excellent and the buds are particularly beautiful. It can be treated as a bush or trained along a low fence. It is good in any aspect, but particularly against a north wall. It is also suitable for an arch. *See* Recipe 37.

'Crimson Shower': 5 m (16½′) high. Introduced in 1951. Trusses of bright crimson flowers appear in July and continue into September. The foliage is dark and shiny. *See* Recipe 16.

'Leontine Gervaise': 5 m (16½') high. Introduced in 1903, also by Barbier in France. It has dark green glossy foliage with a hint of red in the stems and leaves in early summer, followed by a marvellous display of salmon flowers, tinged yellow and red in July. It is good grown near 'Albertine', as it has similar colouring but will flower two or three weeks apart, thus prolonging the main season. *See* Recipe 37.

'May Queen': 4.5 m (15') high. Introduced in 1898. This is a free-flowering rose with clusters of lilac-pink blooms in June and July; these have a lovely delicate fragrance. The rose has dark green foliage. It thrives in a sunny spot but will also tolerate shady north walls. It looks perfect with delphiniums, catmint and white mock orange. *See* Recipe 38.

'Paul's Himalayan Musk': 10 m (33') high. Introduced probably in the late nineteenth century. This is a vigorous rose suitable for planting in the orchard at the base of a tall fruit tree. Bury a bottomless bucket at least 60 cm (2') from the base of the tree, and plant the rose in it. This way the rose can be carefully watered in its infancy. It produces long trails of pretty pale pink flowers in July. The fragrance is carried on the wind. *See* Recipe 23.

'Rambling Rector': 6 m (19½') high. This is a very old rose, probably dating back several centuries. The small creamy white double flowers are produced in large clusters in June and July. The musk scent is delicious. It is a versatile rose which grows against a shady north wall. It is also suitable to train up a tree, or it can be grown over a substantial pergola, where the hips will be appreciated in the autumn. *See* Recipe 39.

'Wedding Day': 6 m (19½') high. Introduced in 1950. This is a vigorous grower which produces arching sprays of flowers, apricot in bud and white when open in June and July. The two-toned effect is enchanting. The foliage is neat and glossy. Small hips show colour in September. It can be grown as a mounding shrub or allowed to cascade through a weeping birch. *See* Recipe 24.

See also list:
13 dog rose and sweet briar.

6 Climbers

Climbers form an integral part of the cottage garden and make use of the boundary walls as well as those of the cottage itself. They add another dimension, so important where the garden is small and often close to neighbouring homes. They are useful for pergolas and arches, creating entrances and divisions, barriers and cosy spaces, and lending so much character.

Often the climbers bring interest at different seasons. Ivy and winter-flowering jasmine give colour in winter. Spring clematis, followed by May honeysuckle and wisteria, give a glorious show. Later clematis and roses prolong the visual feast. Autumn comes with fiery Virginia creeper, pyracantha and cotoneaster. Many of the climbers are scented, including the clematis and wisteria, but the more obvious scents are those of the honeysuckles, roses and summer jasmine.

CLEMATIS: All those described below are deciduous climbing varieties which cling by means of a twining leaf stalk which attaches itself to wires or trellis-work or other vegetation. They will grow in sun or shade, but if the site is in full sun they like to have their roots protected. Grow an herbaceous plant or a low shrub on the south side. All clematis thrive in alkaline soil, so add lime if necessary.

Clematis alpina 'Frances Rivis', 2 m (6½′) high, was introduced before 1961. It produces large pendulous lavender-blue flowers in April and May. It grows well against a wall through a more vigorous host. *See* Recipe 27.

Clematis alpina 'Ruby', 2.5 m (8′) high, was raised in 1935. It produces pink flowers in April and May. It is suitable for planting against a wall through a host or for training over a low wall. *See* Recipe 20.

Clematis macropetala 'Markhamii' or 'Markham's Pink', 2 m (6½′) high, was in cultivation prior to 1935. It is a rose-pink clematis which flowers a little later than the alpines, otherwise it has a similar slender habit. Flowers appear in May and June, followed by silky flower heads. *See* Recipe 16, where it is planted beside the lavender hedge.

Clematis montana rubens, 6 m (19½′) high, was introduced in 1900. It is one of the old-fashioned montanas with bronze green foliage and pale pink flowers. It is a vigorous clematis which will flower throughout May and into June. It makes a lovely feature up a high wall or draped over a fence. It flowers at the same time as the lilac in Recipe 15.

Clematis montana 'Tetrarose', 7 m (23′) high, is of more recent introduction. It is less vigorous than *rubens*, which may make it a more suitable subject for the front of the cottage wall. It has bronze foliage, and is smothered in lilac and deep pink flowers throughout May and into June. *See* Recipe 6.

Large-flowered garden hybrids:

Clematis 'General Sikorski', 3 m (10′) high, was raised in Poland. It has large mid-blue flowers which are reddish at the base. It flowers in June and July. *See* Recipe 21, where it is growing on the wisteria wall.

Clematis 'Jackmanii Superba', 3 m (10') high, was introduced in about 1873. It has large violet-purple flowers from July to September. It is vigorous. An old favourite, it is excellent for late summer colour on an arch. *See* Recipes 3 and 37.

Clematis 'Miss Bateman', 2.5 m (8') high, was introduced in about 1869. It has large white flowers which have a distinctive and beautiful green band running through the petals when they first open. It is best in shade. Flowers appear in June and July. *See* Recipe 37.

Clematis 'Mrs Cholmondeley', 2.5 m (8') high, was introduced prior to 1873. It has large pale blue flowers from May to October. It is suitable for training up pillars. *See* Recipe 39.

Clematis 'Perle d'Azur', 3 m (10') high, has large azure-blue flowers with creamy green anthers. It flowers in June and July. *See* Recipe 27, where it is growing in shade beneath a white climbing rose.

Clematis 'The President', 2.5 m (8') high, was introduced prior to 1876. It has large purple-blue flowers in June and July. Another old favourite, it looks lovely with a yellow climbing rose. *See* Recipe 26.

Clematis 'Vyvyan Pennell', 3 m (10') high, was introduced in about 1959. It has large double violet flowers from May to July. Single flowers are often produced in the autumn. *See* Recipe 39.

Clematis tangutica, 5 m (16½') high, was introduced in about 1890. It is a vigorous, dense-growing, late-flowering clematis with blue-green foliage and small yellow lantern-like flowers which appear from August to October. The flowers are followed by fluffy seedheads and, because of the long flowering period, the two often appear together. It is lovely on a pergola with late-flowering clematis, white roses and small rose hips. *See* Recipe 39.

Clematis viticella 'Alba Luxurians', 3.5 m (11½') high, is a late-flowering clematis with an abundance of white flowers, tinted mauve, from July to September. This particular cultivar is of recent introduction, although the species has been grown in England since the sixteenth century. *See* Recipe 15.

GOLDEN HOP: *Humulus lupulus* 'Aureus', 5 m (16½') high, has bright golden foliage in early summer which gradually turns mid-green with age. It is best from May to July. The female form will produce some hops in the autumn, although not as freely as the female of the species itself. Derived from our native hop, it is a twining climber best grown in full sun. It is suitable for a pergola (*see* Recipe 39) or for scrambling through ceanothus on a house wall. *See* Recipe 1.

GRAPE VINE: *Vitis vinifera* 'Purpurea', up to 7 m (23') high, is a particularly attractive form often known as the claret vine on account of its leaf colouring, which changes from claret-red to purple as the summer progresses and autumn encroaches. Grapes have been grown in cottage gardens for centuries, although this form has more recent origins. Nevertheless, it was a favourite form used by Gertrude Jekyll in many of her planting schemes. The fruits are small and purple, and in a hot summer they are sweet. The vine can be trained easily, and supports itself with twining tendrils. It looks lovely on an arch with an old-fashioned rose such as the buff-yellow 'Gloire de Dijon'. *See* Recipe 36.

JAPANESE WISTERIA: *Wisteria floribunda*, 9 m (30') high, is the lovely Japanese wisteria. Beautiful, long-scented violet-blue racemes appear from May to June. It was introduced in 1830, and became more popular after the turn of the century. Although it is not self-clinging, it is very vigorous, so it can be trained easily and will grow very low along a wall or very high. *See* Recipe 21. It grows best in sun, but it will tolerate partial shade so long as it does not catch the early morning sun following a frost.

VIRGINIA CREEPER: *Parthenocissus quinquefolia*, 15 m (50') high, is a vigorous self-clinging climber which is excellent for high walls and trees. It is an old favourite, introduced in 1629! Its flowers are fairly insignificant, although seen at close range they look particularly attractive with the curly new leaf of the parsley ivy. Its leaves turn orange and crimson in October. It is best grown in shade or partial shade. *See* Recipe 22.

See also lists:
4 perennial pea.
5 roses.
7 honeysuckle, fragrant summer jasmine and annual sweet pea.
12 runner beans.
13 ceanothus, firethorn and Japanese quince.
14 ivies and winter-flowering jasmine.

7 Fragrant Flowers

Scent is one of the great joys of the cottage garden and is important at all times of the year. It is easy to understand why lily of the valley, honeysuckle, old-fashioned roses, summer jasmine and lavender were such great favourites. Smell the honeysuckle in the evening or after a shower of rain: it fills the air with intoxicating sweetness. Brush past a lavender bush in mid-summer and enjoy one of life's great delights. Just a small posy of summer jasmine will transform a room. Plant heliotrope in a window box and let the sweet fragrance waft inside the house. Plant mignonette around the edge and enjoy the double pleasure. There are so many fragrant plants to choose from; many of them, including the roses, are in other sections.

CHERRY PIE: *Heliotropium* × *hybridum* is a half-hardy shrub which was once a great favourite on account of its long-lasting summer flowering period and its deliciously sweet scent. It was planted out in the garden or used in containers. Heliotrope is delightful mixed with pink geraniums and mignonette in a pot or window box. *See* Recipe 62. Propagate it from root cuttings or grow it from seed. Fortunately, it is becoming more widely available in the garden centres. It can be overwintered indoors and made into a standard bush.

GARDEN PINKS: These are best in a sunny spot beside a path or at the front of a border where the heavy clove scent can be fully appreciated. Or plant them in a raised container and enjoy them at nose level. There are many to choose from, including some of the old ones which are still in cultivation, such as 'Mrs Sinkins' (*see* below), 'Bridal Veil', a double white with a green centre dating from the seventeenth century, 'Charles Musgrave' or 'Green Eyes', a single white with a green centre dating from 1725, and 'Dad's Favourite', a striking semi-double white with chocolate eye in the centre and chocolate lacing dating from 1949. Many modern ones have the lovely scent of the older varieties but have the ability to flower for a longer period of time in the summer. Propagate them by means of cuttings 10 cm (4″) long taken from vigorous side shoots in July and August.

Dianthus 'Letitia Wyatt', 30 × 30 cm (1 × 1′), introduced in 1983, has blush-pink double flowers on stiff stems from May to September. Its growth is compact, and its flowers are heavily scented. *See* Recipe 21.

Dianthus 'Mrs Sinkins', 25 × 60 cm (10 × 24″), was registered in 1810, and was raised by the Master of Slough Workhouse, who named it after his wife. It is still widely available. Though lax in habit, it has an unforgettable clove fragrance and will soon make a lovely big clump. Full double white flowers appear throughout June. *See* Recipe 2.

Dianthus 'Strawberry Parfait', 15 × 10 cm (6 × 4″), flowers continuously from early June until the first frosts. Treat it as a hardy annual. *See* Recipe 73.

Dianthus 'Valda Wyatt', 30 × 25 cm (12 × 10″), introduced in 1981, has very delicate lavender colouring with a rosy lavender centre. It is vigorous and its growth is compact. It flowers from the end of May until the first frosts. *See* Recipe 32.

HONEYSUCKLE: One of the old favourites in the cottage garden, it is perfect for growing amongst a hedgerow, or over a fence or as part of an arch. It produces a glorious mass of flowers that have a rich perfume, which is lovely at any time of day but is especially noticeable at dusk or after rain. All of the four honeysuckles included here are deciduous, easy to look after and prefer a site in partial shade. They flower at different times from early summer to autumn, and so among them they are able to make a valuable contribution to the scented garden over a long period. Although described as climbers, they need support initially. Beware: they will twine round anything they can find. If climbing roses are planted nearby, take special care to keep the growths apart. The honeysuckles have luscious orange-red berries in the autumn which will provide many birds with a veritable feast. Propagate them from 10 cm (4″) stem cuttings in July and August.

Lonicera × heckrottii 'Goldflame', 4 m (13′) high, has striking orange-pink flowers from July to September. It is a distinctive form of honeysuckle which has been grown for a hundred years, and it has good bright colouring. *See* Recipe 27.

Lonicera periclymenum, 5 m (16½′) high, is our vigorous wild honeysuckle of the hedgerows. It has creamy yellow flowers from June to September. *See* Recipe 18.

Lonicera periclymenum 'Belgica', 4 m (13′) high, is an early flowering form of the wild honeysuckle above, but it has bushier growth. It has been cultivated since the seventeenth century. Its flowers are richer in colour with a red/purple flush which then fades to a creamy yellow. They are very highly scented. The flowers appear in May and June, followed by orange berries in autumn. *See* Recipe 35.

Lonicera periclymenum 'Serotina', 3 m (10′) high, is a later flowering bushy variety with purple-tinged foliage and colourful red-purple flowers. It flowers from July to October. *See* Recipe 5.

LAVENDER: This is a favourite shrub for the cottage garden. With its fragrant blue flowers from mid to late summer, it is a choice shrub beside the porch or path. It thrives best in full sun. It prefers limey soil, but it will grow on neutral soils as well. Its sweet nectar attracts the bees and butterflies and makes it an excellent choice for the wildlife garden. It is extremely useful for dried flower arrangements or pot-pourri. Propagate it from ripe non-flowering shoots in August. There are many forms from which to choose.

Lavandula augustifolia 'Grappenhall', 90 × 90 cm (3 × 3′), is often described as 'Old English Lavender'. It is taller and much more vigorous than 'Hidcote', with a broader, greyer leaf. Its pale blue flowers open in late July or early August and last until September. *See* Recipe 2.

Lavandula angustifolia 'Hidcote', 60 × 60 cm (2 × 2′), introduced around 1950, is the smallest and most compact lavender chosen here. Its violet-blue flowers appear from early July to September. It is lovely beside garden pinks. *See* Recipes 43, for the butterfly and bee border, and 73. *Lavandula* 'Nana Atropurpurea' is a similar but older form.

Lavandula angustifolia 'Royal Purple', 80 × 80 cm (32 × 32"), is one of the most highly scented forms. Rich purple spikes appear throughout July and August. It has a narrow grey-green leaf. It makes a good fragrant hedge. *See* Recipes 16 and 21. *Also see* Recipe 44, where it forms the frontispiece in the butterfly and bee border.

LEMON VERBENA: *Aloysia triphylla* is a half-hardy deciduous shrub which needs careful protection over the winter. The leaves have a strong lemon scent when crushed. Tiny pale mauve flowers are produced in July and August. Introduced in the seventeenth century, it has been widely used in pot-pourris; the leaves retain their fragrance for two to three years. It is also used to scent candles, ink and paper and in jellies and cake-making. Try it in a pot with scented geraniums. *See* Recipe 65, where the entire pot may be overwintered without disturbance and put out again the following summer.

LILAC: *Syringa vulgaris* 'Katherine Havemeyer', 5 × 5 m (16½ × 16½'), was introduced in about 1922. It is a deciduous shrub with strongly scented compact flower panicles which open purple but then fade to pink. It has a double flower which blooms in mid-May. *See* Recipe 15.

There are many other varieties to choose from, including the single wine-red 'Souvenir de Louis Späth', introduced about 1833, and the white single 'Vestale', which was introduced in about 1910. They are easy to grow in sun or partial shade. Propagate them from half-ripe heel cuttings in July and August.

LILY OF THE VALLEY: *Convallaria majalis*, 15 cm (6") high, grows from a creeping rhizome and will spread quickly in cool shady conditions. The little white bells which appear in May are richly scented. Grow them beneath the cottage window (*see* Recipe 6), or let them spread to their heart's content beneath the privy – or barn – wall as in Recipe 30. They will grow beneath a hedge. Propagate them by division from October to March.

MADONNA LILY: *Lilium candidum*, 1.5 m (5') high, produces tall stems of fragrant white trumpet-shaped flowers in late June and July. These lilies have been cultivated since ancient times and are one of the most evocative plants of the cottage garden. They form large clumps where they have been left undisturbed. They are basal rooting, and like a sunny spot with limey soil best. They have a winter rosette of evergreen leaves. *See* Recipe 26.

MIGNONETTE: *Reseda odorata*, 30 × 30 cm (1 × 1'), is a charming hardy annual which grows very easily from seed and has a delicate lily of the valley type of scent. It was once universally grown and, though not often seen these days, is even now well remembered by those who knew it as children. Fortunately, the seed is readily available. The plants can be bedded out in the garden or used in summer containers. They are best from June to October. *See* Recipes 1 and 62.

MOCK ORANGE: *Philadelphus* 'Beauclerk', 2 × 2 m (6½ × 6½'), was raised in 1938. It has single milky-white flowers, each with a pale purple blotch in the centre. Its scent is strongly reminiscent of orange blossom, hence its name. This is a medium-sized deciduous shrub which flowers in June and July, just at the time when the old-fashioned roses are in full bloom. *See* Recipe 38. It will thrive in sun or partial shade.

There are many other varieties to choose from, including 'Belle Etoile', introduced in about 1930, and the smaller arching 'Sybille', introduced in about 1913. Both have single flowers. 'Virginal', 3 m (10') high, introduced before 1911, is a large upright shrub with double white flowers. Propagate them by taking 30 cm (1') hardwood cuttings in October or November, and root them outdoors in a sheltered bed.

PEONY: These hardy herbaceous plants have a rich fragrance, which has made them firm favourites in the cottage garden where, undisturbed, they will flourish year after year without fuss or attention. They are happy in full sun or partial shade, as long as the ground is moist. They will also grow in grass. Although the flowers reach perfection for only two weeks in either May or June, depending on the variety, they can be enjoyed for longer periods by using early and late forms. The spring foliage is a warm bronze-red which turns green in summer and often colours in autumn. The flower colour varies from white to pink, lilac or red. Propagate them by division in September.

Paeonia lactiflora 'Pink Delight', 70 × 60 cm (28 × 24"), has single blush-pink flowers with colourful yellow stamens at the centre. It blooms in June. It is well-loved and beautifully scented. *See* Recipe 7, where it is planted at the front of the border.

Paeonia lactiflora 'Sarah Bernhardt', 90 × 90 cm (3 × 3'), introduced around the turn of the century, is deservedly an old favourite. In June and early July it has large double pink flowers which are sweetly scented. *See* Recipe 33.

Paeonia officinalis 'Rubra-plena', 75 × 75 cm (30 × 30"), is the old-fashioned double red, introduced in the sixteenth century. It has a generous number of large sumptuous flowers in May, all with a sweet fragrance. *See* Recipe 33.

SUMMER JASMINE: *Jasminum officinale*, 6 m (19½') high, is thought to have been grown in Britain since 1548. It is a vigorous deciduous climber. From June to

October it produces white flowers which are heavily scented. It is an old favourite for growing up the cottage walls. *See* Recipe 2. Propagate it by layering shoots in September or October.

SWEET PEA: *Lathyrus odoratus* 'Antique Fantasy', 2 m (6½′) high, is an annual climber, which is grown from seed each autumn or spring. The flowers, which appear from June to September, are of mixed colours, ranging from blue and white to pink. They have long strong stems. They will grow up poles in the border, or they can be grown as a screen between the flower garden and the vegetable plot. *See* Recipe 45. They look lovely mixed with purple podded beans in a half barrel. Another old variety is 'Painted Lady'.

SWEET ROCKET: *Hesperis matronalis*, 45 × 15 cm (18 × 6″), is a short-lived hardy perennial with large heads of single white, purple or mauve flowers in June. Once an old cottage favourite, it is much loved by butterflies. It is most fragrant in the evening. *See* Recipes 16 and 43. It will usually self-seed. It likes a sunny position.

WALLFLOWER: *Cheiranthus cheiri* 'Fair Lady Mixed', 30 × 30 cm (1 × 1′), is a hardy biennial which is easy to grow from seed. It produces a fragrant mixture of soft lemon, gold, apricot, salmon, rose-pink, purple, and mahogany flowers in April and May. Wallflowers will often self-seed and naturalise on, or at the foot of, a crumbling old wall. They associate well with late flowering tulips, and are loved by bees. *See* Recipe 1. Perennial wallflowers are not scented, *see* list 3.

See also lists:
  1 hyacinths, daffodils.
  2 forget-me-not, primrose, viola and violet.
  3 day lily and flag iris.
  5 roses.
  6 *Clematis montana* and Japanese wisteria.
  8 herbs, aromatic leaves and flowers.
  9 cheddar pink, cowslip and meadowsweet.
10 butterfly bush and phlox.
13 dog rose, hawthorn and sweet briar.
14 daphne, mahonia, viburnum.

8 Herbs

Herbs are such an important part of the cottage scene. They often have gaily coloured, scented flowers and aromatic leaves. Most of them are very attractive to butterflies, bees and other insects. They are useful in the kitchen for flavourings to stews, omelettes and salads, and as garnishes on pâtés and fish dishes. Sage and hyssop and many others are often used medicinally. Add eau de cologne mint to warm water to create a refreshing bath. Use many in pot-pourris where the sweet aromatic leaves can be enjoyed in the house.

Herbs need not necessarily be planted in a herb garden as such. Most of them will be very much at home amongst other herbaceous plants and roses. Or try them in containers mixed with edible flowers. Most of them like a position in full sun, although chives will tolerate partial shade and sweet woodruff is happy in sun or shade.

The list is far from exhaustive. Many of the salad herbs are included elsewhere, e.g. primroses, violets, cowslips, although nasturtiums and little yellow violas can be found here.

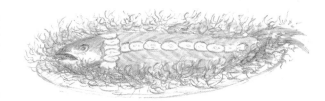

Foeniculum vulgare, 180 × 60 cm (6 × 2'), has bright green foliage rather than bronze, otherwise it is very similar. Both are attractive to insect life. *See* Recipe 8. They seed themselves avidly but are difficult to transplant unless the deep taproot is kept intact. Deadhead flowers to avoid excessive seeding.

CHIVES: *Allium schoenoprasum*, 15 × 15 cm (6 × 6"), has grass-like leaves which taste of onions. They start to grow in early spring and have pretty lavender flowers in June and July. Use the leaves and flowers in

BRONZE FENNEL: *Foeniculum vulgare* 'Purpureum', 180 × 60 cm (6 × 2'), looks attractive with its fluffy mounds of thread-like foliage from May to October. In August and September, it will be topped by a mass of tiny yellow flowers. The leaves, flowers and seeds smell and taste slightly of aniseed. They are a wonderful decoration to salmon. Striking in the herb garden or in a sunny border, it is deep bronze at first and fades a little as the summer progresses. *See* Recipes 28, 36, 44 and 67.

the kitchen with egg and fish dishes. The flowers look lovely separated and scattered on green salads. Chives create an attractive path edging in sun or partial shade. *See* Recipes 29 and 60. Divide them in autumn.

GOLDEN FEVERFEW: *Tanacetum parthenium* 'Aureum', 30 × 30 cm (1 × 1'), with its aromatic yellow-green leaves and white daisy-like flowers in June and July, is a must for the cottage garden. It is excellent for its cheerful winter colouring. It is lovely with hostas and makes a useful edging plant if kept well clipped. It can be used in containers all year round. *See* Recipes 7, 31, 39 and 54. It self-seeds profusely. If it is treated as an edger and its leaves are frequently clipped back, then flowering and seeding will be delayed until September or stopped altogether.

GOLDEN MARJORAM: *Origanum vulgare* 'Aureum', 30 × 30 cm (1 × 1'), is most attractive in early

summer, when its bright gold leaves form a neat hummock of growth. As the summer progresses, it grows taller. It produces pink flowers in July and August. Copper butterflies love it. It is a tasty herb for stuffings, omelettes and salads. It is useful in sun or partial shade, in the border, herb garden or containers. *See* Recipes 28, 29, 59 and 60. Propagate it by division in October or March.

HYSSOP: *Hyssopus officinalis*, 45 × 45 cm (18 × 18"), is an aromatic bushy plant with vivid blue flowers which are loved by bees and butterflies. The flowers, which bloom from July to September, and the leaves may be used in soups, salads or stuffings. *See* Recipes 29 and 44. Propagate it using softwood cuttings taken in early summer.

LEMON BALM: *Melissa officinalis* 'Aurea', 60 × 45 cm (24 × 18"), is a tall herbaceous perennial with strong lemon-flavoured leaves which are best from May to October. It makes a good stuffing for fish when mixed with garlic. In its variegated form, 'Variegata', the leaves have a bright gold splash on them. The colouring is better maintained if the growths are kept clipped back. In this form it is suitable as an edging plant. It likes sun or partial shade. *See* Recipes 29, 59 and 60. Propagate it by division in October or March.

MINT: All these mints will spread rapidly in the garden and need to be watched. For this reason, they are well positioned in containers, where they can be trapped neatly. They smell wonderful when watered. The variegated apple mint has particularly attractive foliage and is an old favourite for planting with late tulips, roses, and herbaceous plants. All the mints

will show good growth from May to October and will flower in late summer, when they will provide a great attraction for bees and other flying insects.

Apple mint, *Mentha* × *rotundifolia*, 60 cm (2') high, spread indefinite, has hairy green leaves and a good minty flavour. It grows early and lasts well into the winter. *See* Recipe 28.

Variegated apple mint, *Mentha* × *rotundifolia* 'Variegata', 40 cm (16") high, is most ornamental with its small cream-edged furry leaves. The minty scent and taste are strong. *See* Recipes 59 and 60.

Eau de Cologne mint, *Mentha* × *piperita* 'Citrata', 45 cm (18") high, has purple-tinged dark green leaves which have a soft spicy aroma. Use some of them to create a lovely scented bath. *See* Recipe 59.

NASTURTIUMS: *Tropaeolum majus* 'Tom Thumb', 45 cm (18") high, is an easy annual, with bright orange, yellow or red flowers and tangy round green leaves. Many parts of the plant are edible, including the colourful petals, the new shoots and the young leaves. It will flower from July to October. Grow it from seed as an edger in the vegetable plot, in a sunny border or in containers. *See* Recipe 45. 'Dwarf Cherry Rose' is used in Recipe 66. Other varieties may be self-coloured, climbing or variegated. All would be quite at home in the cottage garden.

PARSLEY: *Petroselinum crispum*, 30 × 25 cm (12 × 10"), is the well-known culinary herb; its curly rich green leaves are so often used for garnishes and sauces. Its growth is best from May to October. It is wonderful as a path edger, and looks lovely with other herbs or deep red summer geraniums in containers. *See* Recipes 29, 57, 58, 59 and 60. It will grow from seed easily and will seed itself.

ROSEMARY: *Rosmarinus officinalis*, 1.8 × 1.5 m (6 × 5'), is an evergreen shrub. It blooms in April and May with a profusion of pale blue flowers which are much loved by bees. The leaves and flowers are both pungent and useful in flavourings and garnishes. Rosemary likes a sunny sheltered spot: against a wall is ideal. It is useful for both winter and spring containers and for herb hanging baskets. *See* Recipes 28, 52 and 59. Propagate it from heel cuttings taken in summer.

SAGE: Narrow-leaved sage (Spanish), *Salvia lavundulifolia*, 60 × 45 cm (24 × 18″), is an evergreen shrub with narrow grey leaves and striking deep-throated blue flowers in June and July. *See* Recipe 28. The flowers may be used with the leaves to decorate pâtés and to garnish salads. The leaves are very pungent and are excellent when used in a sage and onion stuffing. Propagate it using heel cuttings taken in summer.

Purple sage, *Salvia officinalis* 'Purpurascens', 45 × 60 cm (18 × 24″), also has very pungent leaves with striking blue flowers in June and July, but the leaves are broader and dusky purple-red in colouring. It is a slightly shorter shrub than the narrow-leaved sage, but it is wider spreading. It is colourful in the border as well as the herb garden, and associates well with bronze fennel. *See* Recipes 28 and 36. Propagate it using heel cuttings taken in summer.

SWEET WOODRUFF: *Asperula odorata*, 15 × 30 cm (6 × 12″), is a delightful woodland herb which creates dense light green carpets covered with bright white starry flowers in April and May – enough to brighten any dull corner. It is particularly useful under trees in shade. It will also grow in sun, although the leaf colour fades. It is excellent for containers. *See* Recipe 56. Its dried leaves smell of hay. It can be used to deter insects or as a tea. Propagate it by division either before or after flowering. It is a hardy perennial.

THYME: *Thymus vulgaris*, 12 × 25 cm (5 × 10″), is a small evergreen shrubby herb which loves to be planted in full sun. In June pretty mauve flowers appear, which are much loved by bees. Plant it along paths, as well as in the herb garden. *See* Recipes 28 and 54. It is useful in stuffings or as garnishes: you can use the flowers too. Layer the stems in spring or autumn.

Lemon thyme, *Thymus × citriodorus* 'Aureus', 20 × 30 cm (8 × 12″), also known as golden thyme, is a low-growing evergreen herb, suitable for sunny paving, edging in the vegetable garden or herb garden, and containers. *See* Recipes 29, 54 and 60. The golden leaves have a strong lemony flavour and in June the flowers are pink. Layer the stems in spring or autumn.

VIOLA: *Viola cornuta* 'Prince John', 10 × 25 cm (4 × 10″), is a little yellow viola available as a bedding plant in autumn and early spring. It is so useful in spring and early summer containers along with 'Johnny Jump Up', which is bi-coloured purple and yellow, like our native heartsease, and *Viola tricolor* 'Prince Harry', which is all purple. They are so bright and cheerful, and look beautiful with bellis daisies, parsley and cowslips. *See* Recipes 52, 53, 58, 59 and 60. The flowers are edible and can be scattered on salads or used to decorate trifles or cakes.

See also lists:
  2 bellis daisy, primrose, viola and violet.
  7 lavender.
10 bergamot and evening primrose.

9 Wild Flowers

The cottage garden often received uninvited seeds which would blow in from neighbouring fields and hedgerows or would be introduced by birds. Wild plants would be dug up and brought in either for their culinary or medicinal capabilities or as dye plants. The original purpose may now be rather obscure, even forgotten. Many of our wild flowers are so colourful and fragrant that they are extremely welcome. What could be more enticing and nostalgic than a scented spring carpet of wild primroses and violets beneath the cottage hedge, or a patch of grassland filled with chequered snake's head fritillaries, dainty wild daffodils and nodding yellow cowslips?

Why not preserve the natural beauty of a cottage pond with a colony of sky-blue water forget-me-nots intertwined amongst the sword-like leaves of the scented yellow flag iris? Observe the bees and butterflies paying their respects to the water mint flowers. Watch the wild white water lily blooms open and close each day – a delight to the eye throughout July and August. Grow the soft pink flower heads of hemp agrimony beside tall fluffy meadowsweet and enjoy nature's own very special planting combination. Who could fail to admire the natural beauty of the sweet briar rose, with its graceful arches of pretty pink flowers and apple-scented leaves. Wait awhile and it will be transformed, weighed down by orange hips.

The wild species are often just as attractive as their more sophisticated garden relatives. Indeed, many fit happily into the border context, particularly the bulbs and the nectar plants for the butterflies and bees. Many of them appear in the plant list below, but quite a number will be found in other plant lists, including the spring bulbs and border lists and the butterfly and bee list. Fortunately it is now possible to purchase them all in garden centres or through mail order plant or seed catalogues.

CHEDDAR PINK: *Dianthus gratianopolitanus*, 15 × 30 cm (6 × 12″), is a native pink which produces small pink, fragrant, fringed flowers from May to July. *See* Recipe 33. Propagate it using cuttings taken from vigorous side shoots, from June to early August.

COWSLIP: *Primula veris*, 15 × 15 cm (6 × 6″), is one of our most loved wild flowers thriving in a sunny meadow, in the semi-shade of the hedgebank or on the grass verge beside the cottage gate. The dainty nodding flowers are yellow and sweetly scented. They appear in April and May. *See* Recipes 16, 31, 48 and 59. Once fertilisation has occurred, the flower heads become erect. If left undisturbed they will soon seed themselves to create good colonies. They are an easy hardy perennial. The flowers were once gathered to make wine. Try them in a fragrant salad, scattering them with primroses and violets.

HEMP AGRIMONY: *Eupatorium cannabinum*, 60 × 60 cm (2 × 2′), has lovely big heads of soft pink flowers and looks very attractive throughout July, August and September. It likes damp soil beside a stream or pond and will thrive in sun or extreme shade, so it is useful for dark corners. *See* Recipe 49. It is a perennial plant which can be grown from seed or divided in autumn or spring. It is attractive to butterflies.

MARSH MARIGOLD: *Caltha palustris*, 30 × 25 cm (12 × 10″), is our well-known King Cup, which flowers from March to May. Its large yellow flowers are very distinctive and show off well as they rise above the glossy dark green foliage. It is commonly seen in damp meadows and wet woodland or beside ponds; it is tolerant of sun or shade. *See* Recipe 50. It grows from a rhizome which can be divided and replanted in spring or after flowering either in water to a depth of 15 cm (6″) or on damp soil on land.

MEADOW CRANESBILL: *Geranium pratense*, 60 × 60 cm (2 × 2′) has large pretty purple-blue flowers which appear from June to August. *See* Recipe 48. It is a perennial plant in sunny meadows, where it easily grows from seed; it will spread itself quickly once it is established, and will tolerate semi-shade.

MEADOWSWEET: *Filipendula ulmaria*, 90 × 45 cm (36 × 18″), has creamy white flowers from June to September; they produce a sweet almond-like fragrance. The leaves are ferny and scented too. *See* Recipe 49. Once it was used as a strewing herb, now both flowers and foliage are used in pot-pourri. It is an easy perennial to grow in damp conditions, either in sun or semi-shade. It produces lots of seed. It can be split and divided in autumn.

OX-EYE DAISY: *Leucanthemum vulgare*, 60 × 30 cm (2 × 1′), is sometimes known as the moon daisy for its large white daisy-type flower heads which appear from June to August. *See* Recipe 48. It is a perennial plant which easily grows from seed and will spread quickly. It thrives in sun or semi-shade.

PURPLE LOOSESTRIFE: *Lythrum salicaria*, 90 × 45 cm (36 × 18″), is a tall handsome plant which produces colourful purple spires from June to August. It is an easy perennial and will grow in sun or semi-shade although it flowers better in a sunny spot. It thrives in damp areas. *See* Recipe 50. Divide it in March or take cuttings of new shoots in April.

RAGGED ROBIN: *Lychnis flos-cuculi*, 45 × 45 cm (18 × 18″), bears deeply divided pretty rose-pink flowers from May to August. It likes a sunny spot, but will also grow in semi-shade; it is particularly happy in damp areas. *See* Recipe 49. It is a perennial which will easily grow from seed.

TUFTED VETCH: *Vicia cracca*, 75 cm (30″) or more high, uses its branched tendrils to scramble over other vegetation. It has striking blue flowers which appear from July through to September. *See* Recipe 49, where it is planted at the foot of a sweet briar. It is a perennial which is easily grown from seed.

WATER FORGET-ME-NOT: *Myosotis palustris*, 25 × 25 cm (10 × 10″), is a perennial plant with typical sky-blue forget-me-not flowers produced from June to September. It will grow at the edge of streams or ponds at a depth of about 8 cm (3″), or in damp marshy areas, but it likes to be in semi-shade. *See* Recipe 50, where it is growing around the base of a yellow iris.

WATER LILY: *Nymphaea alba*, is a vigorous perennial which needs to be kept in check in a small pond; this can be done by planting it in a special container. Plant the roots between 45 cm (18″) and 80 cm (32″) deep. The leaves will float. Its lovely white flowers, which appear in July and August, are scented. They open by day and close by night. *See* Recipe 50. The water lily grows from a stout rhizome which may be divided in March.

WATER STARWORT: *Callitriche stagnalis* is an important plant which will help to keep the pond water healthy by producing oxygen. Oxygen, in turn, helps to support pond life and keeps the growth of algae in check. It has a green variable leaf which changes shape according to the state of growth and the depth of the water. It flowers from May to September. *See* Recipe 50.

YELLOW FLAG IRIS: *Iris pseudacorus*, 75 × 60 cm (30 × 24″), has tapering sword-like leaves and attractive large yellow flowers from May to July. They secrete lots of nectar and are pollinated by honeybees and hoverflies. The iris grows in damp marshy areas and in water up to 45 cm (18″) deep. *See* Recipe 50. It is an easy perennial which will grow in sun or semi-shade: the more sun, the better it will flower. Divide the rhizome in spring or autumn.

See also lists:
1 wood anemone, bluebell, wild daffodil and snake's head fritillary.
2 primrose and violet.
3 foxglove, Solomon's seal and Turk's cap lily.
4 ferns.
7 wild honeysuckle.
8 sweet woodruff.
10 common bird's foot trefoil, devil's bit scabious, greater knapweed, lady's smock and water mint.
11 teasel.
13 dog rose, dogwood and sweet briar.
14 snowdrop and ivies.

10 Butterfly and Bee Plants

Planting nectar-rich borders is one way of enticing many different sorts of butterflies and plenty of bees into the garden (*see* Recipes 43 and 44 in particular). The plants are not difficult to choose, as many of the old cottage garden favourites are so fragrant and attractive. It is best to site the flowers in a sunny sheltered spot, because flowers in sunshine will be much more appealing than those in shade. Perhaps the scents are stronger in the sun, or maybe butterflies' wings act as solar panels and need the sun for energy.

For maximum impact, plant not singly but in large numbers so that a mass of the same flowers appears. One or two forget-me-nots in a bed will not achieve very much, but let them run wild through a whole border and they will attract several different kinds of butterfly, including the lovely common blue. The same with valerian. It will self-seed so generously that you are almost bound to have plenty of it. The individual flowers are small but occur in such dense quantities along the flower spikes and are so sweet smelling that even half a dozen plants are bound to attract a whole host of late summer butterflies. Don't be disappointed if you don't see them when the valerian first flowers in June. Cut it back after flowering and it will produce another glorious show in September when the butterfly population will be much greater anyway. Then you will have your reward.

Planting in large groupings does not apply to bigger specimens such as the butterfly bush. It will produce numerous flower spikes so that one mature bush will be enough to feed dozens of hungry butterflies. However, that need not stop you from planting more than one if you have the space.

As a general rule, choose single flowers and, where possible, plant medium to pale colours, not dark ones. Avoid weedkillers or insecticides, fungicides or poisonous chemicals.

Butterflies will find different plants on which to lay their eggs. A sunny patch of nettles will provide food for caterpillars of the comma, red admiral, peacock and small tortoiseshell. Common bird's foot trefoil and clover will provide food for the common blue, holly and ivy for the holly blue, lady's smock for the orange tip and grasses for the wall brown and meadow brown. Buckthorn is needed for the brimstone and brassicas for the large and small whites. The green-veined white prefers the wild members of the brassica family, such as garlic mustard and watercress. The painted lady relies on thistles as a caterpillar food.

GARDEN FLOWERS

ALYSSUM: *Lobularia maritima* has a mass of tiny white flowers which smell like honey. Bees find it a great attraction. It has long been associated in containers with lobelia. *See* Recipe 72. It is an annual, and is easily grown from seed.

ASTER: *Aster × frikartii* 'Mönch', 90 × 40 cm (36 × 16″), was raised in Switzerland in about 1920. It looks rather like a Michaelmas daisy (*see* below), but it flowers for a much longer period from July through to October. It has lavender-blue flowers, 5 cm (2″) across, which the butterflies love to visit in late summer. Although it is quite tall, it is stout and does not normally need staking. Elegant and refined, it is considered to be one of the best asters. *See* Recipes 7, 8 and 9, where it is the link plant in a series of sunny borders. Propagate it by division in March.

BERGAMOT: *Monarda fistulosa* 'Prairie Night', 90 × 45 cm (36 × 18″), was introduced in 1955. It is a tall herbaceous perennial with hooded purple flowers which are produced from June to August. It

attracts butterflies but is better known as a bee plant and is sometimes called bee balm. *See* Recipe 43. Propagate it by division in March. Grow it in a sunny spot. It can tolerate dry conditions.

BUTTERFLY BUSH: *Buddleja davidii* 'Empire Blue', 2.4 × 2.4 m (8 × 8'), has a blue flower with an orange eye, *see* Recipe 38. 'Fascination' has a lilac flower, *see* Recipes 43 and 74. They are strong deciduous bushes which can be pruned to shape as desired. The earlier they are pruned, the earlier they will flower, although the main display is normally in July and August. So if you have several in the garden, stagger the pruning to prolong the flowering period.

The flowers are produced on the current year's growth. They form dense plume-shaped clusters 25 cm (10") or more long. They are sweetly scented, and a great favourite with many butterflies, including tortoiseshells, peacocks and cabbage whites. They act as a Mecca, drawing butterflies from a wide area; so much so that all other so-called butterfly nectar plants will be forsaken whilst the buddleia flowers are abundant. There are many hybrids to choose from, offering a wide range of colours from white through to lilac, pink and dark purple. The lighter colours seem to be preferred by the butterflies, hence the choice of 'Fascination' for the butterfly and bee border. Propagate them using softwood cuttings.

EVENING PRIMROSE: *Oenothera missouriensis*, 25 × 60 cm (10 × 24"), is a favourite bee plant which flowers from June to September. The flowers are yellow and large – up to 10 cm (4") across. They open in the evening and remain open for several days. The main stems lie prostrate. It makes an excellent choice for the front of a sunny border. *See* Recipe 44. Grow it from seed or divide it and replant the roots in March or April.

Oenothera biennis, 60 × 30 cm (2 × 1'), is a hardy biennial which likes a sunny position. It will flower the first year from seed and, if allowed to do so, will self-seed heartily. The erect stems produce fragrant clear yellow flowers from June to September. At first they open only at night; later they stay open all day as well. The butterflies and moths find them very attractive. The leaves and flower are edible. *See* Recipe 74.

ICE PLANT: *Sedum spectabile*, 45 × 45 cm (18 × 18"), is another favourite nectar plant of the tortoiseshell and peacock butterfly. It is an herbaceous perennial which flowers from August onwards. It is green at first, but then it turns a lovely soft pink in September and lasts well into October. Thus it takes over when the butterfly bush has finished its main period of flowering. Each flower head is 8–10 cm (3–4") across, dense and fluffy, and crammed with numerous clusters of small flowers. Authorities say that the paler pink flowers of the species are much

better for attracting the butterflies than the richer pink but common hybrid 'Autumn Joy'. The leaves are thick and fleshy, and of a succulent nature. *See* Recipes 32, 43, 44 and 74. Propagate the ice plant by division from October to March. Frequent division will encourage more upright growth.

Sedum spectabile 'Autumn Joy', 60 × 60 cm (2 × 2'), is a lovely garden plant. The flowers are rich pink, later turning salmon-bronze and then coppery-red. *See* Recipe 19.

LOBELIA: *Lobelia erinus* is the half-hardy perennial so much used in summer containers, in boxes, baskets or pots. It may have upright growth or trail depending on the variety. Its flowers may be light or dark blue, purple, pink or white; its foliage is usually mid-green but it can be bronze in some varieties. Bees love it. It has been available for well over a hundred years. It can be overwintered or grown from cuttings or seed. *See* Recipes 63 and 64.

MICHAELMAS DAISY: *Aster novae-angliae* 'Harrington's Pink', 120 × 60 cm (4 × 2'), has clear pink daisy-type flowers in August and September. This hybrid is just one of many Michaelmas daisies which are a great favourite with many butterflies. *See* Recipe 43. It is a tough garden plant which grows easily. Propagate it by division in March. *Aster novae-angliae* and its varieties seem to be less prone to mildew and aster wilt which often affects the more common *Aster novi-belgii*.

PETUNIA: Petunias became fashionable very quickly, once they were introduced in the 1830s. Soon many bi-colours and double forms were available. By the 1880s they were overshadowed by geraniums and were not quite so widely grown. Many are scented and loved by butterflies, whose long tongues can penetrate the deep nectaries. They are easily grown from seed or cuttings – they would need overwintering in a greenhouse in this case. They make a good combination plant with geraniums in a pot or hanging basket. *See* Recipe 64.

PHLOX: *Phlox maculata* 'Alpha', 90 × 45 cm (36 × 18"), has tall cylindrical heads of flowers in contrast to the pyramid-shaped heads of *Phlox paniculata*. It is not usually attacked by eelworm nor does it need staking, unlike its more common relative. The flowers, in bloom from July to September, are a pretty lilac-pink and scented. They attract butterflies, especially the brimstone. *See* Recipe 43. Propagate phlox by division from October to March.

POACHED EGG PLANT: *Limnanthes douglasii*, 15 × 10 cm (6 × 4″), is a low-growing annual. The flowers open wide, 3 cm (1¼″) across; they have white petals with yellow centres, hence the common name. The leaves are pale green and deeply divided. It makes a charming edging plant which flowers profusely throughout June and July, then it disappears. *See* Recipes 43 and 44. It seeds itself quickly and soon the seeds will germinate so that they will flower the following year. From just a few plants, great white and yellow carpets much loved by bees will appear. Indeed, it was often known as the bee plant, but it is attractive to butterflies as well. It makes an excellent choice for the wildlife border.

SNAPDRAGON: *Antirrhinum majus* 'Yellow Monarch', 45 × 30 cm (18 × 12″), is a perennial plant usually grown as an annual. Many varieties succumb to rust but this one is rust-resistant. It will bloom from June to September with a succession of tall flower spikes. The yellow flowers are scented. Each one is tubular in shape with a rounded upper and lower lip. It snaps open when the sides are pressed. It is an old favourite. Bumblebees like the nectar. If they can weigh down the bottom lip, they will extract it with their long tongues, but if they can't manage like that, they will simply pierce the base of the flower and reach it that way instead. *See* Recipe 44.

SNEEZEWEED: *Helenium autumnale* 'Wyndley', 60 × 60 cm (2 × 2′), produces yellow and copper daisy-like flowers from June to August. The red admiral and comma like the nectar. *See* Recipe 44. It is an herbaceous perennial which enjoys full sun. Propagate it by division between October and March.

THRIFT: *Armeria maritima* 'Dusseldorf Pride', 15 × 30 cm (6 × 12″), is a hummock-forming evergreen perennial which produces a mass of pink flowers from June to August. It is attractive to butterflies. Grow it at the front of a sunny border. *See* Recipes 33, 43 and 74. Propagate it by division in March or April.

VALERIAN: *Centranthus ruber*, 60 × 30 cm (2 × 1′), is a wonderful flower for attracting a great variety of butterflies, including tortoiseshells, peacocks, wall browns, commas and cabbage whites. The first flush of pink or pinky-red flowers appears in June and July, but if these are cut down after flowering, a second flush of flowers will appear in September and October, and will last until the frosts. This is the time when many of the late butterflies may be seen enjoying the warm autumn sunshine, gathering the last of the nectar. The flowers are very small but grow in dense clusters. They are sweetly scented. *See* Recipes 26, 33, 43 and 44. They will self-seed profusely, especially on well-drained chalk or limestone soils. They often grow out of old walls. They are very colourful garden flowers, but they need controlling. They make first-rate butterfly plants.

WILD FLOWERS

COMMON BIRD'S FOOT TREFOIL: *Lotus corniculatus*, 25 × 25 cm (10 × 10″), is a grassland perennial which likes to grow in sunny places, especially where the soil is light. It colonises easily. Its seed pods are arranged like the toes of a bird's foot, hence its familiar name. However, its yellow pea-like flowers are streaked with red; for this reason it is also commonly known as the egg and bacon plant. It blooms from May to August. The leaves are food to the larvae of the common blue butterfly, while the flowers are the main source of nectar to the adult. The iridescent blue marking of the males looks exquisite as they flutter and feed amongst the yellow flowers. *See* Recipe 48.

DEVIL'S BIT SCABIOUS: *Succisa pratensis*, 90 × 60 cm (3 × 2′), is one of the best wild flowers for attracting the late summer butterflies – commas, tortoiseshells and red admirals. It is a caterpillar food plant. It is also a favourite bee plant and attracts seed-eating birds. It flowers from July through to September and has numerous small heads of pink-purple blooms. It is a meadow perennial that grows quite tall but has a dense bushy shape which makes it a good weed suppressor. It will naturalise well in grass or in a border. *See* Recipe 48.

GREATER KNAPWEED: *Centaurea scabiosa*, 90 × 45 cm (36 × 18″), is an easy native perennial which has lots of reddish-purple flowers from July to September. The flowers attract bees and butterflies alike, and later the goldfinches arrive to plunder the seeds. Once the seeds have all been eaten, a pretty silvery fringed cup is left, which is perfect for winter decorations. It adapts to sun or semi-shade. *See* Recipe 48.

LADY'S SMOCK: *Cardamine pratensis*, 15 × 10 cm (6 × 4″), is a perennial native plant of damp meadows, where it produces dainty pale lilac flowers in April and May. It is lovely with snake's head fritillaries, primroses, violets, cowslips and wild daffodils. *See* Recipe 49. It is happy in sun or semi-shade where the soil is moist. It will self-seed profusely and can also be propagated from a single leaf, taken from the base of a stem, kept on the surface of a seed tray of damp compost. It is a favourite nectar plant of the orange-tip butterfly, and is its caterpillar food plant as well.

WATER MINT: *Mentha aquatica*, 30 × 45 cm (12 × 18″), is very fragrant and a favourite nectar plant of both butterflies and bees. Lilac flowers appear from July to October. It will grow in up to 8 cm (3″) of water, in sun or semi-shade. *See* Recipe 50. It propagates easily by division.

The list above gives just some of the flowers which butterflies and bees favour most, but it is by no means exhaustive. There are a host of other plants which should be included as well if your planting space will allow it, *see* below. All of these are much visited by bees, but those marked with an asterisk are particularly important. A rosemary, firethorn or honeysuckle in full flower will literally be alive with bees. Those plants which also attract butterflies are marked (Bu). The distinction is difficult to pinpoint sometimes, for much depends on the density of plants which appear together and what is growing in the neighbouring gardens.

See also lists:
1 anemone, bluebell and hyacinth.
2 alyssum (Bu), aubrieta (Bu), forget-me-not (Bu) and soldiers and sailors*.
3 ageratum (Bu), bellflower, catmint* (Bu), cranesbill*, foxglove* and wallflower* (Bu).
4 caryopteris* (Bu), fuchsia, hollyhock* and sunflower.
7 Cherry Pie heliotrope (Bu), honeysuckle*, lavender*, lilac (Bu), mignonette (Bu), mock orange and sweet rocket (Bu).
8 bronze fennel, golden marjoram, hyssop, mint* (Bu), rosemary* and thyme.
9 hemp agrimony (Bu) and yellow flag iris.
11 globe thistle (Bu), honesty (Bu), sea holly (Bu) and teasel.
12 rotting apples, and plums in the orchard (Bu).
13 dog rose, dogwood (Bu), firethorn*, snowberry (Bu) and sweet briar.
14 *Daphne odora* 'Aureo-marginata', holly (Bu), ivies (Bu), mahonia*, snowdrop and winter-flowering jasmine.

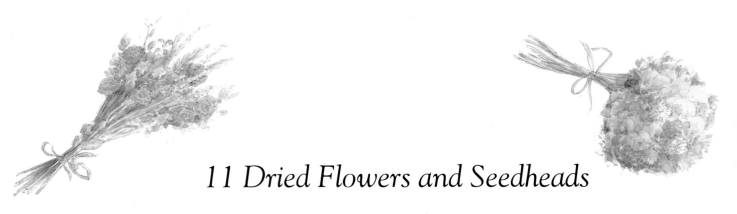

11 Dried Flowers and Seedheads

There are many flowers from the cottage garden which can be picked and dried to make lovely winter arrangements indoors. Some, including acanthus, poppy seedheads, Chinese lanterns and hydrangeas, will be bold and architectural. Together they can make a striking display of their natural colours or gilded or painted for Christmas. Others, such as love-in-a-mist, will be frilly. Some will be dainty fillers, such as lady's mantle and baby's breath. There are a few which retain their colour beautifully, including tea roses and delphiniums. An arrangement of these will bring summer gladness into the home all the year round. Some will be deliciously scented, such as lavender. Tie it in bundles and hang it from the kitchen ceiling or put it in the linen cupboard or weave it around the top of wicker baskets.

Various drying methods exist, but 'air drying' is by far the simplest. Gather the plant material while it is still coming into flower, probably three or four days before it reaches its best. It will open further as it dries. Pick it on a dry day. Remove the lower leaves, and wipe away any moisture. Simply hang three or four stems in small bunches upside-down in a cool, dry, airy atmosphere. The room should be dark so that the colours will not fade. Stagger the heads so that the air can circulate freely. Or stand them in a vase of water, only partly filled, to let them drink it up, but then leave them there until they are needed in an arrangement. Again, cool, dry, dark, airy conditions will be most beneficial.

BABY'S BREATH: *Gypsophila repens*, 15 × 30 cm (6 × 12″), produces masses of tiny pink or white flowers from June to August. Its many divided wiry stems will cascade down a bank or wall. It needs full sun. *See* Recipe 33. Dry it by standing it in a vase of water. Propagate it from basal shoots in April or May.

Gypsophila paniculata 'Rosy Veil', 30 × 45 cm (12 × 18″), produces masses of tiny double flowers which open white and become pale pink between June and September. *See* Recipe 8, where it is used at the front of a border. It likes full sun. For drying and propagation methods *see* above.

Gypsophila paniculata 'Snow White', 90 × 120 cm (3 × 4′), is much larger than the other two varieties mentioned. It flowers from June to September. It is ideal for the front of a large sunny border intermingled with roses or as a contrast to bold acanthus. *See* Recipe 41. For drying and propagation methods *see* above.

BEAR'S BREECHES: *Acanthus spinosus*, 120 × 60 cm (4 × 2′), is a large hardy perennial with spiky dark green leaves and long tapering roots. Beware, as it is a tough invasive plant which will take over a sunny border. The flowers are soft mauve and white, and dry easily. They last from July to September, although they will linger into the autumn if they are not cut. *See* Recipe 41. Hang it in small bunches. Propagate it by root division from October to March.

CHINESE LANTERNS: *Physalis alkekengi franchetii*, 60 × 90 cm (2 × 3′), likes a sunny position but it can be invasive, so it is best kept away from main borders. It is ideal beneath a barn wall. *See* Recipe 30. The orange lanterns appear from September to November but are best gathered early. Dry them hanging. The papery lanterns may be opened up to reveal the orange fruit inside. They are easy to grow and most attractive to use. Propagate them by division in March or April.

GLOBE THISTLE: *Echinops ritro* 'Veitch's Blue', 120 × 60 cm (4 × 2′). It needs a sunny position. Blue flowers appear from June to September; they are attractive to butterflies and bees. *See* Recipe 43. The rounded thistle heads dry well hanging, but they need to be picked before the flower matures. Propagate the plant by division from October to March.

HONESTY: *Lunaria annua* 'Alba', 75 × 30 cm (30 × 12″), is a biennial which flowers in April and May. In autumn, white honesty and purple honesty both produce marvellous seedheads whose outer filaments can be peeled away to reveal silver papery discs adjoining the seeds. *See* Recipes 10, 15, 18, 23, 43 and 44. It will self-seed.

Gather the heads early before the autumn winds spoil the material. Air dry the heads standing in a vase. They are lovely used in an arrangement in front of a window where the light can shine through.

HYDRANGEA: *Hydrangea* 'Preziosa', 75 × 90 cm (30 × 36″), produces large heads of pink flowers which should be cut just as the true flowers in the centre of each floret begin to open. Dry them by standing them in a vase of water. The plant grows well in sun or partial shade, although it likes plenty of moisture and needs a sheltered position. *See* Recipe 4. It will create a dome-shaped small shrub which flowers from July to September. Propagate it using cuttings taken in August or September.

LADY'S MANTLE: *Alchemilla mollis*, 30 × 30 cm (1 × 1′), was introduced in 1874. It is an easy hardy perennial, for sun or shade, which seeds itself. It is excellent near a path or at the front of a border. It produces great sprays of lime-green flowers in June and July which look lovely with deep blue, apricot, pink, peach or white. It sometimes flowers again in September if earlier flowers have been cut back. After it has rained, look at all the little drops of water held in the downy leaves. *See* Recipes 7, 9, 11, 36, 37 and 70.

LOVE-IN-A-MIST: *Nigella damascena* 'Persian Jewels Mixed', 40 × 20 cm (16 × 8″), is an easy annual to grow from seed, thereafter it will often self-seed. Choose a sunny spot. It will flower from June to August. *See* Recipe 16. Dry the flowers or the spherical seedheads by hanging or standing. A warm airing cupboard is the best way to preserve the flower colour.

ORIENTAL POPPY: *Papaver orientale* 'Mrs Perry', 90 × 60 cm (3 × 2′), produces salmon-pink flowers in June and then bears attractive seed pods which may be gathered and dried by hanging. It likes a sunny position. *See* Recipe 8. Propagate it by division in March or April.

SEA HOLLY: *Eryngium alpinum* 'Superbum', 75 × 45 cm (30 × 18″), produces steely blue teasel-like flower heads from June to August which may be cut and hung in small bunches to dry. It grows best in sunny positions. *See* Recipe 7. Propagate it by division in March.

TEASEL: *Dipsacus fullonum*, 200 × 30 cm (6½ × 1′), is the well-known wild flower which produces large spiny mauve flower heads in July and August. It will self-seed easily. Grow it in full sun or in partial shade in grassland, *see* Recipe 49, or as an architectural plant in the front or back of a border. In flower it is very attractive to butterflies and bees, while birds prefer to eat the seeds. Dry it by hanging.

See also lists:
3 delphinium.
7 lavender.

12 Fruit and Vegetables

The cottage garden was always productive, providing the family with fruit and vegetables throughout the year. Favourites among the soft fruit would certainly have been gooseberries and currants, as well as raspberries and strawberries. Rhubarb was important for its early cropping when stocks of fresh fruit from the previous season were getting low. The orchard would have provided apples and pears to last for many of the autumn and winter months, with plums and damsons to preserve and make into jams, jellies and chutneys. The vegetable garden would have yielded copious supplies of cabbages, carrots and parsnips, onions, leeks and potatoes, beans, peas, marrows and tomatoes throughout the season. Many of the potatoes, parsnips and carrots would be stored through the winter months and beans would be salted, while fresh cabbage and leeks would be kept in the garden to pick. Rotation of the crops was, and remains, vitally important.

The food element of the cottage garden is still important but not all these crops have to be grown, and it is not necessary to devote whole specialised areas to them. Lots of gardens will have an apple tree or two without necessarily having an entire orchard.

Many people will grow runner beans but they don't have to be confined to a vegetable garden. A double row would make an excellent screen anywhere they were wanted, perhaps between the flower garden and the compost area, for example. Scarlet runner beans are certainly colourful and make a very attractive feature. The Victorians used them in summer window boxes to train up the sides of the window and act as a living framework. Their bedfellows were not other vegetables, but geraniums, fuchsias and calceolaria!

VEGETABLES
(See the seed catalogues for particular varieties. *See also* Recipe 46.)

BEETROOT: This is best in an open sunny site. Sow the globe varieties between mid-March and July in seed clusters 5 cm (2″) apart. Thin them so that only one seed per cluster is allowed to grow on, then thin again to 10 cm (4″) apart. If you sow more than one row, leave 30 cm (1′) between the rows. Harvest the crop in September and October as needed. The yield from a 3-m (10′) row should be 6 kg (12½ lb).

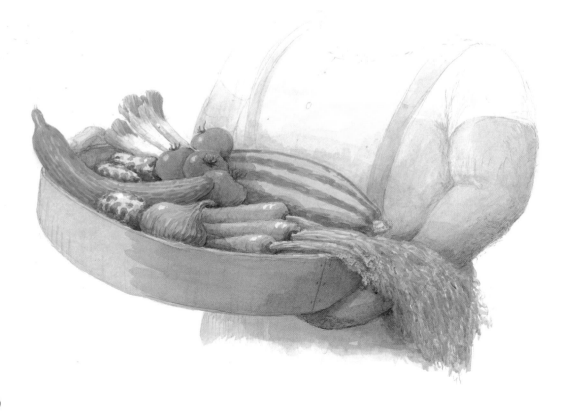

BROAD BEAN: These beans prefer a well-drained soil. Sow the seeds in April, 15 cm (6") apart in a double row 25 cm (10") apart. The beans may need support in exposed spots. When the lowest pod is 8 cm (3") long, remove the tops of the plant. This encourages pod growth development and removes the part of the plant most prone to blackfly. Try harvesting them when they are 5–8 cm (2–3") long in June or July; cook the pod whole. The yield from a double 3-m (10') row should be 9 kg (20 lb).

BRUSSELS SPROUT: Sow the seeds outdoors in May, then thin out the plants when the seedlings are about 3 cm (1¼") high. Transplant them in June 45 cm (18") apart, and leave 45 cm (18") between the rows. Harvest the crop from November to March. Pick the lower sprouts first. The yield from two 3-m (10') rows should be 15 kg (32 lb).

CABBAGE (autumn and winter): Sow the seeds outdoors in April or May, then thin out the plants to 5 cm (2") apart. Transplant them to their permanent site from May to July, 45 cm (18") apart in rows 60 cm (2') apart. The sites for both the seed bed and the final planting should be sunny, open and well drained; the soil should be alkaline. Harvest the crop from October to February. The yield from two 3-m (10') rows should be 11 kg (24 lb).

CABBAGE (spring): Sow the seeds at the end of July or in early August; thin the plants so that they are 5 cm (2") apart. Six weeks after sowing, transplant them to a permanent site, setting them 30 cm (1') apart and leaving 45 cm (18") between rows. Harvest the crop from April to May. The yield from two 3-m (10') rows should be 10 kg (22 lb).

CARROT: A main crop variety should be sown from April to July, leaving 25 cm (10") between each row. Thin the seedlings out, first to 3 cm (1¼") then to 8 cm (3") apart and finally to 15 cm (6"). Harvest the carrots from July to October. They do best on a light well-drained soil in a sunny position. The yield from two 3-m (10') rows should be 14 kg (30 lb).

CAULIFLOWER: Sow the seeds in a seedbed in a sunny and sheltered area elsewhere in the vegetable garden from March to May, then thin the plants to 5 cm (2") when they are large enough to handle. Transplant them to their permanent site from May to July. Plant them 60 cm (2') apart, and leave 60 cm (2') between the rows. Keep the plants well watered. Harvest the crop from July to October. The yield from two 3-m (10') rows should be fourteen cauliflowers.

FRENCH BEAN: These beans prefer a light well-drained soil and a sunny spot. Sow the seeds in pairs 25 cm (10") apart in mid-May in a double row 45 cm (18") apart. Remove the weaker seedlings in early

June. Crop the beans eight weeks after sowing and continue to harvest for another eight weeks. The yield from a double 3-m (10') row should be over 3 kg (just under 7 lb).

GIANT PUMPKIN: Follow the same sowing procedure as for the marrows. One plant will be enough.

LEEK: Sow the seeds outdoors in March. Transplant the young leeks to a permanent bed in June or July, but first trim the tops of the plants to reduce transpiration. Drop the plants into holes 15 cm (6") deep, 25 cm (10") apart, leaving 40 cm (16") between rows. In autumn, draw up the soil around the stems to aid blanching. Harvest the crop from November to March. Leeks are very hardy and provide fresh vegetables even in mid-winter. The yield from 2 rows should be 10 kg (22 lb).

MARROW (bush): These plants prefer a sunny, deep, rich soil. Sow the seeds indoors and plant them out at the end of May, or plant them outdoors directly in mid-May. Sow double the number of plants required and thin the crop in June. The plants should be 60 cm (2') apart. Harvest the marrows from August to October. Three plants will provide lots of meals throughout the autumn, and if stored in an airy frost-free place they can last until the year end.

ONION (main crop): Choose a site in full sun. Sow the seeds in March, directly into a permanent bed in rows 30 cm (1') apart. Thin the plants successively until they are 10 cm (4") apart. Use the thinnings in salad. When the outer leaves begin to turn yellow, bend over the tops to aid ripening. Two weeks later, use a fork to loosen roots. Lift the onions in late September. They will keep well until the following spring. The yield from three 3-m (10') rows may be 7–10 kg (15–22 lb).

PARSNIP: Sow the seeds in March, leaving 40 cm (16") between each row. Thin the plants gradually until they are 15–25 cm (6–10") apart. Harvest the parsnips between September and February. They are extremely hardy and will give fresh vegetables in mid-winter. But they do occupy the ground for a long time. They need sowing thickly because germination is unreliable. Try sowing radishes in the same row. These will be ready for cropping at the same time as the parsnips need thinning. The yield from two rows should be thirty parsnips or more.

PEA (main crop): They prefer a well-drained soil. Sow the seeds in April or May, three seeds across a 10-cm (4″) drill, staggering them so that they are 6 cm (2½″) apart. If you sow more than one row, the rows should be 45 cm (18″) apart. Protect the plants from the birds using cotton or netting. Support young growths with twiggy sticks to encourage the plants to climb. If you are using sugar peas, harvest them when the pods are 5 cm (2″) long and the peas are only just beginning to develop. Otherwise, harvest them when the peas have swollen to a good size but before they are fully mature, from July onwards. The yield will vary between varieties, but one row might provide eight meals for a family of four.

POTATO (1st early): Sprout the potatoes at the end of January and plant them from March to early April, 35 cm (14″) apart in rows 50 cm (20″) apart. Potatoes grow well in most soils, although they do best where the plot has been well manured. Earth them up when the young growth appears and continue to do so each fortnight until the tops meet between the rows. Water them in May and early June if they appear dry. Harvest the crop in late June and July. Four 3-m (10′) rows should yield 80 kg (about 1½ cwt).

RUNNER BEAN: These beans prefer a sunny spot with rich well-manured ground. Sow the seeds in pairs, 30 cm (1′) apart, in mid-May, and grow the plants in a double row, 45 cm (18″) apart, up rustic poles or bamboo canes crossed at the top, linked by a horizontal pole. You can also train them up netting strung between two poles, or grow them up a wigwam of canes as support. Thin them in early June by removing the weaker plants of each pair. They thrive on moisture, so be prepared to water them while in

full growth and at flowering time. Give them a thick mulch to help retain the moisture. Sometimes old newspapers and nettles are laid at the bottom of the trench underneath the beans. Pinch out the growing tips when they reach the top of the poles to encourage side shoots. Pick the beans while they are still young and tender, from July to September. The good news is that the more you pick the more they will produce. There are white-flowering varieties as well as red. The yield from a double 3-m (10′) row should be 18 kg (40 lb).

TOMATO (bush): Grow the plants in a sunny sheltered site. The soil should be rich and moisture-retentive. Start the seeds in the greenhouse in early April and then plant them outdoors 45 cm (18″) apart from the end of May onwards. Even with bush varieties it is advisable to provide each plant with a stout stake and to tie it at regular intervals. Water the plants frequently in dry weather and feed them weekly once the first fruits have set. Pinch out the tops when four fruit trusses have formed. Harvest the tomatoes from August to October. The yield should be about 2 kg (4 lb) per plant.

SOFT FRUIT
(There are many other varieties from which to choose. *See* Recipe 45.)

BLACKCURRANT: 'Wellington XXX' is a mid-season heavy cropper. It is easy to grow and thrives in sun or partial shade, but avoid areas particularly susceptible to late spring frosts. The bushes are long-lived. Crop the fruit from late June to July. Propagate them from 20-cm (8″) hardwood cuttings – with the top softwood removed and some from the bottom, just below a bud – taken in early October and planted from October to March into open ground, 1.2 m (4′) apart, with two buds showing above soil-level, and 1.5 m (5′) between rows.

GOOSEBERRY: 'Lancer' is both a green dessert and cooking variety which will thrive in sun or partial shade, but avoid sites which are susceptible to late spring frosts. This is a mid-season cropper which will ripen at the end of June or early July. Propagate it from 25-cm (10″) hardwood cuttings – with the top softwood removed and some from the bottom, just below a bud – taken in October. Plant them from October to March in a vertical trench, 1.2 m (4′) apart with 1.5 m (5′) between rows, so that two buds show above ground-level.

RASPBERRY: 'Malling Jewel' is an early to mid-season variety which bears a heavy crop with an excellent flavour. Choose a sheltered sunny site, or one that has only a few hours' shade. Plant the canes from November to March, 40 cm (16″) apart in 1.8-m (6′) rows. Harvest the fruit in July. New canes

can be raised from suckers in November. Replace them with new virus-free stock every eight years and use a new site. Raspberries need a moisture-retentive soil and benefit from additions of manure or compost.

REDCURRANT: 'Red Lake' is a mid-season cropper which will thrive in sun or partial shade, but avoid sites which are susceptible to late spring frosts, as they flower early. They are attractive grown as a cordon, trained on wires, and used as an edging or dividing plant in the cottage garden. Plant them 1.2 m (4') apart with 1.5 m (5') between rows. Harvest the fruit from the end of June to July. Propagate them as for the gooseberries above.

RHUBARB: 'The Sutton' is a good variety that rarely runs to seed as some others are likely to do. It has a height and spread of 1 m (3¼'). Harvest it from March to July, although it can be forced earlier. Propagate it by dividing the roots in February or early March. It is tolerant of sun or shade, but it likes soil with plenty of manure or added humus. Lift and divide it only every five to eight years.

ORCHARD FRUIT
(There are many other varieties to choose from. Both of these apple and pear trees need pollinators; however, the second-named variety is a suitable pollinator in each case. The apple and pear tree sizes are for bush fruit trees. *See* Recipe 47.)

APPLE: 'Worcester Permain', 3.5 × 3.5 m (11½ × 11½'), is ready to harvest from the end of August through to September. The fruits are golden yellow streaked with crimson and make a colourful display. It is a good regular cropper, providing juicy, crisp sweet apples, but they do not store well into the winter. It is tip-bearing, so only light pruning is required.

'Sunset', 3.5 × 3.5 m (11½ × 11½'), is ready to pick at the end of September for use from October to December. It is yellow with an orange-red flush. It forms a crisp dessert apple with an excellent flavour. It often fruits well where 'Cox's Orange Pippin' does not. It has an attractive blossom, and is spur-forming with compact growth.

DAMSON: 'Merryweather', 4.5 × 3.5 m (15 × 11½'), flowers in early spring. If it is not caught by frost, it will produce a heavy crop of deep purple damsons in September. It does not need another pollinator. Alternatively, try gages.

PEAR: 'Williams Bon Chrétien', 3.5 × 3.5 m (11½ × 11½'), is one of the best flavoured golden September pears, although it should be picked in late August to ripen in September. It keeps for only a short time.

'Conference' pears, 3.5 × 3.5 m (11½ × 11½'), will keep much longer. Pick the dark green fruits in September for eating in October and November. It is a regular cropper and is excellent for bottling. These two varieties are suitable pollinators for each other.

PLUM: 'Victoria', 4.5 × 3.5 m (15 × 11½'), also flowers in early spring. If it is not caught by late frosts, it will produce a bountiful crop of delicious red and yellow plums in late August or September. They can be used for dessert or cooking. It is self-fertile so it does not need a pollinator. Alternatively, try gages.

13 Small Trees, Shrubs and the Cottage Hedgerow

Many of the trees and shrubs listed here will find their way into the boundary hedgerows of the cottage, creating shelter for the garden. Typical examples might be hawthorn, wild roses, dogwood, snowberry, yew and holly, though these latter two might be left to grow up as specimen trees in the hedge or be planted in the lawn. Some, such as the firethorn and cotoneaster, can be grown up the cottage wall to give colour and interest even in the autumn and winter months.

The evergreen holly, yew and box will give the best and densest shelter. But they are often trimmed to shape and made into many weird and attractive features. Others are good deciduous varieties which are colourful in flower or attractive in fruit and leaf in autumn. The common hawthorn is hard to beat for its wonderful show of scented May flowers. What is more, its haws and leaves are vivid from September through to November. The wild roses and the dogwood are bright with colour too.

The small trees and shrubs are a very important element in the cottage garden, setting the scene and providing some of the backbone. The more varieties that can be introduced the richer the tapestry will become. Most of them provide valuable food for native wildlife. Nectar, berries and nuts are borne in profusion.

BOX: *Buxus sempervirens* 'Pyramidalis', 100 × 60 cm (3¼ × 2′), is a small-leaved evergreen shrub suitable for hedging and many kinds of topiary work. For this reason, box has been common in cottage gardens for centuries. It will thrive in sun or shade. Its flowers are insignificant. Clip it in August or September, and propagate it using cuttings taken at the same time. *See* Recipes 13 and 14.

CEANOTHUS: *Ceanothus* 'Delight', 3 m (10′), is one of the hardiest of the evergreen forms, with bright blue flowers in May and early June. It gained popularity in the 1930s. *See* Recipe 1, where it is trained against a sunny wall.

Ceanothus 'Gloire de Versailles', 2 × 2 m (6½ × 6½′), is a hardy deciduous form which can easily be clipped smaller if required. It is an old favourite, and has been cultivated since the last quarter of the nineteenth century. Its flowers are borne in panicles up to 20 cm (8″) long, from June to October. They are soft powdery blue and fragrant, hence the attraction for butterflies and bees. *See* Recipe 44.

COTONEASTER: *Cotoneaster horizontalis*, 2 × 2 m (6½ × 6½'), is a familiar low-growing deciduous shrub with small leaves and a neat herring-bone pattern of growth. It has little white flowers in summer, followed by small orange berries from October to March. It is useful for north- and east-facing walls. It was introduced in about 1870. *See* Recipe 30.

DOG ROSE: *Rosa canina*, 2.5 × 2.5 m (8 × 8'), is an old favourite, with delicate pink or white flowers in June and July but without the aromatic foliage of its cousin the sweet briar. Egg-shaped scarlet hips transform the bush from August to November. It is useful for hedging. *See* Recipe 17.

DOGWOOD: *Cornus sanguinea*, 2.5 × 1.8 m (8 × 6'), is a native deciduous shrub with white flowers in June and July, followed by black fruit from September to November. It can be used in the cottage hedgerow, where the strong autumn colouring adds a dark richness to the scene. *See* Recipe 17.

FIRETHORN: *Pyracantha rogersiana*, 3 × 3 m (10 × 10'), can be free-standing or trained up a wall. It is useful for a north- or east-facing position. It will tolerate a windy spot. Flowers appear in June, and it is covered in a marvellous display of orange berries from September through to March – depending on the audacity of the blackbirds. It was introduced from China in 1911. There are many varieties from which to choose. *See* Recipe 4. It is evergreen.

FORSYTHIA: *Forsythia suspensa* grows to a height and spread of 2–3 m (6½–10'), although it can be restricted. It favours any aspect, but it is particularly happy on a north wall. It was introduced in 1833. Familiar yellow flowers appear on the slender pendent branches in March and April. *See* Recipe 30. There are many other forsythias from which to choose.

GUELDER ROSE: *Viburnum opulus* 'Notcutt's Variety', 5 × 4 m (16½ × 13'), is a selected form of our familiar native shrub with larger flowers and fruits. It became popular in the 1930s. The blossom is white and appears in May; the fruit is scarlet and translucent, and is borne from August to October. It is a great favourite with birds. The leaves colour well in autumn before dropping. It is a good hedging shrub where it can be clipped to shape. *See* Recipe 17.

HAWTHORN: *Crataegus monogyna*, 8 × 5 m (26 × 16½'), is the common hawthorn of our hedgerows with deliciously fragrant flowers from May to June, followed by red haws August to November, and often fiery colouring of the leaves in autumn. It makes a good dense hedge – a welcome refuge to all sorts of wildlife. *See* Recipe 17. It can be allowed to grow into a full-sized tree.

HAZEL: *Corylus avellana*, 7 × 5 m (23 × 16½'), is our native deciduous nut bush, which produces long dangling yellow catkins in February and sweet-tasting hazel nuts in September and October. Plant it either as a tree or clipped to shape as a hedging plant. This has been an old favourite in gardens for centuries. *See* Recipe 17.

JAPANESE QUINCE: *Chaenomeles speciosa* 'Apple Blossom', 2 × 2 m (6½ × 6½'), produces pretty white flowers, tinged with cream and pink, in March and April before the new leaves appear. It was introduced in about 1932. It can be grown as a tree or against a wall, and is suitable for any aspect. The green fruits are useful for making jelly. *See* Recipe 30.

LABURNUM: *Laburnum anagyroides*, 7 × 7 m (23 × 23'), is sometimes known as the golden rain tree on account of its beautiful long yellow racemes which appear towards the end of May and into June. It likes a sunny position but will tolerate shade as well. It has been cultivated since about 1560. *See* Recipe 15.

SHRUBBY MALLOW: *Lavatera* 'Barnsley', 1.8 × 1.8 m (6 × 6'), is a deciduous shrub with delicate pale pink flowers which appear from June right through to the frosts. It is an amazing display. It is invaluable for any warm sheltered late summer cottage border, and is liked by butterflies and bees. *See* Recipe 43. Propagate it using softwood cuttings in early summer.

SNOWBERRY: *Symphoricarpos albus* 'White Hedger', 2 × 2.5 m (6½ × 8'), is a non-suckering form of our hardy deciduous shrub. Tiny pink flowers appear from June to September, followed by large round white berries from September through to February. Birds don't like the berries but the holly blue butterfly likes the flowers in August. *See* Recipe 17. The berries show up well against the other hedgerow plants intermingling with the colourful hips and haws. They also show up well against a dark green background such as box, conifer or yew.

SWEET BRIAR: *Rosa rubiginosa*, 2.5 × 2.5 m (8 × 8'), is a strong-growing medium-sized native shrub which produces arching sprays of beautiful pink single flowers in June and July. The leaves are aromatic. Oval orange hips adorn the bush from August to November; the sepals stay on the ripening fruit. It is useful as a deciduous hedging specimen or in the wild garden. *See* Recipes 17 and 49.

WEEPING BIRCH: *Betula pendula* 'Youngii', 7 m (23') high, known as Young's weeping birch, makes a deciduous dome-shaped tree of graceful habit with weeping branches. It makes an excellent specimen for a lawn. It will bear both female and male catkins in April and May. The male catkins are the more significant of the two; they are pale yellow and grow 3–7 cm (1¼–3") long. *See* Recipe 24.

YEW: *Taxus baccata*, 5 × 5 m (16½ × 16½'), is an old cottage favourite. Hardy and evergreen, it provides good shelter for the cottage garden. The flowers are insignificant but the fleshy red berries are to be admired. The yew makes a good if moody lone tree; it can also be used as a dense hedging subject, clipped in keeping with the rest of the hedge, or it can be treated as a topiary specimen. *See* Recipe 13.

See also lists:
  4 caryopteris and fuchsia.
  5 shrub roses.
  7 lavender and mock orange.
  8 hyssop, rosemary and sage.
11 hydrangea.
12 cottage fruit trees.

14 The Winter Garden

This is a time of contrasts between the stark skeletons of the deciduous trees and shrubs and those of the evergreens with their prickly, pointed, divided or rounded, glossy or dull leaves. All are accentuated by frosty edges. It is a time to marvel at the dainty flowers. Nodding snowdrops show up well against the bold outline of elephant's ears. The delicate autumn cherry blossoms look lovely against a wintry sunset. Every flower is welcome now. Even the smallest bloom will be enjoyed. What surprising scents there are at this time of year. The daphnes are so sweetly fragrant; the mahonias and viburnums are too.

These plants are not just to be found in the recipe for the winter garden but in many other schemes as well, including the privy, the cottage porch, the shady border, the front gate in shade, the evergreen hedge and the holly tree.

SHRUBS/TREES

AUTUMN CHERRY: *Prunus subhirtella* 'Autumnalis', 7 × 8 m (23 × 26'). It was introduced in about 1900. It is a small tree which produces pretty white blossoms from November through to March and so is an extremely welcome addition to the winter scene. The stems can be brought indoors for winter arrangements. 'Rosea' has blush-pink flowers. It will grow in sun or shade. The leaves colour well in the autumn before dropping. *See* Recipe 14.

DAPHNE: *Daphne odora* 'Aureo-marginata', 1.5 × 1.5 m (5 × 5'), is a small bushy evergreen shrub with variegated leaves. It is hardier than the green form. It has clusters of pale reddish-purple flowers which are sweetly scented and appear from February to April. It will thrive in sun or shade, so long as the position is sheltered. *See* Recipe 40.

Daphne mezereum, 150 × 90 cm (5 × 3'), is known as the winter-flowering daphne. It is a small deciduous shrub which was introduced in about 1561. It is an old favourite, well loved for the delicious scent produced from the bright pink flowers which smother the previous year's shoots from February to March. Scarlet berries appear in late summer. These are poisonous but are loved by birds. *See* Recipes 10 and 14.

GARRYA: *Garrya elliptica*, 4 × 3 m (13 × 10'), is an evergreen shrub which has long green catkins from January through to March. It is a lovely sight in the wintry sun, although it needs a sheltered position and is best near a protective wall or bigger shrubs. It was introduced in 1828. Plant the male form which has the longer catkins. If you are unsure about the sex of your new plant, buy it in winter with the catkins well displayed. *See* Recipe 40.

HOLLY: *Ilex aquifolium* 'Pyramidalis', 6 × 5 m (20 × 16½'), is one of the more recent forms with bright green leaves and a reliably good display of red berries from October to December. *See* Recipe 25.

Ilex aquifolium 'Argenteo-marginata' (broad-leaved silver holly) is another female free-fruiting tree, but it has white-margined leaves. It has white flowers in April and May and produces berries from September to December. It is useful as a hedging plant, because the young leaves are pink. *See* Recipes 13 and 17.

MAHONIA: *Mahonia japonica*, 3 × 3 m (10 × 10'), is an evergreen shrub with deep green pinnate leaves and lovely yellow racemes produced from January through to March. The tiny flowers look like little daffodils but have a rich lily of the valley scent. In full flower it is absolutely glorious. It could be included in the wildlife border as the bees adore it. *See* Recipe 40. It makes a good winter container specimen.

VIBURNUM: *Viburnum tinus*, 3 × 3 m (10 × 10'), is an evergreen winter-flowering shrub which has been cultivated in Britain since the late sixteenth century. It likes sun or shade. It has flat clusters of scented tiny white flowers from November through to April – a remarkable timespan which makes it deservedly popular. *See* Recipe 68.

Viburnum tinus 'Eve Price' is similar to the above, though more compact, but with more attractive flowers from November to April. They are carmine in bud, then pink-tinged. *See* Recipe 15.

Viburnum × bodnantense 'Dawn', 3 × 2 m (10 × 6½'), is a deciduous shrub which produces lovely clusters of pink richly scented flowers on naked stems from November through to February. *See* Recipe 40. Its foliage is bronze at first. It colours well in autumn.

WINTER-FLOWERING JASMINE: *Jasminum nudiflorum*, 3 × 2 m (10 × 6½'), was introduced in 1844 and has come to symbolise the cottage door in winter. As a climber it needs support. Yellow flowers appear on naked stems from November through to March. It can be grown in sun or shade. *See* Recipes 5, 22, 30, 68 and 69.

WINTER HEATHER: *Erica carnea* 'Springwood White', 20 × 45 cm (8 × 18"), is a low-growing evergreen shrub which produces a mass of white flowers from January through to March. It is tolerant of lime. *See* Recipe 40. This is an old favourite. It can be grown in sun or partial shade, and is useful in winter containers.

BULBS/CORMS
CYCLAMEN: *Cyclamen coum*, 5 cm (2") high, has dainty pink flowers sometimes as early as December, but mainly in January and February. The leaves appear the previous autumn and last until spring. They are variously mottled and marked and

exceedingly beautiful. Tolerant of sun or shade, they make a good subject for the winter garden and look lovely beside snowdrops. *See* Recipes 14 and 25.

SNOWDROP: *Galanthus nivalis*, 10 cm (4") high, is a universal favourite with its dainty drooping white flower which appear from the end of January through to March. *See* Recipes 14, 24, 40 and 69.

Galanthus nivalis 'Flore Pleno', 10 cm (4") high, has double white flowers produced mainly in February and March. *See* Recipes 2, 5, 10 and 23.

Neither of these two snowdrops is easy to get established, but given time they will multiply and self-seed, and will create lovely white carpets of flower. They are happy in sun or shade, in the border or in grass. Plant dry bulbs immediately after they become available from a garden centre, or in spring after flowering 'in the green', with leaves intact.

WINTER ACONITES: *Eranthis hyemalis*, 8 cm (3"), provides a lovely splash of yellow from February to March. It is happy in sun or shade and can grow in a border or under deciduous trees. *See* Recipes 12 and 24. The leaves are very divided and attractive. They will quickly self-seed, particularly in a border.

HERBACEOUS
CHRISTMAS ROSE: *Helleborus niger*, 30 × 30 cm (1 × 1'), is deservedly an old cottage favourite, sometimes flowering just before Christmas in a sheltered sunny position, but welcome whenever it decides to produce its array of pure white flowers. They often last right through to March. The dark green leaves are highly divided. The Christmas rose looks lovely beside bold round elephant's ears. Propagate it by division in March. *See* Recipes 5 and 10.

LENTEN ROSE: *Helleborus orientalis*, 45 × 60 cm (18 × 24"), is a hardy evergreen. Throughout February and March it produces nodding flowers with striking maroon, pink or white colourings. They are spotted inside. It was first introduced in 1839; now there are many lovely hybrids. Propagate it by division in March. *See* Recipe 40.

IVIES
Ivies form an important part of the cottage scene. As hardy evergreens they were very commonly grown. Indeed, almost every cottage garden would have

grown one or more. Their distinctive leaf shapes meant that they were all individually attractive, and when they flowered and fruited they were particularly so. They would be gathered at Christmas and used to decorate the home. But they looked good all year round, including in the spring when the new glossy leaves appear. Some thought that by clothing the house walls, the cottage was kept warm and dry.

Most are easy to place and many will tolerate very difficult dry and shady conditions. They are very simple to look after. All the ivies listed below are self-clinging and will climb as far as they are allowed, but they are easily pruned to shape and so can be contained if necessary. There are a great many to choose from.

Hedera helix 'Buttercup' (buttercup ivy), 1 m (3¼') high, has light green leaves that turn yellow in full sun. It is perfect for a sunny wall or bank. *See* Recipe 19.

Hedera helix 'Heise', 3 m (10') high, is an attractive variegated silver-leaved ivy for a shady site. Use it as a climber up a north-facing cottage porch. *See* Recipes 5, 68 and 69.

Hedera helix 'Manda's Crested', 2 m (6½') high, is just one of several 'parsley' ivies with crinkly leaves. This one turns a coppery shade in winter, but the new growth is attractive too. *See* Recipe 22.

Hedera hibernica (Irish ivy) will berry freely when it has reached the top of the gateway. *See* Recipe 13.

See also lists:
  1 crocus.
  2 elephant's ears, primrose, soldiers and sailors and violet.
13 box and yew.

ACKNOWLEDGEMENTS

I would like to express my sincere gratitude to Simon Buckingham for his wonderful interpretation of the garden plans and also to Juliette Wade for her artistic photography. I am particularly grateful to them both for their enthusiasm and patience. My thanks also to Arianne Burnette for her painstaking skills in editing the text, and to Peter Barnes, botanist at the Royal Horticultural Society, who updated the script with the latest botanical names.

Very special thanks go to John and Theresa Scarman of Cottage Garden Roses, who have given me considerable support and help with this project. I would like to extend my sincere thanks to John Taylor and John Walker of O. A. Taylor Bulbs Ltd of Holbeach, Lincolnshire for their botanical advice. Thanks also go to Max Robinson and Tina Whitney of Hinwick Hall Horticulture, Noel Mellish of Norfolk Lavender, Michael Marriott of David Austin Roses, Philip Read of Podington Nurseries, Tony Fry of Bressingham Gardens and Ursula Key of Fibrex Nurseries. I am also indebted to Frank Clarkson, Pru Dempster, David Smart, Tony Smith and Mollie Wain.

I would like to thank Badgers Hill Farm of Chilham, Kent for providing wooden barrels for me to use. I am grateful to many people in lending containers or providing sites for my containers to be photographed. Here thanks go to Barbara Cattermole, Sandra and Michael Frampton, Paula and Alex Gray, Barbara Humphriss, Catherine Moran, Margaret and Roy Pryn, Brian and Claire Stapleton, Sara and Nicholas Tusting. I am particularly grateful to others for allowing their gardens to be painted and for providing such a source of inspiration. Deserving special mention are Pat Barker and Rosamond Brown, also Tom Davies, Jean Edwards, Jane and Chris Eagle, Bill Harris and Mrs Warwick. For help in so many other ways, my thanks go to John Arnold, Frank Barratt, Suzanne Bullerwell, Joanna Cree, Sue and David Gorham, Penny Hamp, Isobel Hart and Jane O'Connor.

As always, the greatest thanks go to my husband Simon, for his unfailing encouragement, and to my children Jonathan and Suzanna. Lastly, to my mother who died so tragically just as this book was conceived. By her example and teaching she nurtured my love of cottage garden plants.

SPECIALIST SUPPLIERS OF PLANTS

This list is by no means exhaustive. For further names and addresses, look among the advertisements in the gardening magazines and in the Sunday newspapers. Many of the suppliers listed below provide a very good mail order service.

Bulbs: Walter Blom and Son Ltd, Primrose Nursery, Sharnbrook, Bedfordshire, MK44 1LW. Telephone: 01234 782424

Broadleigh Gardens, Bishops Hull, Taunton, Somerset, TA4 1AE. Telephone: 01823 286231

Foxgrove Plants, Enbourne, Newbury, Berkshire, RG14 6RE. Telephone: 01635 40554

Fuchsias: Arcadia Nurseries, Brass Castle Lane, Nunthorpe, Middlesbrough, TS8 9EB. Telephone: 01642 310782

Garden Pinks: Three Counties Nurseries, Marshwood, Bridport, Dorset, DT6 5QJ. Telephone: 0129 77 257

Geraniums, Ferns and Ivies: Fibrex Nurseries Ltd, Honeybourne Road, Pebworth, Nr Stratford-on-Avon, CV37 8XT. Telephone: 01789 720788

The Vernon Geranium Nursery, Cuddington Way, Cheam, Sutton, Surrey, SM2 7JB. Telephone: 01813 937616

Herbaceous and Alpine: Bressingham Gardens, Diss, Norfolk, IP22 2AB. Telephone: 01379 687464

Margery Fish Plant Nursery, Lambrook Manor, South Petherton, Somerset, TA13 5HL. Telephone: 01460 240328

Hopleys Plants, Much Hadham, Hertfordshire, SG10 6BU. Telephone: 0127 984 2509

W. E. Ingwersen Ltd, Birch Farm Nursery, Gravetye, East Grinstead, West Sussex, RH19 4LE. Telephone: 01342 810236

Peter Jones, Manningford Nurseries, Mannington Abbots, Pewsey, Wiltshire. Telephone: 01672 62232

Plants From The Past, 1 North Street, Belhaven, Dunbar, East Lothian, EH42 1NU. Telephone: 01368 863223

Rushfields of Ledbury, Ross Road, Ledbury, Herefordshire, HR8 2LP. Telephone: 01531 632004

Southview Nurseries, Eversley Cross, Basingstoke, Hampshire, RG27 0NT. Telephone: 01734 732206

Lavender: Norfolk Lavender Ltd, Caley Mill, Heacham, Norfolk, PE31 7JE. Telephone: 01485 570384

Roses: David Austin Roses, Bowling Green Lane, Albrighton, Wolverhampton, WV7 3HB. Telephone: 01902 373 931

Cottage Garden Roses, Woodlands House, Stretton, Nr Stafford, ST19 9LG. Telephone: 01785 840 217

Seeds: Thompson and Morgan Ltd, London Road, Ipswich, Suffolk, IP2 0BA. Telephone: 01473 688588

Shrubs and Trees: Hillier Nurseries Ltd, Ampfield House, Ampfield, Romsey, Hampshire, SO51 9PA. Telephone: 01794 368733

Notcutts Nurseries Ltd, Woodbridge, Suffolk, IP12 4AF. Telephone: 01394 383344

INDEX